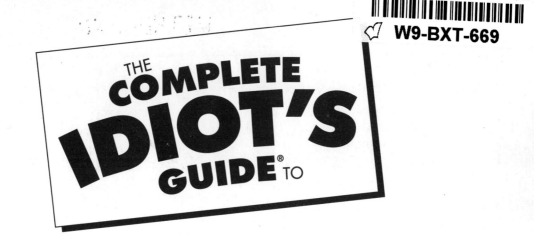

THE

COMPLETE IDIOT'S GUIDE® TO

Options and Futures

Second Edition

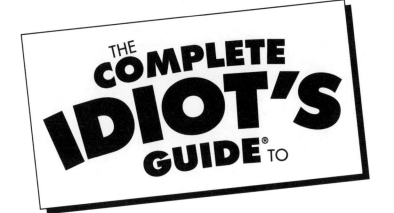

THE COMPLETE IDIOT'S GUIDE® TO

Options and Futures

Second Edition

by Scott Barrie with Lita Epstein

A member of Penguin Group (USA) Inc.

ALPHA BOOKS

Published by the Penguin Group

Penguin Group (USA) Inc., 375 Hudson Street, New York, New York 10014, U.S.A.

Penguin Group (Canada), 10 Alcorn Avenue, Toronto, Ontario, Canada M4V 3B2 (a division of Pearson Penguin Canada Inc.)

Penguin Books Ltd, 80 Strand, London WC2R 0RL, England

Penguin Ireland, 25 St Stephen's Green, Dublin 2, Ireland (a division of Penguin Books Ltd)

Penguin Group (Australia), 250 Camberwell Road, Camberwell, Victoria 3124, Australia (a division of Pearson Australia Group Pty Ltd)

Penguin Books India Pvt Ltd, 11 Community Centre, Panchsheel Park, New Delhi—110 017, India

Penguin Group (NZ), cnr Airborne and Rosedale Roads, Albany, Auckland 1310, New Zealand (a division of Pearson New Zealand Ltd)

Penguin Books (South Africa) (Pty) Ltd, 24 Sturdee Avenue, Rosebank, Johannesburg 2196, South Africa

Penguin Books Ltd, Registered Offices: 80 Strand, London WC2R 0RL, England

International Standard Book Number: 1-59257-548-X
Library of Congress Catalog Card Number: 2006929095

08 07 06   8 7 6 5 4 3 2 1

Interpretation of the printing code: The rightmost number of the first series of numbers is the year of the book's printing; the rightmost number of the second series of numbers is the number of the book's printing. For example, a printing code of 06-1 shows that the first printing occurred in 2006.

Printed in the United States of America

Publisher: *Marie Butler-Knight*
Editorial Director: *Mike Sanders*
Managing Editor: *Billy Fields*
Acquisitions Editor: *Paul Dinas*
Development Editor: *Michael Thomas*
Production Editor: *Kayla Dugger*
Copy Editor: *Jennifer Connolly*

Cartoonist: *Richard King*
Cover Designer: *Bill Thomas*
Book Designers: *Trina Wurst/Kurt Owens*
Indexer: *Heather McNeill*
Layout: *Brian Massey*
Proofreader: *Mary Hunt*

Contents at a Glance

Contents

Foreword

The commodity futures and options markets are "the last bastions of pure capitalism left on Earth." The futures markets are a zero sum game, meaning that for every dollar made, someone else loses a dollar. For every winner, there is a loser. The commodity futures and options markets are a financial jungle, where only the strong survive and the slow are eaten for breakfast.

At Gecko Software, Inc., we have made it our business to help people become more familiar with this jungle. Our premier product, Gecko Charts, is a time machine of sorts, which allows one to have access to over two decades of historical market data. Access to this data, and the ability to test out trading ideas, allows those new to the world of futures and options to put their ideas and trading acumen to the test, without money on the line. Experienced speculators use Gecko Software products to try out new ideas and as historical reference tools to help them be more efficient in the fast-paced world of commodity futures and options trading. Gecko Software is an educational tool which allows people to learn from their mistakes, before they are too costly.

As the head of a market educational firm, I found Scott Barrie's *The Complete Idiot's Guide® to Options and Futures* a refreshing change from many of the introductory books on the subject. Risk and reward are covered equally, giving the reader a true look at the potential of using futures and options. Advanced concepts are presented in such a user-friendly manner that they seem easy. The reader is presented with a clear look at the production and consumption cycles and how these factors affect the pricing of traditional commodities, such as corn, crude oil, silver, soybeans, cocoa, and cattle. This book also covers the financial markets, providing the reader with a guide to examining the economy, and how changes in the economy should affect interest rates, currencies, and the stock market. New markets, such as single stock futures, are covered as well, giving a complete up-to-date guide and reference for anyone interested in participating in the futures and/or options markets.

Because the advice and knowledge contained within the pages of *The Complete Idiot's Guide® to Options and Futures, Second Edition*, is so simple, yet so valuable, I am advising many of the so-called industry experts to read it. For the beginning trader, however, I consider it an absolute must read.

Lan H. Turner, CEO
Gecko Software, Inc.
www.geckosoftware.com

Lan Turner is also known as "The Pitmaster" and mediates one of the most popular options and futures trading educational websites on the Internet, www.pitnews.com.

Introduction

In life as in the marketplace there are two types of people: the risk takers and the risk avoiders. The futures market serves both because the heart and purpose of these markets are to transfer risk from risk avoiders to risk takers.

The risk avoiders use the futures market to secure prices and lock in profit margins through a process known as hedging. Inside these pages you will be shown how to use the futures market to avoid unnecessary risks, allowing you to operate your business more effectively.

The hedgers transfer their risk to speculators, who assume this risk for the likelihood of a profit. The futures markets offer the perfect vehicle for one to speculate on a variety of markets from Corn to Crude Oil, or Soybeans to the Standard & Poor's Stock Index.

The nuts and bolts of hedging and speculating are laid out inside these pages, giving the reader a general overview of how the futures and options markets work, as well as practical advice on the opportunities and pitfalls associated with these fast-moving markets.

How This Book Is Organized

The book is divided into five parts. We start with a basic introduction to the futures markets, followed by a discussion of the risk involved. Then we look at the role of options on futures followed by an overview of the how the markets work. We end with a part that focuses on trading tips.

Part 1, "Introduction to Futures and Exchanges," outlines how and why the futures markets developed. By thoroughly understanding how these markets developed, you get a great appreciation for how the market functions.

Part 2, "Using Futures to Take or Alleviate Risks," shows how the futures markets transfer risk from those wishing to avoid it (hedgers) to those who embrace risk in the hopes of profit (speculators). The uses and regulation of the futures markets are explained in plain English, so you can understand how these markets function.

Part 3, "Options on Futures," explains the options markets. The use of put and call options on futures are explained, and the reader is shown how to use these instruments to either protect against unwanted price changes or how to profit from changing prices.

Part 4, "Understanding What Makes Markets Tick," is, as the title implies, about the forces that cause prices to change. General supply and demand themes are laid out for the Grain, Food, Livestock, Metals, Petroleum, and Financial markets. This part is designed to help you to not only understand prices and their direction, but to anticipate them.

Part 5, "Applying Your Knowledge … Getting Ready to Trade," takes the reader through the steps necessary to develop a trading plan. If your goal is to actually speculate in the futures market, this section will help you to develop a well-thought-out plan on how to profit from these exciting markets.

Some Things to Help Out Along the Way

To add to the material in the main text of the book, a series of shaded boxes throughout the book highlight specific items that can help you understand and implement the material in each chapter:

def•i•ni•tion

Like any industry, profession, or vocation, the world of futures and options has its own language or lingo. Inside these sections you will find translations into English for terms and **buzz words.**

Trading Tips

Tips and techniques to help you implement some of the ideas you pick up in this book. These represent the collective wisdom of a decade in the business, and are taken from personal experience, as well as many other fine publications written about the markets.

Trading Time Bomb

These are things that can cause you to lose serious money. Pay attention and learn from them or pay the price!

Commodity Corn

Tidbits that might add to your knowledge or just amuse you.

Acknowledgments

We would like to thank Great Pacific Trading Company; Lan Turner and Gecko Software, Inc.; Jim Zalesky; and John J. Lothian, President of The Price Group Electronic Trading Division; for their help with this publication.

Special Thanks to the Technical Reviewer

The Complete Idiot's Guide® to Options and Futures, Second Edition, was reviewed by an expert who double-checked the accuracy of what you'll learn here, to help us ensure that this book gives you everything you need to know about options and futures. Special thanks are extended to Ken Kaplan.

Kenneth Kaplan resides in Port Washington, NY, with his wife Janet. Kenneth has spent over 30 years as a financial analyst on Wall Street. He has a daughter who is in graduate school in New York and a son attending college in Florida. Kenneth was born and raised in New York.

Trademarks

Part 1

Introduction to Futures and Exchanges

Before jumping into the futures and options markets, it is important to understand how these markets developed and why.

By understanding how the commodity futures and options markets developed and why, you can gain an appreciation for their uses both as a risk-taking and risk-transference tool. Armed with an understanding of the history of these markets, you will have a more thorough understanding of the mechanics of how they work.

History and Development of the Futures Market

In This Chapter

- ◆ How the markets developed
- ◆ A forward step with forward contracts
- ◆ Why standardized futures make trading possible
- ◆ Why standardized futures are better

Inside these pages you will learn how to trade in the fast-paced and exciting world of the futures markets. This market is not for the timid or meek. The futures markets are known for their extreme volatility, and the amount of leverage involved makes these markets extremely risky. You can parlay a small amount of money into a fortune because of the amount of leverage involved, but you can also lose more than your original investment. Get started on the journey by reading this first chapter on how past history shaped the current futures markets.

The World's Developing Markets

Today's futures markets are the result of principles and practices that are centuries old. Dating to the ancient Greek and Roman markets, formalized trading practices began with a fixed time and place for trading, a central marketplace, and a common currency system, as well as a method to store and deliver goods in the future.

The Forum in Rome was originally established as a trading center, while the Agora in Athens was a major commercial market for the ancient world. Despite the fall of the Greek and Roman civilizations, centralized marketplaces continued. During the Dark Ages, when centralized commerce was disrupted, products were bought and sold in scattered local marketplaces.

By the twelfth century, the scattered local marketplaces had evolved into large and quite complex fairs. These medieval fairs grew near major cities, and began to specialize not only in products but also in trade among nations. By the thirteenth century, transactions for later delivery had begun, with merchants, craftsmen, and politicians setting standards of quality to be adhered to.

> **Commodity Corn**
>
> The old medieval fairs were a place where the rule "buyer beware" was prevalent. Often, unscrupulous merchants would substitute the baby pig purchased with a cat when it was bagged to go home. When the buyer got home, he or she would "let the cat out of the bag"!

The major advances made in the medieval fair were the practices of self-regulation and arbitration, and the result they had in formalizing trading practices. In medieval England, a code known as the Law Merchant established standards of conduct acceptable to local authorities. In most cases the standards were minimal, but they formed the backbone of common practices in the use of contracts, bills of sale, freight and warehouse receipts, letters of credit, transfer of deeds, and other bills of exchange. Violators of the standards were forbidden to trade with fellow merchants, and often the punishment involved torture.

To resolve disputes between buyers and sellers, the English Merchant Association was granted the right to administer its own code of conduct by local and national authorities. By the fourteenth century, the English Merchant Association was recognized under common law as the arbitrator of trade disputes among members, allowing their assessments of penalties and awards to supersede those of local magistrates and courts. In Japan by the 1700s, *forward contracting* was done on rice. Forward contracting is a cash transaction in which a buyer and seller agree upon price, quality, quantity, and a future delivery point and time for a specific commodity. Since nothing in these forward contracts was standardized, each term of the contract was negotiated between the buyer and seller. While these forward contracts were enforceable by law, in practice they were only as good as the word of the parties involved.

The principles of self-regulation found in English Common Law followed settlers to the American colonies. Commodity markets existed in the United States as early

def•i•ni•tion

A **forward contract** is a contract between a buyer and seller in which the seller agrees to deliver a specific commodity to the buyer at some time in the future.

as 1752 and traded domestic produce, textiles, hides, metals, and lumber. Most of the transactions in the markets were simple cash transactions for immediate delivery; they greatly increased the ease and scope of trading in all types of commodities.

Chicago and the Birth of Futures

The history of modern futures trading and that of the city of Chicago are closely tied. Incorporated as a village in 1833, Chicago became a city in 1837 with a population of 4,107. Chicago's strategic location on Lake Michigan and easy access to all of the Great Lakes (as well as the fields of the Midwest) contributed to the city's rapid growth as the nation's Grain Terminal. However, problems with supply, demand, transportation, storage, and delivery led to a chaotic marketing situation, which resulted in the need for modern futures trading.

For producers and consumers in the 1800s, supply and demand was chaotic. Farmers brought grain and livestock to regional markets at certain times of the year, often finding that the supply far exceeded the demand, and the resulting prices were poor. Millers and meat packers often found supply difficult to obtain at other times of the year, which resulted in extremely high prices. Often, immediately after harvest, supply so far outweighed demand that grains were dumped in the street because of a lack of buyers at a reasonable price.

Trading Tips

Even today, much of the raw materials produced in the United States are moved by barge along the nation's waterways. The bulk of the grains and meats produced in the Midwest is moved to the East Coast by barge through the Great Lakes and up the St. Lawrence Seaway. Grain moved to the West goes down the Mississippi to New Orleans. Transportation problems today are serious, often causing short-term gaps between supply and demand, resulting in price volatility.

The glut of commodities at harvest time was only part of the problem. In some years, droughts and/or crop failures caused extreme shortages. Even in years when supply was abundant at harvest, supplies became exhausted later in the year, prices soared, and people often went hungry. Businesses lacked raw materials and faced bankruptcy, which then resulted in workers being laid off. Though rural farmers usually had enough to eat, they lacked a mechanism to sell their crops, and therefore, did not have the income necessary to pay for manufactured items such as tools, building materials, and textiles, which they needed to keep their operations running smoothly.

Transportation difficulties and a lack of adequate storage facilities aggravated the situation. Throughout most of the year, snow and rain made the dirt roads from farmlands to Chicago impassable. Although roads of wooden boards enabled farmers to bring wagonloads of grain to the city, transportation was extremely expensive and time consuming. It often cost a farmer as much to transport a wagon of wheat to Chicago as it did to produce the crop in the first place. Once the commodities reached the city, inadequate storage facilities and the lack of a developed harbor impeded the shipment of the grain to eastern markets and the return of needed manufactured goods to the West.

In response to these conditions, farmers and merchants began to contract for forward delivery. The most common early user of the forward contract was the river merchant. River merchants would buy corn from farmers in the fall and early winter at harvest. Because corn has high moisture content and the rivers were often impossible to navigate at that time of year, they would store the grain through the winter. Seeking to avoid price risk, or declining prices in the winter, river merchants would travel to Chicago and forward contract with processors for delivery of the grain in the spring. This allowed them to dry the corn during the winter and to avoid potential declining prices during the winter.

The first recorded forward contract traded in Chicago was made on March 13, 1851. The recorded contract called for the delivery of 3,000 bushels of corn to be delivered to Chicago in June at a price of one cent below the price on March 13th.

Forward contracting began in wheat slightly later. However, in the Wheat market it was the processors and Chicago merchants who faced the price risk in storing grain. Thus, the Chicago merchants sold forward contracts to wheat millers and distributors on the East Coast.

Standardized Futures

From this humble beginning, 82 merchants banded together to form the Chicago Board of Trade (CBOT) in 1848. The purpose of the Board of Trade was to establish a centralized meeting place for buyers and sellers of commodities as well as to promote the commerce of the city. During the early days of the Board, forward contracts were used.

But forward contracts had their drawbacks. They were not standardized according to quality or delivery time, and merchants and traders often did not fulfill these forward commitments. But, in 1865, the Chicago Board of Trade took the first step to making futures contracts by creating a standardized agreement—known as a *futures contract*.

Futures contracts, in contrast to forward contracts, are standardized as to quality, quantity, and time and place for delivery of the commodity being traded. A margining system was initiated that same year to

def•i•ni•tion

A **futures contract** is a legally binding agreement, made on the trading floor of a futures exchange, to buy or sell a commodity or financial instrument some time in the future. Futures contracts are standardized according to quality, quantity, and delivery time and location for each commodity. The only variable is price, which is discovered on an exchange trading floor.

eliminate the problem of buyers and sellers not fulfilling their contracts. A margining system requires both the buyer and seller of the futures contract to deposit funds with the exchange or an exchange representative to guarantee performance. This is similar to earnest money deposited on a house, where the party who backs out of the contract gets to keep the deposits. By continually adjusting the amount of money being held in margin, both sides of the futures contract are guaranteed funds equivalent to the price exposure of the underlying commodity.

Specific quality *grades* are acceptable for delivery against futures contracts. Sampling and testing of part of the deliverable commodity arrive at the quality of a commodity. A complex system of standards and safeguards protects buyers from unscrupulous sellers and low quality, while producers have a standard to meet, making selling their product easier. More accurate sampling methods and weighing measures ensure that quantity and quality issues are met on all futures contract deliveries.

def•i•ni•tion

The standard **grades** of commodities or instruments are listed in the rules of the exchange that must be met when delivering against a futures contract. Grades are often accompanied by an exchange set schedule of discounts and premiums allowable for delivery of commodities of lesser or greater quality than the standard called for by the contract rules.

Time for delivery also was standardized with the futures contract. Months were chosen—or more precisely, gradually agreed upon—by grain merchants and farmers based on harvesting and transportation conditions:

◆ March was a logical choice because the end of winter made transportation possible.

◆ May also became a delivery month because of the clean-up of old-crop oats and wheat (those harvested the previous summer).

◆ July was established as a delivery month for the same reason as May.

◆ September was agreed upon as a grain delivery month because this gave farmers a chance to sell early-harvested grains.

◆ December was chosen because it was after the fall harvest and usually the last month before winter made transportation impossible.

Standardization and a margining system also allowed speculators to enter into the grain trade.

Standardization vs. Forward Contracting

Because futures contracts are standardized, contracts are no longer between individuals, but part of the exchange. Each contract on the same commodity and delivery month is interchangeable. This is a key concept in standardization vs. forward contracting. Because each contract is the same, one can establish a futures position and exit out of it without ever accepting delivery, with the only variable being price.

For example, assume you buy one contract of Corn for March delivery, where one contract of Corn is equal to 5,000 bushels (for more details on contract specification, see Chapter 4). If at a later time, before March, you (the holder of the futures contract) wish to exit your position, you can simply sell the same futures contract, which will result in either a profit or loss depending upon the pricing at entry and exit. At no point in this process do you have to actually handle the physical grain, as the futures contract represents an obligation to make or accept delivery

Trading Tips

Most financial instruments are a commodity in the sense that they are an article of commerce or a product that can be used for commerce. For example, Treasury Bonds are a commodity because they are indistinguishable from each other, as long as the length of time to maturity is equal. Stock certificates, too, are a commodity, as one share is the same as the next. Hence we have financial instruments as commodities now.

of a specific amount and quality of a commodity at a specific point in the future. Until the futures contract enters into a delivery period, the contract can simply be offset by entering an opposite position in the futures market.

Enter the Speculator

The advent of speculators entering into the futures market allowed the market to become more efficient. Doctors, lawyers, and others not connected with the grain trade began to enter into the futures trading arena with the hopes of securing an honest profit through correctly forecasting prices in the future. Because these speculators buy or sell contracts that may not have otherwise been traded, speculators make the market larger (more liquid) and help to minimize price fluctuations.

Through standardization, growth in futures trading increased dramatically. In the late nineteenth and twentieth centuries, new exchanges were formed. Many types of commodities were traded on these exchanges, including cotton, cocoa, coffee, soybeans, sugar, cattle, hogs, orange juice, and lumber to name a few. In addition to the traditional agricultural commodities, new futures contracts have evolved on crude oil, unleaded gasoline, heating oil, gold, silver, copper, platinum, and palladium to name a few.

As the world's financial structure changed because of new monetary policies, the futures industry has expanded its contract offering so businesses and financial institutions could continue to manage price risk. In the 1970s, futures contracts on government debt (first Ginnie Mae's mortgage bonds, then treasury bonds, notes, and bills) were started. In 1975, futures contracts on foreign currencies such as the British Pound, Canadian Dollar, Swiss Franc, and Japanese Yen were conceived. Other financial instrument–based futures contracts have been invented including Stock Index futures and single stock futures contracts.

In 1982, the Chicago Board of Trade introduced another market innovation—options on futures. In contrast to futures, options on futures allow speculators and risk managers to set a predefined amount of risk in the form of the amount paid for an option and still have a chance at profits or minimizing risk. I talk more about how options on futures are bought and sold in Part 2.

Today's futures markets are larger in total dollar volume traded than all of the world's stock markets. It is truly amazing how 82 far-sighted merchants in Chicago established all of this.

The Least You Need to Know

- ◆ A forward contract is a contract between a buyer and seller in which the seller agrees to deliver a specific commodity to the buyer at some time in the future.

- ◆ A futures contract is a legally binding agreement, made on the trading floor of a futures exchange, to buy or sell a commodity or financial instrument some time in the future.

- ◆ Futures contracts are standardized according to quality, quantity, and delivery time and location for each commodity. The only variable is price, which is discovered on an exchange trading floor.

- ◆ Futures contracts are advantageous over forward contracts because they are standardized so the contract is no longer between two individuals—as in a forward contract—but between individuals and the exchange which guarantees all transactions.

- ◆ Because futures contracts are standardized, they are interchangeable, allowing positions to be entered and exited on the exchange floor without ever having to make or accept delivery of the underlying commodity.

- ◆ Futures contracts represent more than just Corn and Soybeans; today we have futures contracts on traditional commodities ranging from corn and crude oil, to contracts on Treasury Bonds, foreign currencies, and Eurodollar deposits, as well as single stock futures contracts.

How Futures Trading Works

In This Chapter

◆ The purpose of the futures markets

◆ How standardization makes for an easy "in and out"

◆ The long and short of buying and selling

◆ Learn to minimize risk with futures: hedging

◆ Speculating in the futures market

◆ How margin guarantees safety and honesty

The futures market makes it possible for those who wish to manage price risk (hedgers) to transfer that risk to those who are willing to accept it in the hopes of a profit (speculators).

Futures markets are first and foremost a risk transference vehicle. Futures markets also provide price information that the world looks to as a benchmark in determining value of a particular commodity or financial instrument on any given day or at any specific time of the day. These benefits—risk transference and price discovery—reach every sector of the economy of the world where changing market conditions create economic risk, including such diverse areas as agricultural products, foreign exchange, imports, exports, financing, and investment vehicles.

This chapter will explain how standardized futures work, and the margining system implemented to ensure that the contract is fulfilled.

Futures Contracts

As described in Chapter 1, futures contracts are standardized to meet the specific requirements of buyers and sellers for a variety of commodities and financial instruments. Quantity, quality, and delivery locations—all the essential ingredients—are pre-established. The only variable is price, which is set through an auction-like process on the trading floor of an organized futures exchange.

def•i•ni•tion

Offset is taking a second futures or options position opposite to the initial position or opening position. To offset the purchase of a futures contract, a second futures contract on the same commodity with the same delivery month is sold. To offset the sale of a futures contract, a second futures contract on the same commodity with the same delivery month is purchased.

Because futures contracts are standardized—with the only variable being price—buyers and sellers are able to exchange one contract for another and actually offset their obligation to deliver or take delivery of the commodity underlying the futures contract. *Offset* in the futures market means taking an equal and opposite position in the futures market to one's initial position.

For example, assume an individual buys one contract of March Corn at $2.25 per bushel on January 2nd, initiating a long position. This contract calls for the delivery of 5,000 bushels of #2 yellow corn seven days before the last business day of the delivery month (March) at an exchange-recognized facility.

If on February 15th, the purchaser of the March Corn contract wishes to exit his position, he can do so buy selling one March Corn contract.

Assuming that the contract was sold at $2.45 per bushel, the holder of the March Corn contract would receive $1,000.00 before brokers' commissions and fees for holding the position for six weeks:

Profit or Loss = Sale Price − Purchase Price × # of bushels

$2.45 − $2.25 = $0.20 × 5,000 = $1,000.00

Our person in this example is $1,000 richer for the experience, and has no further obligation in the Corn market because the sale of the March Corn futures contract at $2.45 per bushel offset the earlier purchase at $2.25 per bushel.

Notice in this example, that all of the features of the contract were predetermined by the exchange except price.

♦ Quantity: 5,000 bushels for Corn futures

♦ Quality of the corn: #2 Yellow

♦ Delivery time: seventh to last business day of the contract month

♦ Location: exchange-recognized warehouse or transfer station

This whole system is held in place because eventually the futures price and the cash price of the commodity will converge. For example, assume that going into delivery the March Corn futures are trading $0.05 per bushel higher than the price at which you could purchase similar corn. Farmers would rush to sell futures contracts, earning an extra $0.05 per bushel (or $250.00 per contract). However, their resulting sales would drive futures prices down and into line with the *cash market*. (The cash market will be explained more specifically in Chapter 5.)

If the futures contracts were trading at a price less than the underlying cash market, buyers would rush to the futures market to secure cheaper supply, and the resulting buy orders would drive the futures prices back up to the cash market. This process, known as *arbitrage*, ensures that the futures market always reflects an accurate price.

def•i•ni•tion

The **cash market** refers to physical commodities, which you can touch—be they corn, wheat, beef, bonds, or stock. **Arbitrage** is when you buy something in one market and sell it in another in order to profit by exploiting price differences. For example, if Corn futures were overvalued relative to the cash market, arbitragers would sell Corn futures and sell cash corn, waiting to take delivery of the corn from the futures to deliver the physical corn, pocketing the price differential. However, usually as the arbitragers buy or sell futures, they drive the price back in line with the physical market. They offset their positions at a profit.

Standardization of contract terms and the ability to offset contracts led to the rapid increase in the use of futures contracts by commercial firms and speculators. Commercial firms were quick to realize that futures markets offered them protection against price volatility without the need to make or take delivery of the physical commodity, because they could be offset. Speculators found that standardization added trading appeal to the contracts because contracts could be bought and sold, or sold and bought, at a profit if they were correct in their forecasts of price movement, without ever having to deal with the physical commodity.

The Long and Short of It

There are two basic positions one can have in the futures markets:

◆ A *long position* entails the purchase of futures contracts in anticipation of rising prices.

◆ A *short position* entails the sale of futures contracts in anticipation of lower prices.

Long Position

A long position is entered into by purchasing a futures contract. Long positions are profitable if the underlying futures contract increases in price during the holding period. A long position is offset by selling the same quantity and contract month that one initially purchased. For example, if you buy one March Corn at $2.35 per bushel, this position could be offset later by selling one March Corn contract. If the resulting sale price is higher than the entry price, then a profit is earned. If the resulting sale price is less than the original purchase price, then a loss occurs. Long positions are typically used by consumers to hedge against rising prices, and initiated by speculators in anticipation of higher prices.

def•i•ni•tion

A **long position** entails the purchase of futures contracts in anticipation of rising prices. A **short position** entails the sale of futures contracts in anticipation of lower prices.

Short Position

A short position is entered into by initially selling a futures contract. In the futures market, unlike the stock market, it is just as easy to establish a short position as a long position. Short positions are profitable if the underlying futures contract decreases in price during the holding period. Short positions are offset by buying the same quantity and contract month that you initially sold. For example, if you sell one March Corn at $2.35, this position could be offset by buying one March Corn at a later time.

If the resulting purchase price is less than the original sale price, a profit is achieved. However, if the resulting purchase price is greater than the original sale price, a loss is incurred.

Commodity producers (those who actually grow or make the product that underlies the futures contract) who wish to *avoid* potentially lower prices—as a short position increases in value as prices decline—usually establish short positions. Speculators *anticipating* lower prices in the future establish short positions.

Risk Transference: Hedging

Hedging, a major economic purpose of the futures markets, is buying or selling futures contracts to offset risks of changing prices in the cash markets. This risk transference mechanism has made futures contracts virtually indispensable in the effort to control costs and protect profits.

Commercial firms, producers, consumers, merchandisers, warehousers, and processors of commodities use futures contracts to protect themselves against changing cash prices. They are able to do so because the cash market and the futures markets usually respond to the same economic factors and tend to move in the same direction over extended periods of time. For example, news of bad weather is immediately reflected in higher cash prices as well

def•i•ni•tion

Hedging is the practice of offsetting the price risk inherent in any cash market position by taking an equal but opposite position in the futures markets. Hedgers use the futures market to protect their businesses from adverse price changes.

as futures prices as consumers seek to buy more and store it in anticipation of future supply shortages. The futures prices will also act in unison, as participants use this market to secure future supply. Hence the futures market will stay in line with the cash market, allowing the use of futures contracts to offset risks in the cash market.

For example, assume Kellogg's agrees to sell 500,000 pounds of corn meal to a European company in six months. Both agree on today's price even though the meal will not be delivered for another six months. Kellogg's does not own the corn needed at present and is concerned that prices may rise between now and when it has to purchase the 10,000 bushels of corn to process into meal and deliver. To hedge against the possibility that Corn prices may rise in the next several months, Kellogg's buys two Corn futures. When it comes time for Kellogg to buy the corn, if prices have risen, Kellogg's will have to pay more for the corn, but this loss should be mostly offset by the increase in the futures contract. However, if Corn prices decline, Kellogg's gain from purchasing a cheaper raw material (corn) will be offset by losses on the futures contract. Hence, by purchasing futures contracts, Kellogg's has "locked in" today's price, avoiding potential losses from rising raw material prices and at the same time sacrificing windfall profits from declining raw material costs.

In this example, a processor was able to secure his profit margin by locking the price of the raw material. If Corn prices had risen, the forward contract entered into may have resulted in a substantial loss. In order to guard against this, the processor entered into a long hedge by buying the futures contract to guard against rising prices. Specific examples of this are given in Chapter 5.

News of higher than expected supplies or low usage is immediately registered in lower prices, as producers rush to unload inventories before prices decrease more and consumers lower their bids for the commodity to reflect increased supply. This, too, is reflected in the futures price decreasing as buyers lower their bids and sellers rush to lock in declining prices.

For example, assume a farmer is expecting to produce a bumper crop this year and fears by harvest time the price of corn will be substantially lower (remember, greater supply = lower prices). To protect against falling prices, the producer can sell five December Corn futures, which should give him plenty of time to harvest his crop and sell it to his local co-op before the contract calls for delivery. If the farmer was correct and prices do fall in the ensuing months to harvest, he will receive a lower price for his corn from his local co-op. However, this will be offset by the gains made on the short futures position. On the other hand, if prices rise, the potential gains the farmer could have made by the increasing Corn prices will be offset by losses on his short futures position. So when the farmer sells his corn to his co-op at the beginning of November, the price he receives will be similar to today's price because any changes in the cash price will be reflected by a similar change in the futures price. In order to lock in today's price, the farmer entered into a short hedge by selling the futures contract to guard against declining prices.

For example, in August 1999, Corn prices were hovering near $2.30 per bushel nationally in the cash market, and December Corn futures were trading at $2.40 per bushel. By harvest time in mid-November, cash corn was trading at roughly $1.85 per bushel nationally, and December Corn futures were trading at $1.90. A farmer who did not hedge his crop sold his corn for –$0.35 per bushel less in mid-November than in August. The hedged farmer would have been able to recoup this –$0.35 difference by selling a futures contract, locking in the $2.40 price. On a per-contract basis, this represents a price differential of $1,750 per 5,000 bushels of corn. This could seriously affect the profitability of an operation.

In all hedging transactions, the basic idea is to establish, in advance, an acceptable price or rate of interest. Every business, regardless of whether it performs a service, produces goods, or processes commodities, is exposed to price risk in some shape or form. Without the ability to offset this risk, the prices of all the goods and services we enjoy in the economy today would be more expensive.

The ability to offset this risk allows producers and consumers to act more efficiently, and deliver their goods and services at lower prices with more attractive profit margins. It is the risk transference of futures from those wishing to avoid risk (hedgers) to those willing to accept it (speculators).

Risk Acceptance: Speculating

Speculators assume the risk that hedgers try to avoid. Profit is the motivation for *speculation*. Often viewed as a pariah feeding off of others' misery and blamed for market irregularities, speculators are an essential element in the marketplace. By being on the opposite side of hedging transactions, they provide depth to the market so it is less volatile.

Although speculators have no commercial interest in the underlying commodity, the potential for profit is what motivates them to trade commodity futures. Successful speculators gather information regarding supply and demand so they can anticipate changes, which will affect pricing. By buying and selling futures contracts, speculators also help to provide information about the impact of current events on expected future demands. In essence, speculators make the market more fluid and efficient, bridging the gap between buyers and sellers with a commercial interest. Specific examples of speculation are given in Chapter 6.

def•i•ni•tion

The dictionary defines *speculate* as follows: (1) To meditate on a subject; reflect. (2) To engage in a course of reasoning often based on inconclusive evidence; synonym: think. (3) To engage in the buying or selling of a commodity with an element of risk on the chance of profit.

Potential commodity traders should think of **speculating** as engaging in a thought process to reach a conclusion, based on incomplete facts, for the purpose

Middleman to Everything: Clearinghouses

A party to every transaction is the exchange, or more specifically the clearinghouse branch of the exchange. A clearinghouse is an agency or separate corporation of a futures exchange that is responsible for settling trading accounts, clearing trades, collecting and maintaining margin monies, regulating delivery, and reporting trading data. Clearinghouses act as third party to every futures transaction, the buyer for sellers, the seller for buyers, and guarantor of every trade.

The clearinghouse is an essential piece of the risk transference puzzle. In the days before futures contracts, forward contracts were used and negotiated between individuals. However, sometimes individuals would not honor the contract. This made the forward contract market only as good as the parties involved. Bankruptcies and widespread disasters made fulfillment of contracts difficult in some circumstances. This risk that the other side of the contract will not fulfill—known as counter-party risk—is eliminated by the clearinghouse.

Trading Tips

Though funds on deposit with a futures broker are not federally protected—like money in the bank is—all of the exchange's clearinghouses enjoy the highest quality credit ratings from rating agencies such as Standard and Poor's, Moody's, and the like. The rating for the Chicago Board of Trade Clearing Corporation is higher than the rating given to the country of Japan.

Exchange clearinghouses are able to guarantee all trades because they require all parties to make a transaction to deposit performance bond margins. Performance bond margins are financial guarantees required of both parties (buyers and sellers) of futures contracts to ensure fulfillment of the contract obligations. That is, buyers and sellers are required to take or make delivery of the commodity or financial instrument represented by the futures contract unless the position is offset before contract expiration.

Performance Bonds: Margins Guarantee Safety and Honesty

Margins are determined on the basis of market risk. Because margins are adjusted to risk, they help to assure the financial soundness of futures exchanges and provide valuable price protection for hedgers with a minimum tie-up of capital. Margins are typically set at 3 to 18 percent of the value of the commodity underlying the futures contract and are assessed each day depending upon the settlement of the underlying futures market in a process known as mark to market.

The exchange has set two types of margin requirements:

♦ Initial margin requirement is the amount of money a party must have on account with a clearing firm (your broker) at the time the order is placed. Initial margin funds must be on deposit before any trade can be accepted.

♦ Maintenance margin is a set minimum margin (per outstanding futures contract) that a party to a futures contract must maintain in his or her margin account to hold a futures position.

For example, let's assume a speculator wishes to buy March Corn at $2.10 per bushel. The Chicago Board of Trade (where Corn futures are traded) has set the initial margin requirement at $338 per contract and the maintenance margin at $250 per contract. In order to enter this order, our speculator must have at least $338 in his or her margin account before the order can be placed. In order to maintain this position, the value of the account must stay above $250. Basically, for $338 you can control $10,500 worth of Corn ($2.10 × 5,000 bushels = $10,500 contract value). This represents a deposit of 3.2 percent to control a contract of Corn.

Trading Tips

If a customer fails or is unable to meet a margin requirement, then the customer's brokerage must deposit the funds. If the brokerage firm is unable, then the broker's clearing firm must deposit funds. If the clearing firm is unable, then the exchange clearing corporation makes up the difference. In the last century, very few times has the exchange clearing firm had to cover debts, but every time it has had to, it has been up to the task.

Assuming that our speculator has $1,000 in his account, he can purchase one Corn futures contract because he has more than the initial margin of $338. Our speculator buys one March Corn futures contract at $2.10 per bushel. Because he has $1,000 in his trading account, which is more than the maintenance margin requirement at the end of the day, he can hold this position overnight. At this time, $250 of his account is transferred to the exchange's clearing firm as a guarantee of the futures contract. This money will be held by the exchange clearinghouse the entire time the position is open. Thus our speculator has an available balance in his account of $750, as $250 dollars is held by the exchange's clearinghouse to guarantee performance on the futures contract (maintenance margin).

Assume the next day that Corn prices drop because the USDA announced that corn production had increased. The price of March Corn drops from $2.10 to $2.00 per bushel in response to increasing supply. Our speculator has an open position loss of $500 in his account ($0.10 × 5,000 bushels = $500 per contract loss). His available account balance drops from $750 to $250. He can continue to hold this position because he still has an available account balance of $250, which leaves an excess of $250 beyond the maintenance margin requirement of $250 per contract. The $500 loss accrued in this trade to date is removed from his account and deposited with the exchange clearinghouse, in addition to $250 already deposited for maintenance margin.

However, if on the next day, March Corn were to trade below $1.95 per bushel, his total open position loss would be $750 (or $0.15 × 5,000 per bushel = $650 loss per contract). With a $650 loss on his futures contract, the available account value would

Trading Tips

An old market axiom is that a margin call is best left unanswered. This does not mean to not pay money you owe to your broker; this means that if you receive notice about a margin call, you should exit the losing position, as you obviously speculated wrong. The most basic concept of speculation is to maximize your winners and cut your losses. If you receive notice about a margin call, you have not sufficiently cut your losses! A margin call is best left unanswered!

be $0 ($1,000 initial – $750 loss – $250 Maintenance Margin = $0 account balance). At this point the speculator's account balance would no longer be greater than the maintenance margin level of $250 and his broker would contact him asking for him to either deposit additional funds or to offset (liquidate) his position by selling one March Corn contract. Deposits of additional funds can be required immediately—sometimes requested to be wired and received before markets are closed—but usually overnighting a check or wiring funds the next business day will suffice.

If our speculator wished to deposit more funds—not a wise thing to do—then he would have to deposit $89 to bring his account balance back above the initial margin requirement ($250 account balance + $89 deposit = $339 which is greater than the initial margin of $338).

If our speculator exits the position at $1.95, he would have an account balance of $250, as the maintenance margin funds would be returned to his account. The margin funds are always returned to the account after a position is closed, less any losses that are greater than the amount of money in the account. For example, if our speculator were to lose $0.16 per bushel, the total loss would be $800, and only $200 of the $250 maintenance margin would be returned, and the remaining $50 would be applied to the loss.

Basically, the margin system assures that each party has the financial wherewithal to be trading by first setting up a minimum standard to enter a market (initial margin) and a minimum standard to maintain an open position (maintenance margin). Think of initial margin as the little cartoon characters at Disneyland, which say you have to be at least *this* tall to ride this ride. Initial margin is the exchange's way of saying you have to be at least *this* rich to trade in this market. Maintenance margin is like the amount of money in your checking account—when it runs out, you had better stop writing checks.

In summary, initial margin is the minimum amount of money you must have in your account to open up a futures position. Maintenance margin is the minimum amount of money you must have in your account to maintain the position. So in our corn example, the initial margin was $338, meaning that a trader must have at least $338 per contract in his or her margin account before a Corn futures position can be entered into. After the position is entered into, a balance of $250 or the maintenance margin must be maintained in order for the position to be left open. If the available funds in the account—funds deposited + open position profit or loss – maintenance margin requirement—is less than zero, then more funds must be deposited or the futures positions will be closed out or offset by taking an opposite position in the futures market (long or buy positions are offset or closed by selling, while short or sell positions are offset or closed out by buying).

In our previous example, it was not necessary for the speculator to have $1,000, as $338 would have sufficed because maintenance margin requirements are taken *in the place of* initial margin requirement, not *in conjunction with*. One does not need to deposit $338 and $250 to satisfy margin, as the $250 maintenance margin is taken from the initial margin, leaving a buffer amount for safety.

Do note that in the futures market it *is* possible to lose more than your initial investment! Using the previous example, if Corn prices had dropped below $1.90, our speculator would have lost his entire $1,000 initial account balance. For example, if Corn were to trade at $1.80, our speculator would have lost his initial investment of $1,000 as well as an additional $500.

From a clearing standpoint though, the additional $500 would be paid for by the speculator's brokerage firm immediately, and credited to the exchange's clearinghouse. As you can see, margin funds ensure that everyone has enough capital to participate, and that funds are available so all transactions are paid in full. In standardized futures contracts there is no counter-party risk, as the exchange clearinghouse is the opposite side of all transactions, and all transactions are backed by margin on a daily basis.

Margins Can Vary

As you can see, the margining system is key to making futures trading viable. By requiring funds to back up positions, and the exchange clearinghouse acting as middleman to all transactions, the margining system allows contracts to offset and all counter-party risk is removed.

Margin levels are set by the exchange in accordance with the potential risk involved in the futures contract (refer to the following figure).

For example, if you wished to establish a position in the Gold market, you would have to have $2,363 in your account before placing an order to enter the market for a standard Gold contract initial margin. In order to maintain a position, the account balance would have to stay above the $1,750 maintenance margin. From this, a participant in the commodity futures market can ascertain that Gold is about seven times more risky than Corn, as Gold requires seven times the amount of margin required initially to enter this market.

Some markets, such as Natural Gas (NAT. GAS), have extremely high margin requirements for a standard contract, due to extreme volatility in the market at the current time. For example, the margin of Natural Gas was $12,150 in February 2006 because of changes in the supply and demand relationships in the gas market and the large run-up in prices. This is more than twice what it was just five years ago. Increases like these in margin requirements—though rare—can happen and are required to keep the performance bond in line with the price of the commodity. By adjusting the performance bond margin to reflect market conditions, the exchanges can guarantee that only those with sufficient funds can participate in the market, ensuring that all contracts will be honored.

Margin Requirements of 25 Popular Commodities as of February 20, 2006

Commodity	Initial Margin	Maintenance Margin	Contract Size
Metals			
Comex Gold	$2,363	$1,750	100 TROY OZ
Comex Silver	$3,038	$2,250	5000 TROY OZ
Platinum	$2,700	$2,000	50 TROY OZ

Currencies			
Dollar Index	$1,283	$950	1000 × INDEX
B Pound	$2,025	$1,500	62,500 BP
J Yen	$3,105	$2,300	12.5 MIL JY
Swiss Franc	$2,160	$1,600	125,000 SF
Grains			
Wheat	$608	$450	5,000 BU
Corn	$338	$250	5,000 BU
Oats	$540	$400	5,000 BU
Rough Rice	$513	$380	2,000 CWT
Soybeans	$1,148	$850	5,000 BU
Bean Oil	$675	$500	60,000 LBS
Softs			
Cocoa	$980	$700	10 MET. TONS
Coffee	$2,800	$2,000	37,500 LBS
Sugar	$1,400	$1,000	112,000 LBS
Cotton	$1,400	$1,000	50,000 LBS
Orange Juice	$980	$700	15,000 LBS
Lumber	$1,080	$800	110,000 BFT
Meats			
Cattle	$945	$700	50,000 LBS
Lean Hogs	$1,050	$800	40,000 LBS
Pork Bellies	$1,620	$1,200	40,000 LBS
Energies			
Crude Oil	$4,725	$3,500	1,000 BBL
Heating Oil	$6,750	$5,000	42,000 GALS
Natural Gas	$12,150	$9,000	10,000 MM BTU

The Least You Need to Know

◆ A futures position can be offset by taking a second futures or options position opposite to the initial position or opening position.

◆ The purchaser of a futures contract is said to have a long position in the futures market. The seller of a futures contract is said to have a short position in the futures market.

◆ Hedging involves taking a position in the futures market opposite your interests in the physical commodity.

◆ Initial margin is the amount of money you must have in your trading account before a position can be taken in a specific market. Maintenance margin is the amount of money you must maintain in your account in order to keep a futures position.

◆ Margin levels are set by the exchanges to guarantee performance of the futures contract. They are subject to change without notice.

◆ It is possible to lose more than your initial account balance or margin deposit in a futures position.

Chapter 3

Price Discovery and the Floor

In This Chapter

- ◆ Life in the pits: exchanges and their role
- ◆ What is all that yelling and screaming about?
- ◆ Floor traders
- ◆ The flow of a typical order, from customer to pit

Futures exchanges provide a centralized location for buyers and sellers to meet, and through an open outcry auction process, discover a price for a specific futures and/or options contract. The exchanges are also responsible for disseminating these prices and guaranteeing fulfillment of traded contracts.

The larger trading floors in the United States are the Chicago Board of Trade, Chicago Mercantile Exchange, New York Mercantile Exchange, and New York Board of Trade, plus the smaller regional exchanges—Kansas City Board of Trade and Minneapolis Grain Exchange. Everyone has indirect access to the trading floors of the world through their brokers; only exchange members have the privilege of actually trading on the floor of the exchange proper. Each exchange is unique in size, shape, governing principles, and rules, but all the exchanges in the United States have a few common characteristics.

In this chapter, we'll show you how the exchanges work, who is on the trading floor, how your orders flow through the process, and other details that will help you understand how the system operates.

Commodity Corn

A great rivalry exists between the two Chicago exchanges. For example, members of the Chicago Board of Trade refer to Chicago Mercantile Exchange members as "Merc Jerks," while the Chicago Mercantile Exchange refers to the Chicago Board of Trade as the "Board of Thieves." The rivalry between the exchanges is similar to the rivalry between baseball fans. (Don't even get me started on why the Cubs are a better team than the White Sox.)

Where It All Happens

Exchange members stand in octagonal and/or polygonal trading pits or rings, with steps descending to the center of the pit. Traders stand in groups inside the pits according to the contract month they are trading. Buyers and sellers stand throughout the pit, as any trader can be a buyer or seller at any given moment. They communicate with each other through their booming voices and hand signals developed to communicate what they are buying or selling (quantity, contract month, and price). In most cases each pit trades a particular commodity.

Adjacent to the trading pit (or sometimes in its center) are market reporters who are employed by the exchanges to record price changes as they occur (refer to the section "Order Flow from Customer to Pit" later in this chapter for more information). The recorded prices are then displayed on computerized display boards. These prices are also sent outside the exchanges to more than 50 different vendors of financial information, who in turn retransmit the information in a variety of different formats to hundreds of thousands of different subscribers. This important function of the exchange, where prices are arrived at on the floor of the exchange but disseminated to the world, is known as price transparency.

The exchanges on the web are as follows:

- ◆ www.cbot.com—Chicago Board of Trade—Trades Corn, Wheat, Soybean Complex, Treasury Bonds and Notes, and the Dow Jones Stock Indexes.

- ◆ www.cme.com—Chicago Mercantile Exchange—Trades Eurodollars, S&P Stock Index, NASDAQ Stock Index, Cattle and Hogs, Foreign Currencies, and Lumber.

- www.nymex.com—New York Mercantile Exchange—Trades Gold, Silver, Platinum, Palladium, and Petroleum Products (Crude Oil, Heating Oil, Gasoline).

- www.nybot.com—New York Board of Trade—Trades Coffee, Sugar, Cocoa, and U.S. Dollar Index.

- www.kcbt.com—Kansas City Board Of Trade—Trades Wheat and Value Line Stock Index.

- www.mgex.com—Minneapolis Grain Exchange—Trades White and Spring Wheat futures.

The futures exchanges allow the world to know what the specific commodity—based on the futures contract—is trading at any time during the exchanges' operating hours.

The Auction Market

Within each trading pit, offers to buy and sell are shouted out in an auction style known as *open outcry*. The vocalization of prices is key to the whole exchange as it allows every trader an equal opportunity to participate (in theory), allowing for a smoother flow of prices and opportunity.

def•i•ni•tion

The **bid** is the highest price the floor is quoting for the purchase of a commodity contract. The **offer** is the lowest price the floor is quoting for the sale of a commodity contract; also known as the **ask**. The difference between the bid and offer (or ask) is the **bid/ask spread**. This is known as the market. Typically when people think of a market, they think of a single price. However, markets are made up of bids and offers. The combination of a bid and offer is a market.

Traders wishing to buy a futures contract shout out *bids*, while traders wishing to sell a futures contract verbalize their offers. This is what is referred to as the market price, the highest bid and lowest offer. The *spread* between the bid and ask is how most of these guys and gals make a living, buying the bid and promptly selling the offer, hopefully pocketing the difference before prices can change against them.

The bid represents the highest price the floor is willing to pay. This is the price that the public sells at and the floor buys at. The bid is always lower than the offer or asking price. Being able to buy at the bid and sell at the offer is one of the privileges of exchange membership.

The *ask*, or offering price, is the price the floor is willing to sell contracts at. This is represented as the lowest price, which they are willing to sell at. If one were to buy a futures contract, more than likely this would be the price they would pay.

Most of the shouting one hears on the exchange floor is the posting of bids and offers. For example, trader A may yell "215 for 10!" while trader B would respond "10 at 216." Trader A has indicated that he is willing to buy 10 contracts at 215 ($2.15 per bushel), while trader B responded that she is willing to sell 10 contracts at 216 ($2.16 per bushel). This jockeying for position is carried out thousands of times a day, with trader C maybe bidding 215½ on 30 contracts and trader D responding with an offer of 50 contracts at 215¾. If trader X hears that trader D is willing to sell at 215¾, trader X may yell "Sold," indicating that he is willing to pay (buy) 50 contracts at 215¾, and a trade is consummated.

The tendering of bids and offers makes up much of the noise and mayhem on the trading floor. Bids and offers are yelled out as loud as possible, so everyone can hear. Traders in the pit have to pay attention to others' bids and offers as the highest bid and the lowest offer must be fulfilled before another bid or offer can be placed.

Using our example, trader X buys 50 contracts from trader D at 215¾. Trader X then may bid to buy more at 215½—the highest bid in the pit—or higher. If he bids 216, then trader B, who was offering to sell at 216, would sell his or her contracts to him. Or, given that trader X bought 50 at 215¾, trader B may change his or her offer to 216¼ and the shouting continues.

Trading Tips _____

If you ever find yourself in Chicago, be sure to visit the Chicago Board of Trade and Mercantile Exchanges. Both exchanges have a visitor's gallery that overlooks the trading floor. If you place your hand up to the glass of the visitor's gallery you can feel the noise. Seeing the action in the trading pits gives you a new understanding of how a market operates, and the jobs of floor brokers, traders, and others who keep the markets moving.

This system, which seems clumsy and chaotic at first, is highly effective once it is understood. Because all transactions are done in open outcry, everyone has an equal shot at the orders, ensuring fair pricing in the commodities markets. Although this system is extremely effective, in recent years a move has been underway to end the open outcry trading pits, replacing them with electronic screen-based trading. The shouting of bids and offers would be replaced by bids and offers posted on screens. Though much less glamorous, screen-based trading is effectively the same system, with microchips and processors replacing the loud voices of exchange members.

Types of Floor Traders

Exchange members can be broken down into two main categories—floor brokers and locals. These men and women who trade on the floor of the world's futures exchanges perform a variety of different functions.

Floor Brokers

Probably the most important person on the floor to readers of this book is the floor broker. Floor brokers are in the business of filling outside orders for different firms such as commission houses (like your broker), commercial interests, financial institutions, portfolio managers, processors and exporters, and the general speculating public. For each contract that the floor broker trades (buys or sells), he or she generally receives $1.00. Floor brokers generally cannot trade for their own accounts, and strictly fulfill the orders that they are handed. The floor brokers on the U.S. futures exchanges work very hard to get the best price for their customers in the fastest amount of time. They have to pay attention to all of the bids and offers, working hard to make sure that all of their orders are filled at the best possible price in the shortest amount of time. With most pits having in excess of 50 people shouting bids and offers, this can be a daunting task.

Locals

Another group of traders, known as *locals*, trade for their own accounts or the accounts of their firms (private brokers). These are the speculators who generally post bids and offers in the auction market. A bid is the highest price the trading pit is willing to pay while the offer or ask is the lowest price the pit is willing to sell at. For example, assume that March Corn is $2.15 bid and $2.15½ offer. This means that currently the traders on the floor of the Chicago Board of Trade are willing to buy March Corn at $2.15 per bushel.

There are generally three types of locals who trade for themselves:

- Day traders
- Position traders
- Scalpers

Day traders normally buy or sell several times during the day, hoping to buy ahead of rising prices and sell ahead of falling prices. They generally hold positions for several minutes to several hours. Day traders usually risk their own money, though day traders on the floor of the major exchanges manage some commodity funds. These traders are called day traders because they usually offset all of their positions at the end of each day, going home without any futures contract positions, or *flat* as it is known on the floor.

Position traders tend to hold positions for days or weeks. They are called position traders because they tend to hold positions (either long or short) overnight, taking positions home with them. Position traders range from locals trading for their own accounts, to those actively hedging positions for their firms, to large institutions speculating on the future direction of prices.

Trading Tips

Though scalpers make money being middlemen, they perform a vital function in the markets. Scalpers, because they have such a short-term outlook on prices, are always willing to buy or sell, making a market for the rest to trade against. They are the sellers to our buying and the buyers to our selling. They provide liquidity to the market.

The most essential cog in the pit is the scalper. Scalpers are ultra short-term traders who post bids and offers, always trying to buy the bid and sell the offer, *scalping* the difference. For example, assume trader D is a scalper. He yells out a bid of 215½ and an offer of 216. "215½ bid … 216 offer for 50" would be his battle cry. Assume that he managed to buy 50 at 215½ from trader Z at 9:35 CST. After buying 50 contracts of March Corn at 215½, he may then say "50 at 215¾," undercutting the 216 offers in the pit. With trader X buying 50 at 215¾, trader D was able to make $625 in less than a minute (215¾ – 215½ = ¼ cent × 250,000 bushel [50 contracts of 5,000 bushels] = $625 before commissions and fees).

Because our scalper, trader D, is an exchange member, he pays commissions of roughly $0.20 per contract—membership has its privileges—so he would make roughly $605 in a very short time by buying at the bid and selling at the offer and pocketing the difference of $12.50 per contract. After this trade is written up, and reported, trader D may bid 215¾ on 20 and offer 20 at 216¼, hoping to repeat the experience as many times as possible during the day. Essentially, a scalper strictly makes a market, with no directional bias, hoping to always buy the bid and sell the offer.

Because the scalpers are always willing to buy or sell, they ensure that the market is always two-sided—both a bid and an offer. Because he or she has always bought the bid and is always selling the offer, the scalper hopes that if prices go against them, they can get out of the trade at an equal price or a slight loss. For example, assume trader D, bids 215¾ on 20 contracts and offers 20 at 216. If someone buys 20 from him at 216, trader D may turn around and bid 216 on 20 and offer 20 more at 216¼. Being an active market-maker, trader D may be one of the first people to be able to buy at 216, getting out of the trade for profit or loss. However, if the market is rising, trader D may sell 20 more at 216¼, giving him an average price of 216⅛. If he can buy 40 at 216¼, then his losses would be $250 before commissions.

This process of buying the bid and selling the offer is repeated thousands of times each day, and hopefully at the end of the day the scalper has an average buying price less than his average selling price. In essence, by always making a two-sided market, with sufficient order in the pit, he can make a nice living just making the middle between the bid and offer.

Order Flow from Customer to Pit

The open outcry auction market of the futures exchanges is an efficient system where prices are discovered and transmitted to the outside world through the interaction of many different individuals.

The perimeter of most U.S. futures exchanges is flanked with long desks covered with computer terminals and rows of telephones. These trading desks are staffed by member firms, which act as order-taking and informational portals for the markets.

Trading Time Bomb

Many traders are tempted at the very beginning of trading to use electronic order placement via the Internet. Because a simple error can cost you thousands of dollars, beginning traders should consider a reputable full-service broker until they get their feet wet. The extra money you pay in commissions is small compared to what you could lose if you place an order wrong yourself. But, after you are comfortable with order placing, use whatever system you wish.

Assume Farmer Brown is growing corn. Seeing the price of Corn at $2.15 for May delivery, Farmer Brown decides he wishes to sell 5,000 bushels of his corn in storage to finance his planting efforts in March. Farmer Brown calls his broker, Mark at Great Pacific Trading Company (GPTC). Mark writes down Farmer Brown's order to sell one contract of May Corn (5,000 bushels) at $2.15 per bushel or better, checks to make sure that Farmer Brown has sufficient funds (initial margin), and quickly hands the order to his firm's central order desk. The order desk inputs this *ticket* (industry jargon for an order) into its computer system, which is hooked up to a computer system on the Chicago Board of Trade, where Corn futures are traded.

The order to sell one contract (5,000 bushels) of May Corn is printed out at GPTC's clearing firm's booth on the Chicago Board of Trade. The order is taken from the printer and handed to the *runner*, who quickly brings the order to the floor broker in the Corn pit. The floor broker assesses the current price of Corn; seeing that May Corn is $2.15 bid and $2.15½ offer, he sells one contract to trader D at $2.15 and writes up the trade on a ticket, which is handed back to the runner, who brings it back to his desk. The trade is punched back into the computer as "Selling one May Corn at $2.15" and sent back to GPTC. The GPTC order desk writes this up and hands the order back to Mark, who calls Farmer Brown to tell him he sold one contract of May Corn at $2.15.

The amount of time the order spent at GPTC was probably less than two minutes. After spending two minutes at GPTC, the order is on the floor, and in the pit in another two minutes, before the floor broker executes it. Usually about five minutes will pass in between the order being filled and the runner bringing it back to the desk. So within 10 minutes, the order is executed and reported back to the brokerage firm. Mark will call his client back immediately, and the entire process can take place in about 12 minutes.

In other pits, like Treasury Bonds or the Stock Indexes, orders are *flashed* into the trading pit using a complex set of hand signals from the clearing firm desk, and orders can be executed and reported back to the order desk in one to two minutes.

In the fledgling electronic markets, like the Chicago Mercantile Exchange's E-Mini S&P Stock Index Futures, orders can be filled and reported back using the computers in less than 30 seconds.

Some Final Thoughts on the Trading Floor

Futures exchanges are free markets where many different factors that influence supply and demand converge on the trading floor and through the open outcry auction market are translated into a single price. Exchanges—like the Chicago Board of Trade and Chicago Mercantile Exchange—act as barometers for price, registering the impact of the many worldwide forces on specific commodities and financial instruments being traded.

Because the same economic forces are at play in the cash and futures markets similarly, futures prices parallel the actual cash values of the commodities and financial instruments. This characteristic of futures prices allows hedgers and speculators to gauge the value of the underlying instrument in the near or distant future.

Millions of people all over the globe use the price information generated by futures exchanges to make marketing decisions—whether or not they actually participate in the futures markets. Thus, the importance of risk transference in the futures markets is magnified, because the futures markets act as a price discovery mechanism as well. By being able to access a price reference, buyers can be more competitive in their pricing of commodities, and sellers have a better reference point with which to price their goods. This translates into a more efficient market for all goods and services, and is made possible by the price discovery function of the U.S. futures markets.

Thus, the nation's futures exchanges are not only a place where risk can transferred from those wishing to avoid it (hedgers) to those willing to accept it (speculators), but they also serve a price-finding and -reporting purpose, allowing consumers and producers to reference a single price for most actively traded commodities.

The Least You Need to Know

- Futures exchanges provide a centralized location for buyers and sellers to meet and, through an open outcry auction process, discover a price for a specific futures and/or options contract.

- Floor traders can be broken down into two main categories: floor brokers (who fill customer and institutional orders) and locals, which includes private traders (who trade for their own accounts).

- Buy orders are executed on the floor's bid—or the highest price the floor is willing pay. Sell orders are executed on the floor's offer—or the lowest price the floor is willing to sell a futures contract or option for. The bid is always lower than the offer. The difference is referred to as the bid/ask spread.

- Millions of people all over the globe use the price information generated by futures exchanges to make marketing decisions—whether or not they actually participate in the futures markets.

- Orders tend to go from the client to the broker, from the broker to the Exchange trading floor desk, and from the desk to the trading pit to be executed by a floor broker and sent back to the desk to be reported to the broker who informs the client.

Chapter 4

Reading Prices

In This Chapter

◆ Letters, numbers, and symbols: reading futures quotes

◆ Dollars, and making sense of it all

◆ Reading grain, livestock, currency, metals, and financial quotes

◆ Understanding how a market is quoted

The only variable in a futures contract—as delivery time, place, quantity and quality are all specified in the contract—is price, which is discovered on an exchange trading floor. In Chapter 3, we examined how floor brokers and locals make bids and offers, creating a continuous market for buying and selling. In this chapter, we will examine how futures prices are quoted, so you can make sense of those prices and know the difference between points and cents, and dollars and digits.

Futures Quotes

Throughout the day, the price of exchange-traded futures contracts fluctuates, sometimes by a small amount and other times by a large amount. Since each futures contract is on a different commodity, ranging from corn to crude oil, soybeans to silver, or the Standard and Poor's Stock Index futures, we will break down each of the most popular commodities and how prices are quoted.

The Prices

For each commodity we will present a table with some active delivery months and prices you might expect to find in a given month. Remember, commodity trading can be very volatile, so the prices you see when you look at charts today may be very different than those quoted here. We're just showing how to read the charts, not giving actual trading numbers in any given year. Also, not all commodities are quoted the same way, with some quoted in cents, others in dollars, and yet others in fractions of a point or just points on the index. In each of our examples, we will present four prices: open, high, low, and close.

The *open* is the price which the exchange in question signifies as the opening price. Many commodities have an opening range, not a single price opening like stocks, so this is somewhat confusing. But generally the price signified as the opening is the midpoint of the opening range or a single price designated by the exchanges.

The *high* is the highest price the particular contract traded at during the trading session. This is the maximum price paid by any buyer and the maximum price received by any seller during the particular trading session.

Trading Tips

With the advent of electronic trading, many exchanges and newspapers post the open as the open of the electronic night session, not the start of the daily trading session. Before using a quote service, find which price they use, as this can alleviate some confusion down the road when placing orders or receiving price quotes on orders, as the electronic night trading sessions have some restrictions on order placement.

The *low* is the lowest price the futures contract in question traded at during the particular trading session. This represents the lowest price paid by a buyer and the lowest price received by a seller during a particular trading session.

The *close*—sometimes called the settlement—is the price at which the contract is settled at the end of the day. Like the open, the close is usually a range of prices, with the exchange designating a single price close or settle so that margin requirements can be marked to market each night. Usually the close is the average price received during the last three minutes of trading.

The *change*, which is usually quoted along with the price, is the difference between that day's close and the previous day's close.

The Commodity and Month

Above each Commodity Quote table, we will give the name of the commodity and the most common symbol used to quote it. Because futures have many different contract months that are all trading simultaneously, each futures contract receives a standard letter code along with its symbol signifying the contract month. These codes make no apparent sense, but are used throughout the industry and on TV tickers as the standard, so traders may wish to memorize them. Usually quotes appear as symbol + month + year.

The following is a list of contract month codes:

F = January	N = July
G = February	Q = August
H = March	U = September
J = April	V = October
K = May	X = November
M = June	Z = December

For example, March 2006 Corn may be quoted as CH6, with C being the symbol for Corn, H being the symbol for March, and the 6 signifying 2006. Sometimes the year is signified by two numbers such as 06 for 2006 and sometimes not. In this chapter, we're showing you how to read price quotes for the various commodities. Commodity prices won't be related to a specific year. Remember, commodity prices are volatile and can vary greatly year to year.

On some exchanges, like the New York ones, traders refer to months as holidays, so December Gold may be referred to as Christmas Gold. It is not necessary for a trader to know these, as long as when communicating with a broker you speak clearly, as September and December can sound very similar if you are eating breakfast during the conversation. (In Chapter 6, we will discuss communicating with your broker and tips about order placing.)

In the following pages, we will break down each commodity, and learn how to read the prices that are quoted. Since we have been using corn as our example to date, we will start off with the Grain Futures and move on, covering all the major commodity groups.

Preceding each sample quote, the name of the commodity, and the units of trade and contract size will be given. This information is necessary so you can compute profits or losses.

Grain Futures

Corn, Winter Wheat, Soybeans, Soybean Oil, Soybean Meal, and Oat futures are all traded on the Chicago Board of Trade. Generally the grains—except Soybean Meal and Soybean Oil—are quoted in cents per bushel. Because grain trading is extremely old, Grain prices are typically quoted including $\frac{1}{8}$ of a cent increments.

On this day, March Corn futures had an opening price of $2.15¾ cents per bushel, a high of $2.18 cents per bushel, a low of $2.15¾ cents per bushel, and a close of $2.17½ cents per bushel, up +1¼ cents per bushel on the day. Corn, like the rest of the grains, is usually quoted in cents per bushel, so you would quote the closing price of March Corn as 217½ cents, meaning the price per bushel is two hundred and seventeen and one-half cents per bushel. The +2 in the prices—like in the opening of September Corn—is $\frac{1}{8}$ of a cent or $\frac{1}{4}$ cent or $0.0025 per bushel. Grain futures are quoted in $\frac{1}{8}$ of a cent increments, even though the minimum fluctuation is $\frac{1}{4}$ of a cent.

Chicago Board of Trade Corn (C)–5,000 Bushels per Contract

	Open	High	Low	Close	Change
March	215.6	218.0	215.6	217.4	+1.2
May	223.6	226.0	223.6	225.6	+1.4
July	231.6	234.0	231.6	233.2	+1.0
September	240.2	241.4	240.2	241.2	+1.2
December	251.2	253.0	251.2	252.2	+0.6

A trader who had bought March Corn on the previous day's settlement at 216¼ would have made $62.50 before commissions and fees on his long position, as each 1-cent move in Corn is worth $50.00 ($0.01 × 5,000 bushels = $50.00).

Like Corn, Chicago Board of Trade Wheat (Soft Red Winter Wheat, to be specific) is quoted in cents per bushel. For example, March Wheat opened at 284 cents, had a session high of 285½ cents, a low of 282¼ cents, and settled at 282½ cents per bushel, down –2¾ cents on the session. Had a speculator bought March Wheat at the previous session's closing price of 285¼, he or she would have an open position loss in his or her account of –$137.50 per contract before commissions and fees (–$0.0275 × 5,000 bushels = –$137.50).

Chicago Board of Trade Wheat (W)—5,000 Bushels per Contract

	Open	High	Low	Close	Change
March	284.0	285.4	282.2	282.4	–2.6
May	295.4	297.0	293.6	294.2	–2.6
July	306.0	307.6	304.4	304.6	–2.2
September	316.4	316.6	314.6	314.6	–2.0
December	329.4	330.2	329.0	329.0	–1.4

Traders should be aware that Wheat futures are traded on the Kansas City Board of Trade as well as the Minneapolis Grain Exchange. The difference in these contracts is the type of wheat being traded. Kansas City trades Hard Red Winter Wheat, which usually trades at a higher price than the Soft Red Winter Wheat on the Chicago Board of Trade. Minneapolis trades Spring Wheat and White Wheat futures. All of these different variations on Wheat are quoted the same, in cents and $\frac{1}{8}$ of a cent per bushel. It is accepted in the industry that when one says wheat, they usually mean Chicago Board of Trade Wheat futures. Usually the other types of wheat are referred to as the city in which they are traded, such as Kansas City Wheat and Minneapolis Wheat for the Spring Wheat, while White Wheat (not very popularly traded) is referred to as White Wheat.

Like the other grains, Soybeans are quoted in cents and $\frac{1}{8}$ of a cent per bushel increments. For example, suppose March Soybeans opened at 476½ (476.4), traded as high as 479¾ (479.6) and as low as 471½ (471.4), to finally settle the trading session at 472¾ (472.6), down –4¾ cents. As with the other Grains, Soybeans are worth $50.00 per cent per contract, so a –4¾ cent move is equal to a $237.50 change, or a $237.50 profit for a short position and a loss of –$237.50 for a long position.

Chicago Board of Trade Soybeans (S)—5,000 Bushels per Contract

	Open	High	Low	Close	Change
March	476.4	479.6	471.4	472.6	–4.6
May	482.4	485.6	478.6	479.4	–4.0
July	489.4	492.6	486.2	487.0	–3.0
August	486.4	490.0	484.6	484.6	–3.2
September	481.4	483.4	479.0	479.6	–2.6
November	485.0	488.2	483.0	483.6	–2.0
January	493.4	496.0	492.4	493.0	–2.0

The Chicago Board of Trade also trades the soybean products, Soybean Oil, and Soybean Meal. Unlike the other members of the grain markets, these markets are quoted very differently and the contract sizes are radically different based on the normal increments in which they are sold.

Soybean Oil, which is a by-product of processing soybeans, is traded in cents per pound. For example, suppose March Soybean Oil opened at 14.69, or $0.1469 cents per pound. Therefore, a 1-cent move in Soybean Oil is worth $600.00 ($0.01 × 60,000 = $600.00). Prices are typically read without the decimal point, so the March Bean opening of 14.69 would be read aloud as 1469, or "fourteen sixty-nine." March Bean Oil had a high of 14.78 cents (read as 1478), a low of 14.50 (read as 1450), and settled at 14.52 cents (read as 1452), settling down –0.10 cents (down 10) on the session. The change from the previous close of 14.62 to this session close of 14.52 would equate to a loss of $60.00 on a long position and a gain of $60.00 on a short position.

Chicago Board of Trade Soybean Oil (BO)—60,000 Pounds per Contract

	Open	High	Low	Close	Change
March	14.69	14.78	14.50	14.52	–0.10
May	15.09	15.18	14.89	14.92	–0.09
July	15.50	15.56	15.30	15.32	–0.09
August	15.71	15.71	15.45	15.47	–0.05
September	15.87	15.87	15.62	15.62	–0.07
October	16.05	16.05	15.85	15.85	–0.05
December	16.27	16.33	16.15	16.15	–0.06
January	16.50	16.50	16.35	16.35	–0.02

Finally, we have a quote that actually makes perfect sense. Soybean Meal is quoted in dollars per ton, so a price of 176.4 is actually $176.40. Soybean Meal quotes are spoken just as money is, just dropping the currency, so the opening price of 176.4 on the March contract would be spoken as "one hundred and seventy-six forty" or 176.40. Because a contract of Soybean Meal calls for delivery of 100 metric tons of Meal, each 10-cent price change is worth $10.00. So March Soybean Meal opened at 176.40, had a high of 177.00—pronounced as "one seventy-seven even"—and a low of 175.60, and settled at 176.30, up 70 on the day. The holder of a long futures position in March Soybean Meal would have made $70.00 per contract on this day, while a person with a short position would have lost $70.00 per contract based on the closing price.

Chicago Board of Trade Soybean Meal (SM)–100 Metric Tons per Contract

	Open	High	Low	Close	Change
March	176.4	177.0	175.6	176.3	+0.7
May	171.8	173.0	171.3	172.1	+0.6
July	170.8	172.4	170.3	171.0	+0.8
August	169.5	170.8	169.3	169.9	+1.1
September	168.5	169.5	168.0	168.8	+1.0
October	166.0	167.8	166.0	166.8	+0.8
December	166.5	167.5	165.5	166.5	+0.6
January	166.2	166.2	166.2	166.2	+0.1

Like the other grains, Oats, too, are quoted in cents and ⅛ of a cent per bushel incre-ments. For example, suppose March Oats opened at 107 (107.0), traded as high as 107¾ (107.6) and as low as 106 (106.0), to finally settle the trading session at 106¼ (106.2), unchanged on the session (0.0). As with the other grains, Oats are worth $50.00 per cent per contract, but since Oats settled unchanged from the previous session, an open position in the Oat market would be worth as much as it was on the previous day.

Chicago Board of Trade Oats (O)–5,000 Bushels per Contract

	Open	High	Low	Close	Change
March	107.0	107.6	106.0	106.2	0.0
May	113.2	114.0	112.0	112.2	0.0
July	118.6	119.6	118.0	118.0	0.0
September	123.6	124.0	123.0	123.0	0.0
December	129.4	129.6	129.0	129.0	0.0
March	135.0	135.0	135.0	135.0	0.0

With a little practice, understanding grain quotes is not that difficult. One just has to remember that Corn, Wheat, Soybeans, and Oats are all traded in cents and one-eighths of a cent. Each 1-cent move is worth $50.00 per contract. Soybean Oil and Meal are quoted slightly differently and are worth different amounts based on their contract sizes ($600 per cent and $100 per dollar, respectively). Some of the other contracts are even more confusing.

Meat Futures

Meat complex futures are generally quoted in cents per pound and include the Live Cattle, Feeder Cattle, Lean Hog, and Pork Belly futures and are all traded on the Chicago Mercantile Exchange. The difficult part about making sense of Meat market quotes is that they are traded in 0.02½ cent increments, but the quotes are generally rounded down to the nearest 0.01 cent increment. Each 0.02½ cent increment is valued at $10.00 ($0.00025 pound × 40,000 pounds = $10 per contract minimum move).

Chicago Mercantile Live Cattle (LC)—40,000 Pounds per Contract

	Open	High	Low	Close	Change
February	80.07	80.32	79.35	79.62	−0.57
April	79.65	79.82	79.05	79.52	−0.33
June	73.85	73.92	73.20	73.52	−0.37
August	73.60	73.67	72.95	73.30	−0.30
October	74.90	74.95	74.37	74.62	−0.27
December	75.70	75.80	75.35	75.55	−0.27

For example, suppose February Live Cattle futures had an opening price of $0.80075 cents per pound, a high of $0.80325 cents per pound, a low of $0.7935 cents per pound, and a close of $0.79625 cents per pound, down −$0.00575 per pound on the day. However, prices are read in cents, so an opening of 80.07 would be 80.07½ cents per pound, with the final 0.00½ cent increment dropped from the quote. Because the Meat Complex futures are quoted in 0.02½ cent increments, whenever you see a price in the meats ending in either a 0.02 or 0.07, the actual price is 0.02½ cents and 0.07½ cents. This 0.00½ increment is equivalent to $2.00 per contract, and who doesn't care about an extra $2.00?

Instead of February, let's look at the October contract. October Live Cattle opened at 74.90 cents (said as "seventy-four ninety"), had a high of 74.95 cents ("seventy-four ninety-five") and a low of 74.375 cents ("seventy-four thirty-seven and a half"), and settled at 74.625 cents ("seventy-four sixty-two and a half"), down 0.275 cents ("down twenty-seven and a half"). Notice how on the low of 74.37 the extra ½ (0.0005) was left off, as well as on the close of 74.62.

A trader who happened to have bought October would have lost $110.00 today before commissions and fees, while a person with a short position would have made $110.00 ($0.00275/pound × 40,000 pounds = $110.00).

Chicago Mercantile Feeder Cattle (FC)–50,000 Pounds per Contract

	Open	High	Low	Close	Change
January	88.30	88.45	88.25	88.35	−0.45
March	88.90	89.25	88.85	89.15	−0.35
April	88.65	88.90	88.65	88.80	−0.47
May	88.10	88.15	88.00	88.08	−0.22
August	88.35	88.60	88.35	88.50	−0.15
September	88.30	88.30	88.25	88.25	0.00
October	88.27	88.27	88.27	88.27	+0.02
November	88.50	88.75	88.50	88.67	−0.07

Feeder Cattle futures are quoted the same way as Live Cattle futures, in cents per pound. Like Live Cattle, Feeder Cattle trades in 0.02½ cent increments, though the last 0.00½ is dropped from price quotes for simplicity (0.02 = 0.02½ and 0.07 = 0.07½). So, looking at the January Feeder Cattle futures, they opened at 88.30 cents, had a high of 88.45 cents, a low of 88.25 cents, and settled at 88.35 cents, up +0.45 cents. The +0.45 cent move is worth $225.00 ($0.0045 × 50,000 = $225.00). Traders in a long position would see this amount debited from their accounts at the end of the day, while traders in a short position would see this amount credited to their account.

Chicago Mercantile Lean Hogs (LH)–40,000 Pounds per Contract

	Open	High	Low	Close	Change
February	56.60	57.20	56.40	56.80	+0.47
April	59.40	59.75	59.10	59.65	+0.57
June	64.45	64.80	64.40	64.65	+0.25
July	61.55	61.90	61.55	61.75	+0.30
August	59.40	59.60	59.35	59.60	+0.35
October	51.70	51.95	51.70	51.95	+0.27
December	48.75	49.00	48.70	51.95	+0.27

Lean Hog futures are quoted the same way as Live Cattle futures, in cents per pound. Like Cattle, Lean Hogs trade in 0.02½ cent increments, though the last 0.00½ is dropped from price quotes for simplicity (0.02 = 0.02½ and 0.07 = 0.07½).

So looking at the February Lean Hog futures, they opened at 56.60 cents, had a high of 57.20 cents, a low of 56.40 cents, and settled at 56.80 cents, up +0.47½ cents. The +0.47½ cents move is worth $190.00. Traders in a long position would see this amount credited to their accounts at the end of the day, while traders in a short position would see this amount debited from their accounts (losses are taken out just like gains are put in each night).

Chicago Mercantile Pork Bellies (PB)—40,000 Pounds per Contract

	Open	High	Low	Close	Change
February	70.00	70.40	69.20	69.65	+0.92
March	70.50	70.80	69.80	70.00	+0.90
May	71.10	71.20	70.95	70.95	+1.35
July	70.00	71.30	70.00	70.40	−0.70
August	69.50	69.50	69.50	69.50	−1.50

Pork Belly futures trade the same way as the rest of the Meats, in 0.02½ cent increments, with the final 0.00½ cent dropped. For example, February Pork Bellies opened at 70.00 cents, traded as high as 70.40 cents and as low as 69.20 cents, and finally settled at 69.65 cents, up 0.92½ cents on the day. The holder of a long position would be credited $370.00 ($0.00925 × 40,000 = $370.00) while the holder of a short position would be debited $370.00, as the position is marked to market at the end of the session.

Metals Futures

Gold, Platinum, and Palladium futures are quoted in dollars per troy ounce, while Silver futures are quoted in cents per troy ounce, and Copper futures are quoted in cents per pound. This market group's quotes are straightforward, with decimal pricing and no digits dropped.

New York Mercantile Gold (GC)—100 Troy Ounces per Contract

	Open	High	Low	Close	Change
February	266.3	267.2	265.5	265.7	+0.9
April	268.9	269.4	267.9	268.2	+1.0
June	271.1	271.5	270.5	270.5	+1.1
August	272.0	272.0	271.1	271.3	+0.1
October	273.0	273.0	273.0	273.0	+0.1
December	276.3	276.3	276.0	276.0	+1.4

February Gold settled on this day at $265.70 per troy ounce, for a contract value of $26,570 worth of Gold per contract. This quote is read exactly as it appears, so it would be quoted as "two hundred and sixty-five seventy" with the decimal dropped, just like amounts are quoted in the rest of the world—the last numbers are implied as cents. So Gold for February delivery opened at $266.30 per ounce, traded as high as $267.20 per ounce and as low as $265.50 per ounce, to finally settle at $265.70 per ounce, up +$0.90 (90 cents). The holder of a long position would be credited $90.00 for this day's movement while the holder of a short position would be debited $90.00 per contract ($0.90 × 100 ounces = $90 per contract).

New York Mercantile Platinum (PL)—50 Troy Ounces per Contract

	Open	High	Low	Close	Change
January	623.0	623.0	623.0	617.0	+7.4
April	622.5	622.5	618.0	618.0	+10.4
July	607.8	607.8	607.8	607.8	+8.2
October	605.8	605.8	605.8	605.8	+8.2

Platinum trades in the same fashion as Gold futures, except that the contract calls for delivery of only 50 ounces of Platinum versus the 100 ounces for Gold. Platinum for April delivery opened this trading day at $622.50 per ounce, traded as high as $622.50 per ounce and as low as $618.00 per ounce, to finally settle the session at $618.00 per ounce, up $10.40 per ounce. The contract value at settlement for Platinum would be worth $30,900 per contract ($618/ounce × 50 ounces = $30,900). The gain of $10.40 per ounce would result in a gain of $520 per contract for the holder of a long position and a loss of $520 per contract for the holder of a short position.

New York Mercantile Silver (SI)–5,000 Troy Ounces per Contract

	Open	High	Low	Close	Change
January	474.9	474.9	474.9	474.9	–4.5
March	479.5	481.0	474.0	475.5	–7.0
May	483.5	483.5	477.5	480.0	–6.6
July	487.0	487.0	480.5	483.0	–6.7
September	494.0	494.0	490.0	490.0	–3.2
December	498.0	498.0	489.50	489.5	–7.2

Unlike the other metals discussed so far, Silver futures trade in cents per ounce. For example, suppose the March Futures settled this day at a cost of $4.75½ cents per ounce, though the futures are quoted in cents, so the quote would be read as 475.5 cents per ounce. The contract value for Silver is $23,775, or $4.755 × 5,000 ounces.

New York Mercantile Copper (HG)–25,000 Pounds per Contract

	Open	High	Low	Close	Change
January	86.00	86.00	85.25	85.30	–1.40
February	86.20	86.20	85.10	85.15	–1.35
March	86.10	86.10	84.65	84.75	–1.40
April	85.05	85.05	84.30	84.30	–1.25
May	85.30	85.30	84.00	84.05	–1.20
June	84.15	84.15	83.95	83.95	–1.20
July	84.70	84.90	83.90	83.90	–1.15
August	83.80	83.080	83.80	83.80	–1.15
September	84.80	84.80	83.75	83.75	–1.15
October	84.20	84.20	83.70	83.70	–1.15
November	83.75	83.75	83.75	83.75	–1.15
December	83.75	83.75	83.75	83.75	–1.15

Copper, or more specifically High Grade Copper futures (now are the symbols making a little sense?), trades similarly to Silver and is quoted in cents per pound. For example, suppose February Copper futures settled at $0.8515 cents per pound. The February contract opened at 86.20 cents, traded as high as 86.20 cents and as low as

85.10 cents, before settling at 85.15 cents, down –1.35 cents. The contract value of the February Copper contract would be $21,287.50 cents. The holder of a long position would have their account debited –$337.50 from the $1.35 cent loss, while a short position holder would have their account value increase +$337.50 when the position is marked to market for margin purposes.

Petroleum Futures

The New York Mercantile Exchange trades futures contracts on Crude Oil, Heating Oil, and Unleaded Gasoline. Do not try to equate the prices you see at the pump with those at the futures exchanges, as the United States gasoline taxes and state taxation on fuels is not considered in the futures contract price. Taxes account for almost half the cost per gallon, so this exercise will only serve to frustrate you if you are anything like me.

Petroleum futures are quoted in dollars per barrel for Crude Oil and dollars per gallon for Heating Oil and Unleaded Gasoline. Since Unleaded and Heating Oil typically trade for less than two dollars per gallon (remember, this is before Federal and State taxes), they are usually displayed with a decimal point or in cents.

New York Mercantile Crude Oil (CL)—1,000 Barrels per Contract

	Open	High	Low	Close	Change
February	30.50	32.40	30.14	32.19	+1.74
March	28.65	30.30	28.38	30.19	+1.52
April	27.80	29.50	27.51	29.29	+1.51
May	27.15	28.80	26.92	28.56	+1.39
June	26.65	28.05	26.44	27.98	+1.29
July	26.29	27.50	26.25	27.50	+1.22
August	26.15	27.06	26.15	27.06	+1.14
September	25.70	26.66	25.70	26.66	+1.08
October	25.60	26.30	25.60	26.30	+1.01
November	25.99	25.99	25.99	25.99	+0.96
December	24.60	25.68	24.60	25.68	+0.89
January	24.81	25.43	24.75	25.43	+0.85

Crude Oil is quoted in dollars per barrel, so the quotes are very straightforward to read. February Crude Oil futures settled this trading day at $32.19 per barrel, gaining +$1.74 per barrel for the session. Because Crude Oil trades in 1,000 barrels per contract, a $1.00 move in Crude Oil futures is worth $1,000 and the contract value of the February Contract would be $32,190 on this day. The holder of a long position would see an increase of $1,740 in his account, while a short position holder would have lost an equal amount when this was marked to market for margin purposes ($1.74 per barrel × 1,000 barrels = $1,740).

New York Mercantile Heating Oil (HO)—42,000 Gallons per Contract

	Open	High	Low	Close	Change
February	0.8775	0.8820	0.8625	0.8725	+0.0310
March	0.8390	0.8430	0.8275	0.8350	+0.0325
April	0.7904	0.7970	0.7850	0.7890	+0.0275
May	0.7550	0.7560	0.7550	0.7560	+0.0280
June	0.7390	0.7390	0.7330	0.7350	+0.0230
July	0.7280	0.7330	0.7240	0.7270	+0.0210
August	0.7280	0.7280	07280	0.7280	+0.0210
September	0.7195	0.7354	0.7195	0.7354	+0.0244
October	0.7240	0.7399	0.7240	0.7399	+0.0244
November	0.7400	0.7400	0.7400	0.7400	+0.0205
December	0.7400	0.7400	0.7400	0.7400	+0.0160
January	0.7400	0.7400	0.7400	0.7400	+0.0180

Heating Oil is quoted in dollars per gallon, so the above prices are in fractions of a dollar. For example, February Heating Oil settled this trading day at $0.8725, or 87.25 cents per gallon. With a contract size of 42,000 gallons, the February Heating Oil contract controls $36,645 worth of Heating Oil. Each 1-cent move (0.0100) represents a change of $420 per contract. The holder of a long Heating Oil position on this day would have seen a gain in their account of $1,302 based on the +$0.0310 increase in Heating Oil prices, while the holder of a short position would have seen an equal loss.

New York Mercantile Unleaded Gasoline (HU)—42,000 Gallons per Contract

	Open	High	Low	Close	Change
February	0.8580	0.8900	0.8500	0.8812	+0.0232
March	0.8396	0.8700	0.8320	0.8611	+0.0237
April	0.8738	0.9100	0.8670	0.8966	+0.0247
May	0.8603	0.8880	0.8603	0.8816	+0.0231
June	0.8470	0.8680	0.8470	0.8626	+0.0221
July	0.8360	0.8450	0.8300	0.8386	+0.0211
August	0.8200	0.8200	0.8116	0.8116	+0.0201
September	0.7816	0.7816	0.7816	0.7816	+0.0196
October	0.7350	0.7460	0.7350	0.7406	+0.0186
November	0.7200	0.7231	0.7200	0.7231	+0.0181
December	0.7100	0.7136	0.7100	0.7136	+0.0176
January	0.7100	0.7111	0.7100	0.7111	+0.0171

Unleaded Gasoline trades in the same fashion as Heating Oil, in dollars per gallon. For example, suppose February Unleaded Gasoline settled at $0.8812 per gallon, or 88.12 cents per gallon, up 2.32 cents per gallon. With a contract size of 42,000 gallons—the same as Heating Oil—this represents a gain of $974.40 per contract held long and a loss of an equal amount per short contract. The February contract represents $37,010.40 worth of Heating Oil.

Food and Fibers (or the Softs)

All of the groups of futures contracts we have discussed so far have been based on similar commodities like Grains, Meats, Metals, and Petroleum. The Food and Fiber futures, also known as the Softs, are a hodgepodge of commodities ranging from Coffee to Cocoa, and Sugar to Orange Juice. Though the rules for reading these quotes are not homogenous, the same basic principles apply.

Many members of the Softs are traded on the New York Board of Trade (NYBOT) including Coffee, Sugar, and Cocoa, as well as Cotton and Orange Juice futures.

NYBOT Coffee Futures (KC)—37,500 Pounds per Contract

	Open	High	Low	Close	Change
March	67.25	68.70	67.00	68.30	+1.55
May	69.90	71.40	69.80	70.95	+1.35
July	72.75	74.10	72.75	73.65	+1.25
September	75.50	77.00	75.40	76.25	+1.25
December	79.50	80.75	79.50	80.35	+1.45

Coffee futures are traded in cents per pound. Suppose March Coffee futures settled at 68.30 cents per pound, or $0.6830 per pound. Each 1-cent move in Coffee is worth $375.00. Based on this, one can see that the contract value of the March futures is $25,612.50; the holder of a long Coffee futures contract would have gained $581.25 per contract and a short position holder would have lost an equal amount per contract based on the +1.55 cent gain in Coffee futures during this session.

NYBOT Sugar #11 Futures (SB)—112,000 Pounds per Contract

	Open	High	Low	Close	Change
March	9.83	10.16	9.83	10.09	+0.22
May	9.53	9.83	9.53	9.74	+0.21
July	8.93	9.17	8.93	9.10	+0.21
October	8.53	8.74	8.53	8.70	+0.21

The most actively traded Sugar futures contract is for Sugar #11, which specifies the grade of Sugar to be delivered. This is also known as "Domestic Sugar" in some circles, as opposed to "World Sugar" futures, which also trade, but very sporadically. World Sugars are based on Sugar in the World Sugar Federation quota system and is subject to changes in the quota system, which is why it is not traded as much as Sugar #11 futures on the NYBOT.

Sugar futures are quoted in cents per pound, with a Sugar contract calling for the delivery of 112,000 pounds of refined sugar—either cane or beet. Prices are read as such. Suppose March Sugar futures settled at 10.09 cents per pound, or $0.1009 per pound. Based on this day's settlement, one contract of Sugar #11 futures controls $11,300.80 worth of Sugar. Holders of a long position in Sugar on this day would have gained $246.40 per contract while holders of a short position would have lost an equal amount per contract, based on the +0.22 cent gain. Each 1-cent move in Sugar is equal to $1,120 per contract.

NYBOT Cocoa Futures (CC)—10 Metric Tons per Contract

	Open	High	Low	Close	Change
March	960	975	935	957	–39
May	960	968	935	958	–38
July	960	969	947	968	–33
September	973	980	960	980	–30
December	990	1003	985	1003	–33

Cocoa futures are very straightforward to read, with Cocoa trading in dollars per metric ton. Each $1 move represents a gain or loss of $10.00. For example, suppose March Cocoa futures settled this session at 957 dollars per ton, down –39 dollars per ton. Trading is done in $1 increments. This contract represents control of $9,570 worth of Cocoa. The holder of a short position in this contract would have gained $390 during this trading session while those with long positions would have lost an equal amount (–$39/ton × 10 tons/contract = –$390 per contract).

NYBOT Orange Juice Futures (OJ)—15,000 Pounds per Contract

	Open	High	Low	Close	Change
March	78.35	79.00	76.95	76.95	–1.80
May	81.80	82.25	80.50	80.60	–1.45
July	84.40	84.40	83.55	83.55	–1.30
September	86.50	86.50	86.30	86.30	–0.80
November	88.70	88.70	88.70	88.70	–0.85

Though we think of orange juice in the form of gallons, it is sold in solid frozen state (which is why it is quoted in pounds). Each Orange Juice contract represents 15,000 pounds and is quoted in cents per pound. For example, suppose March Orange Juice futures settled at 76.95 cents per pound ($0.7695 per pound), losing –1.80 cents. The March contract controls $11,542.50 worth of Orange Juice; the holder of a short position would have gained $270 per contract while the holder of a long position would have lost an equal amount based on the loss of –1.80 cents per pound during this session.

NYBOT Cotton Futures (CT)—50,000 Pounds per Contract

	Open	High	Low	Close	Change
March	60.15	61.35	60.15	60.63	+0.13
May	61.55	62.70	61.55	61.82	−0.15
July	62.80	63.80	62.80	63.01	−0.17
October	62.45	62.60	62.25	62.25	−0.25
December	62.45	62.60	62.25	61.90	−0.34

Cotton futures are traded in cents per pound. For example, suppose March Cotton futures settled this session at 60.63 cents per pound, or $0.6063 per pound. Each 1-cent move is equal to $500 per contract. The holder of a long position in March Cotton would have gained $65.00 per contract while the holder of a short position would have lost an equal amount based on the +0.13 cent gain in Cotton futures on this day. The March contract would control $30,315 worth of Cotton based on current prices.

Financial Futures

Up until this point we have concentrated on commodity futures contracts. But, starting in the 1970s, futures contracts have been expanded to include financial instruments ranging from interest rate vehicles (Eurodollars and Treasury Bonds) to Currencies (Japanese Yen, British Pound, and Canadian Dollar) and Stock Index Futures (Dow Jones Average, S&P Futures, S&P E-mini Futures).

The same basic principles apply to these instruments as to standard commodities. Each of the financial instruments is standardized as to amount, time, and delivery points. These quotes can be a little more difficult to read, but these markets offer some fantastic trading opportunities.

Interest Rate Vehicles

The most heavily traded interest rate vehicles in the world of futures are Eurodollar futures and Treasury Bonds. Both of these markets represent interest rates, but how they are quoted certainly shows the difference between them.

CME Eurodollars (ED)—Yield on 3-Month $1,000,000 Deposit

	Open	High	Low	Close	Change
March	94.7400	94.7800	94.7400	94.7450	+0.1000
June	95.0100	95.0700	95.0100	95.0200	+0.0350
September	95.0600	95.0900	95.0450	95.0650	+0.0150
December	94.8400	94.8700	94.8050	94.8350	−0.0350

Eurodollars is the term used for U.S. Dollars on deposit in foreign banks. Eurodollar futures represent the yield to maturity of these deposits. The applicable yield can be calculated by subtracting the futures value from 100 (100 − Futures = Yield). Because Eurodollars are a yield-based instrument, they move in the opposite direction of interest rates. If interest rates are rising, Eurodollar futures decline and vice versa.

The quotes for Eurodollar futures are easy to read, as they are read just as they appear. For example, suppose the March Eurodollar futures settled at 94.7450 (read as "ninety-four seventy-four fifty"). They trade in 0.0005 increments representing 0.005 percent. Each 0.01 incremental change is worth $25 per contract, as the contract calls for $1,000,000 deposit and the yield is on a 3-month deposit (0.0001 × 1 million × .25 = $25.00 per contract). For example, suppose March Eurodollars settled at 94.7450 (yield of 5.255 percent), gaining +0.1000 basis points for a gain of $250 per contract held long and an equal loss on short positions (.01 × 100 × 25 = $250.00).

CBOT Treasury Bonds (US)—$100,000 of 30-Year Bonds per Contract

	Open	High	Low	Close	Change
March	103.14	103.20	103.01	103.06	−1.18
June	103.04	103.10	102.26	102.29	−1.19
September	102.21	102.21	102.21	102.21	−1.20
December	102.11	102.11	102.11	102.11	−1.21

Unlike Eurodollars, 30-Year Treasury Bonds are price denominated and trade in basis points and $1/32$ of basis points. For example, suppose the March Treasury Bonds settled at 103⁶/₃₂, or 103.06. Treasury instruments are quoted in fractions, but the denominator (bottom number) is left off. Hence, when you see the −06, it means $6/32$. Usually when quotes are given, the denominator is also left off, so the March settlement value would be read as "one hundred and three zero six," but it is also not uncommon for the denominator to be given by brokers, as in "one hundred and three and six thirty-seconds." Each $\frac{1}{32}$ move in the Treasury Bond contract is worth $31.25 per contract. So a trader in a short March Treasury Bond futures contract position would have made $1,562.50 while a trader with a long position would have lost an equal amount based on the bond contract declining $1^{18}/_{32}$. Usually price changes are given in full points and "–" fractions, or $^{32}/_{32} + {^{18}/_{32}} = 1^{18}/_{32}$.

Currency Futures

Though the start of a common European Currency Unit (also known as the "Euro-dollar" or "Euro FX" so as to not confuse this futures contract with the interest rate vehicle) has put a damper on currency future trading, it is still a fairly popular avenue of trading.

Currency futures are quoted in terms of dollars per foreign currency.

CME Euro FX Futures (EC)–$100,000 per EC, per Contract

	Open	High	Low	Close	Change
March	0.9369	0.9409	0.9283	0.9390	+0.0028
June	0.9405	0.9409	0.9298	0.9409	−0.0066

Reading and understanding Currency futures quotes can be a little difficult. First, a foreign currency quote represents an exchange rate. For example, the above quote says that one Euro FX is worth $0.9390 (roughly 94 cents to buy one Euro FX). All Foreign Currency futures are quoted in dollars per foreign currency. For world travelers this can be confusing, as you are used to thinking the other way around. As a U.S. traveler, you usually seek a quote of how many Euros you can get for a dollar.

Reading the March Quote table, it settled on this day at 0.9390, or "ninety-three ninety," gaining 0.0028 points. Each 0.0100 move is worth $1,000 per contract, so on this day the holder of a long futures position would have gained $280.00 per contract while a short position holder would have lost an equal amount per contract.

CME Canadian Dollar Futures (CD)–$100,000 per CD per Contract

	Open	High	Low	Close	Change
March	0.66313	0.6639	0.6600	0.6612	+0.003
June	0.6633	0.6645	0.6601	0.6616	+0.002

Canadian Dollar futures are read the same way as Euro FX futures. Each 0.01-point change is worth $1,000 per contract. The above quote signifies that it takes roughly 66.12 cents to buy one Canadian Dollar, or $1.51 Canadian to equal one U.S. Dollar.

CME British Pound Futures (BP)—$62,500 per BP, per Contract

	Open	High	Low	Close	Change
March	1.4664	1.4664	1.4664	1.4644	+0.0004
June	1.4530	1.4650	1.4520	1.4636	−0.0074

As one can see from the previous quotes—which are read the same as the rest of the currency quotes—the British Pound is worth more than $1.00. Using the March futures contract as a basis, it takes roughly $1.46 to buy one Pound Sterling (God save the Queen!). The other interesting thing about British Pound futures is the unique contract size, or $62,500 worth of Pounds. Each 0.0001 move in the British Pound is worth $6.25. So reading the March futures, which settled at 1.4644, up +0.0004, a speculator with a long futures position would have gained $25.00 while a short positioned trader would have lost an equal amount.

CME Japanese Yen Futures (JY)—$1,250,000 per JY, per Contract

	Open	High	Low	Close	Change
March	0.8668	0.8668	0.8668	0.8668	+0.0062
June	0.8775	0.8775	0.8735	0.8763	+0.0119

The Japanese Yen futures are quoted the same way, though they should really be displayed as with two leading zeros first (0.008669 versus 0.8668 for the March futures contract) as it takes roughly 8 U.S. cents to buy 1 Yen. However, with the larger contract size, the Yen futures are worth $12.50 per 0.0001-point move. For example, the March futures settled at 0.8668, gaining +0.0062 points, equating to a gain of $775.00 for the holder of a long position per contract and a similar loss for the holder of a short position per contract.

Index Futures

An index is a representative grouping. Futures contracts are traded on Stocks Indexes, like the Dow Jones Industrial Average, as well as a Dollar Index. Indexes are quoted in terms of points, and contract sizes are based on number of indexes.

NYFE Dollar Index (DX)—1000 Times Index Value

	Open	High	Low	Close	Change
March	109.96	110.68	109.52	110.65	+0.76
June	109.99	110.68	109.99	110.68	+0.76

A division of the New York Cotton Exchange, the New York Financial Exchange (NYFE) trades a futures contract based on a compilation of the U.S. Dollar versus a basket of 35 different currencies. This index is quoted in points, and profits and losses are based on 1,000 times the Index value. Quotes are simply read exactly as they appear above. Each 0.01-point move is worth $10 per contract. For example, the March futures closed at 110.65, gaining +0.76 points. The holder of a long futures contract would have made $760 per contract while a short position holder would have lost an equal amount based on a change of +0.76 points.

CME S&P 500 Stock Index (SP)—250 Times Index Value

	Open	High	Low	Close	Change
March	1347.50	1364.20	1341.00	1358.50	+10.00
June	1363.00	1380.00	1360.50	1374.00	+10.00

The Standard and Poor's 500 Stock Index is a basket of the 500 largest companies in America with listed securities. This widely quoted proxy for the U.S. Stock Market also has futures traded on it. The S&P 500 Index contract is a popular trade with day traders as it allows for position in the stock market itself, as opposed to individual stocks. Add in the attractive margins on this index versus buying an equivalent amount of stock and you can see why speculators love this contract and its cousin, the E-mini. Quoted in terms of points, with each full point being worth $250.00, the S&P is an excellent proxy for the stock market. Reading the quotes is easy. For example, suppose the March futures settled at 1358.50, up +10.00; that equates to a gain of $2,500 per contract for those with long positions and a loss of an equal amount for short positions.

The E-mini S&P futures are quoted the same way, except the contract size is only $50.00 per point. For example, a holder of a long E-mini futures contract would have netted only $500 per contract with a corresponding 10.00 point gain on the day.

Understanding Financial Displays

Understanding how a market is quoted is a slightly daunting task, but with a little practice reading the financial section of your paper or visiting your favorite website, it will become second nature.

Each futures contract has its own way of displaying prices, with the Grains showing prices in $\frac{1}{8}$ of a cent increments, the Meats showing prices in .02$\frac{1}{32}$ of a cent increments, and Bonds showing prices in $\frac{1}{32}$ of a point increments.

However, once you understand how each contract is quoted, figuring out your profit or loss due to a change in pricing is easy. Simply multiply the contract size times the price change in dollars per unit. The following is a quick-and-dirty cheat sheet you can use.

It is also imperative that users of the futures markets understand how quotes are given before they start trading. Misquoting prices can cause serious loss of capital. In Chapter 5, we will detail the popular order types for placing commodity positions. Using this information in conjunction with the knowledge we learned in this chapter, we will walk you through how to hedge your obligations in the futures markets or how to start speculating in the futures markets, by devoting example-filled chapters to both hedging and speculating.

Minimum

	Symbol	Contract Size	Units	$/Unit	Fluctuation
		METALS			
COMEX GOLD	GC	100 TROY OZ	$/OZ	1PT = $1	10 PT = $10
COMEX SILVER	SI	5,000 TROY OZ	CTS/OZ	1CT = $50	½CT = $25
PLATINUM	PL	50 TROY OZ	$/OZ	$1 = $50	10CTS = $5
COMEX COPPER	HG	25,000 LBS	CTS/LB	1PT = $2.50	5PTS = $12.50
PALLADIUM	PA	100 TROY OZ	$/OZ	1PT = $1	5PTS = $5
		CURRENCIES			
DOLLAR INDEX	DX	1,000 × INDEX	PTS	1PT = $10	1PT = $10
B POUND	BP	62,500 BP	CTS/BP	1PT = $6.25	2PT = $12.50
J YEN	JY	12.5 MIL JY	CTS/JY	1PT = $12.50	1PT = $12.50
SWISS FRANC	SF	125,000 SF	CTS/SF	1PT = $12.50	1PT = $12.50
CANADIAN $	CD	100,000 CD	CTS/CD	1PT = $10	1PT = $10
		FINANCIALS			
U.S. BONDS	US	100,000	⅟₃₂NDS	1PT = $31.25	⅟₃₂ND = $31.25
EURODOLLARS	ED	1,000,000	BASIS PT	1PT = $25	1PT = $25
S&P 500	SP	250 × INDEX	PTS	1PT = $2.50	10PTS = $12.50
S&P 500 E-MINI	ES	50 × INDEX	PTS	1PT = .50	25PTS = $12.50
		GRAINS			
WHEAT	W	5,000 BU	CTS/BU	1CT = $50	¼CTS = $12.50
CORN	C	5,000 BU	CTS/BU	1CT = $50	¼CTS = $12.50
OATS	O	5,000 BU	CTS/BU	1CT = $50	¼CTS = $12.50
ROUGH RICE	NR	2,000 CWT	$/LB	1CT = $20	¼CTS = $5

	Symbol	Contract Size	Units	$/Unit	Fluctuation
SOYBEANS	S	5,000 BU	CTS/BU	1CT = $50	¼CTS = $12.50
BEAN MEAL	SM	100 TONS	$/TON	1PT = $1	10PT = $10
BEAN OIL	BO	60,000 LBS	CTS/LB	1PT = $6	1PT = $6
		SOFTS			
COCOA	CO	10 MET. TONS	$/TON	1PT = $10	1PT = $10
COFFEE	KC	37,500 LBS	CTS/LB	1PT = $3.75	5PTS = $18.75
SUGAR	SB	112,000 LBS	CTS/LB	1PT = $11.20	1PT = $11.20
COTTON	CT	50,000 LBS	CTS/LB	1PT = $5	1PT = $5
ORANGE JUICE	OJ	15,000 LBS	CTS/LB	1PT = $1.50	5PTS = $7.5
LUMBER	LB	110,000 BFT	$/M BFT	1PT = $1.10	10PTS = $11.10
		MEATS			
LIVE CATTLE	LC	40,000 LBS	CTS/CWT	1PT = $4	2.5PTS = $10
FEEDER CATTLE	FC	50,000 LBS	CTS/CWT	1PT = $5	2.5PTS = $12.50
LEAN HOGS	LH	40,000 LBS	CTS/CWT	1PT = $4	2.5PTS = $10
PORK BELLIES	PB	40,000 LBS	$/LB	1PT = $4	2.5PTS = $10
		ENERGIES			
CRUDE OIL	CL	1,000 BBL	$/BBL	1PT = $10	1PT = $10
HEATING OIL	HO	42,000 GALS	CTS/GAL	1PT = $4.20	1PT = $4.20
UNL. GAS	HU	42,000 GALS	CTS/GAL	1PT = $4.20	1PT = $4.20
NAT. GAS	NG	10,000 MM BTU	$/BTU	1PT = $1	10PT = $10

The Least You Need to Know

- ◆ Each day four main prices are given to sum up the day's futures trading: open, high, low, and close (settle).

- ◆ The close or settlement price is the price at which all futures positions are marked to market for margin purposes.

- ◆ The close is derived by taking an average of the closing range, or typically, the last three minutes of trade.

- ◆ Each futures contract is quoted differently, as each represents a specific commodity.

- ◆ To calculate the dollar value of a change in a commodities price, simply multiply the price difference by the contract size (Dollar Value = Price Change in Dollars × Contract Size).

- ◆ It is imperative to understand how quotes are given before beginning to trade. Misquoting prices can cause serious loss of capital.

Part 2

Using Futures to Take or Alleviate Risks

In this part, you will see how the futures and options markets are used to transfer risk from those who wish to avoid price risk (hedgers) to those who embrace risk for a profit (speculators).

In plain English, concepts regarding different types of risks and relationships between different types of markets are explained. You will understand how a producer can lock in a selling price of their unfinished goods using the futures markets, or how a purchaser can lock in attractive prices on raw materials, ensuring attractive profit margins and future supplies.

You also explore how a speculator, correctly assessing the future direction of prices, can profit from price changes—either up or down.

Hedging in the Futures Market

In This Chapter

- ◆ Hedging your bets and exposure
- ◆ The relationship between cash and futures markets
- ◆ Hedging in the futures markets
- ◆ The long and short of hedging
- ◆ Working with leverage and margin
- ◆ Elements of successful hedging

One of the primary functions of the futures markets is risk transference. Price risk is transferred from those who wish to avoid it (hedgers) to those who embrace it (speculators) in the hope of making a profit. Hedging, in its simplest form, is the practice of offsetting the price risk inherent in any cash market position by taking an equal and opposite position in the futures market.

Hedgers use the futures markets to protect themselves and their businesses from adverse price changes. Speculators assume this risk, often bridging the gap between those who have price exposure to falling prices (producers or "short hedgers") and those who have price exposure to rising prices (consumers or "long hedgers").

In this chapter, we will show you how the futures markets are used to alleviate risk. This is important to understand, because much of the volume in futures trading is done by people using it to transfer risk. If you want to accept this risk, or wish to transfer some risk yourself, you should understand the process.

Hedging

Price risk exists throughout the business world, in commerce and finance. In farming, for example, a prolonged drought can affect farmers' crop supplies as well as the income they receive. But the drought also affects the price paid by the grain companies for corn, wheat, soybeans, and oats. Those prices directly impact the consumer's price paid for cereals, salad dressing, bread, poultry, beef, and a whole host of other items that consumers buy on an everyday basis.

For manufacturers, trade embargoes, labor strikes, and inclement weather can interrupt supplies and lead to sharp price increases for raw materials. These factors directly affect jobs, as well as the price we pay for a whole host of items ranging from gasoline and jewelry to the cost of your house. Sudden price hikes in raw materials can cause manufacturers' profits to diminish, forcing plant closures and such, and, as we all know, costs of production are typically passed down to us on the consumer level.

Financial institutions are not immune to price risks either. Changes in interest rates by the Federal Reserve can increase the cost of lending and borrowing money. A sudden increase in interest rates can cause banks to be strapped with lower interest loans, while at the same time their cost to borrow money (deposits) increases as they are forced to pay out a higher interest rate. Anyone with a variable rate mortgage knows that changes in interest rates can dramatically increase house payments, as well as a whole host of other debt payments. As stock prices fluctuate, wealth is created and destroyed with every tick of the Dow Jones Industrial Average. People's views of their financial safety, and hence their spending habits, are closely tied to how well their employee stock plans, 401(k)s, IRAs, and retirement plans are doing. This has a pronounced effect on their spending habits, and the economy as a whole.

There is no escaping the varying degrees of price fluctuation—price risk—in every sector of today's international economy: agriculture, manufacturing, business, and finance. However, much of this risk is minimized through hedging, as hedging lessens the impact of unwanted price changes.

Hedging is a dominant feature in our everyday lives, though we tend to give it little thought. Homeowners take out insurance policies against their homes to protect their invested money. Banks and Savings and Loans are more willing to loan money to homeowners because the insurance can be purchased for a small fraction of the value of the home and protects the value of the home against fire, storms, and a whole host of other risks associated with homeownership.

Repair warranties are also a form of insurance and hedging, as the buyer of an appliance purchases an extended warranty to guard against the total breakdown of an appliance and having to replace it. Even college savings and retirement plans are a form of hedging, where assets are invested in areas where they should grow to meet a future need (retirement or college), which will most likely be more expensive when met.

These are all examples of consumers protecting against unwanted price changes and the possibility of total loss. Hedging in the futures markets works the same way. It is a conscious effort to reduce the price risk inherent in buying, selling, or even a cash market commodity.

> **Trading Tips**
>
> Though the purpose of hedging is to eliminate risk, hedges are often put on just to minimize risk. For example, you buy collision insurance for your car to protect against the loss of the value of the car. The risk you take in doing so is your deductible plus cost of the insurance. You swap a big risk (cost of a new car) for a smaller risk (cost of insurance and deductible).

Who Are the Hedgers?

Hedgers are individuals or companies that own or are planning to own a cash commodity—Corn, Wheat, Soybeans, Cattle, U.S. Treasury Bonds, Stocks, Foreign Currencies, and so on—and are concerned that the cost of the commodity may change before they either buy it or sell it. Almost anyone who seeks to protect cash market commodities from unwanted price changes can use the futures markets for hedging—farmers, grain elevators, merchandisers, producers, exporters, importers, bankers, bond dealers, brokerage houses, insurance companies, money managers, portfolio managers, airlines, transportation companies, governments, and many others.

For example, assume a jewelry manufacturer agrees to sell gold rings to a major jewelry retailer in six months. Both agree on a price today, even though the rings will not be delivered for six months. The jewelry manufacturer does not yet own the gold to make the rings, and he is concerned about the cost of gold rising in the next six months. The retailer has not yet sold the rings, and is concerned that the cost of gold may fall, lowering the value of the rings he just purchased for delivery in the next six months.

To hedge against this risk, the manufacturer buys Gold futures calling for delivery in six months. After four months have passed, the ring maker can buy the gold he needs to meet his order. If prices have risen, as he feared, the gold will be more expensive, possibly eroding the profit he thought he could make when he agreed to the original order. However, because he hedged in the futures market, the jewelry manufacturer can sell his futures contract at a profit because the futures contract price would have increased also. The profits from the futures position would offset much—if not all—of the losses associated with the higher raw material costs, ensuring his profits on the sale of the rings.

To hedge against the risk of falling prices, the jewelry retailer would sell a futures contract. Because the actual cost of gold is a major component in the price of rings, lower gold prices would mean that he would be forced to sell his rings at a lower price to stay competitive with other jewelers. If prices increase, the jewelry retailer would be able to sell his rings for more money, offsetting most, if not all, of the loss associated with the futures position, keeping his original margin intact. However, if prices had fallen, the loss he would take on selling the rings at a lower price would be offset by the gain in the futures contract, again keeping his profit margin intact.

Hedging works the same way in the financial markets. For example, assume a major manufacturing company has a contract to sell its product to a Japanese distributor in three months. The Japanese firm will pay for the merchandise in Yen. The U.S.–based manufacturer has price exposure to a strengthening Yen, because if the Yen appreciates against the dollar in the next three months, the Yen paid will convert to fewer dollars. To protect itself against this risk, the manufacturer can purchase a Japanese Yen futures contract. If the Yen appreciates, the loss on conversion from Yen to Dollars will be offset by the gain in the futures contract.

Hedgers accept the possibility that they may have to forfeit any windfall profits in return for price stability. Our jewelry manufacturer accepts the fact that he will not make a larger profit from the sale of his product if the price of gold declines because he is more concerned with being able to make his profit margin if prices increase. For hedgers, it is more important to establish a market objective that protects their investment and regular profit margins than it is to miss a possible opportunity for extended profits. Hedgers use the futures markets to offset risk.

The Cash and Futures Market Relationship

Often a difference is equated in the industry and throughout this book between the cash market and the futures market. The cash market refers to physical commodities, which you can touch—be they Corn, Wheat, Beef, Bonds, or Stock. The futures market refers to the right or obligation to make or accept delivery of these physical commodities.

Cash market transactions refer to the purchase and sale of actual commodities at current prices. Delivery of the commodity can be immediate or within several days. For instance, when a miller buys corn from a local elevator, that is a cash transaction.

In the futures market, however, buyers and sellers agree to make or take delivery of a specific commodity (quality, quantity, time, and location are all predetermined and standardized), with the only variable being price. The date of the purchase can be days, weeks, or months away—hence the name futures.

Whereas a cash transaction is between individuals—the buyer and seller—futures contract transactions are between exchange clearing members. For example, the buyer of a Corn futures contract gets the contract for her individual account at an exchange clearing firm, to which she posts performance bond margin to guarantee. The actual transaction between the buyer and the seller of the contract is executed on the exchange floor between clearing member firms, who are ultimately responsible for fulfilling the contract.

One of the major differences between a futures contract transaction and a cash market transaction is that a futures contract transaction has no counter-party risk. Because performance bond margins (initial and maintenance margin) must be posted and maintained in accordance with exchange rules, the transaction is backed by funds. In a cash market transaction, the transaction is only as good as the parties involved. Think about buying a stereo from a street vendor. If the stereo does not work when you get it home, you may not be able to find the street vendor to get your money back. That is counter-party risk.

Basis and the Relationship Between the Cash and Futures Markets

The difference between the cash price of a commodity at a specific location and the price of a specific futures contract is known as *basis*. To calculate the basis, simply subtract the futures price from the cash price:

Basis = Cash Price – Futures Price

For example, if a grain elevator operator in central Iowa buys corn from a local farmer for $2.30 per bushel and the May Chicago Board of Trade Corn futures are trading at $2.40 per bushel, the basis at the elevator would be –$0.10 per bushel. Typically, when referring to basis, it is usually assumed that the closest-to-delivery futures contract (or front month) is used. Basis can be positive or negative, depending upon the location, quality of the commodity, and local market conditions.

def•i•ni•tion

Basis is the difference between the current cash price and the futures price of the same commodity. Unless otherwise specified, the price of the nearby futures contract month is generally used to calculate the basis.

Hedgers use the basis for assessing their local conditions to those on the exchanges. The basis represents a simple way of tracking the difference.

For example, assume that in July a corn farmer can get $2.50 per bushel for his corn from the local elevator. He expects his production to be 20,000 bushels of corn, and wishes to lock in this price. To do so, he would sell four December Corn futures (each Corn futures contract represents 5,000 bushels). At the same time, December Corn futures are trading at $2.65 per bushel. His basis is –$0.15 per bushel ($2.50 – $2.65 = –$0.15).

July

Farmer has 20,000 bushels of corn at $2.50

Farmer sells four December futures at $2.65

Basis = –$0.15 per bushel

By November, the farmer has harvested his corn production. Assume that the local elevator is willing to buy his corn at $2.10 per bushel, and the December Corn futures have declined in value, and are trading at $2.27 per bushel.

November

Cash Corn at $2.10 per bushel

Four December futures at $2.27

Basis = –$0.17 per bushel

By waiting to sell his crop (yes, he did have to wait for it to mature before he could harvest it), the farmer got $0.40 less per bushel (–$8,000 loss) for his corn in November than he could have gotten in July. However, by selling futures contracts against his future production, the farmer made $0.38 per bushel ($7,600 gain).

	Cash	**Futures**
July	Corn Price $2.50/bu	Sold 4 Dec Corn Futures $2.65
November	Corn Price $2.10/bu	Bought 4 Dec Corn Futures $2.27
Net	Loss –$0.40/bu (–$8,000)	Gain +$0.38/bu (+$7,600)

By hedging, the farmer transferred his risk of outright price exposure for basis risk exposure. The basis widened from –$0.15 per bushel ($2.50 – $2.65) to –$0.17 per bushel ($2.10 – $2.17). Hence, the futures contracts tracked all of his price risk except $0.02 per bushel, or $400 on 20,000 bushels of corn. As you can see, this risk exposure is significantly less.

So even though a hedger is trying to avoid risk, she is truly just swapping risk. She is transferring the risk of the loss in the cash market for a risk of loss in the futures market. She is transferring risk exposure for the underlying commodity for basis risk exposure.

The basis cannot be predicted precisely, but it is generally less volatile than either the futures or cash price. By knowing the basis, the hedger replaces the risk of price fluctuations in the cash market with the lesser risk of a change in the basis, or the difference between the cash market and the futures market.

Hedgers must pay close attention to the basis relationship. Without knowledge of the usual basis relationship and basis patterns for a given commodity, it is impossible for a hedger to make a truly informed decision about whether to accept or reject a given price (cash or futures); whether, when, and in what delivery month to hedge; when to close a hedge; or when and how to turn an unusual basis situation into a possible profit opportunity.

Why Hedging Works

The main reason why hedging works is that futures and cash prices of related commodities tend to respond to the same economic factors. As a result, futures contracts tend to converge with the underlying cash market. There are several reasons why this happens.

For starters, futures contracts for traditional commodities, such as Grains, Metals, Foods and Fibers, and Petroleum products, require all participants holding contracts at expiration to make or take delivery of the underlying commodity. This responsibility to make or take delivery of the actual commodity assumes that futures prices will reflect the actual cash value of the commodity.

If the futures contract is trading at too high a price versus the cash commodity, market participants will sell futures and buy the underlying commodity as much as possible, making a profit from the unrealistic difference in a process known as arbitrage. This process will drive the futures price down—as heavy selling occurs—and raise prices on the cash market as supply is snapped up. This will continue until the difference narrows to an economically acceptable level. If the futures are too cheap compared to the cash market, then arbitragers will buy futures contracts and sell the cash market commodity, delivering the underlying commodity when it is delivered from the futures contract.

The fact that many commodities call for making or taking delivery will drive prices together. If it is cheaper for Kellogg's to get their needed supply of corn for Corn Flakes via the futures market, they will. If it is more economical for large producers like Archer Daniels Midland (ADM, known as the "supermarket to the world") to deliver against futures than to sell their production in the cash market, they will. The fact that futures contracts call for making or accepting delivery of a physical commodity aides in the convergence as well.

Some futures contracts are cash settled instead of having a physical delivery (usually financial futures), but the Chicago Mercantile Exchange's Lean Hog futures are also *cash settled*. This means that instead of an actual *commodity* transferring hands at expiration of the futures contract, an equivalent amount of *money* is. This is similar to, for example, getting paid by your employer in necessities rather than cash. Each month you buy food, lodging, insurance, and entertainment with your paycheck. If your employer stocked your cupboards, paid your mortgage (or rent), gave you a car, and sent you to the movies and an occasional night on the town, you wouldn't need a paycheck (unless you actually wanted to save some money for future needs). Another example: Would you rather receive 100 shares of XYZ stock currently trading at $50.00 per share, or $5,000? They are both the same at that particular point in time, and if they are not, arbitragers will buy the undervalued portion and sell the overvalued portion until they are equivalent again.

Like other contractual obligations, predetermined delivery steps must be completed within a specified amount of time to comply with the terms of the contract. For example,

Chicago Board of Trade Corn futures call for delivery of 5,000 bushels of deliverable grade Corn, #2 Yellow Corn, or predetermined substitutions at differentials established by the exchange. This ensures that buyers know what they are getting and when, and sellers know their responsibilities as well. Hence all parties enter into the transaction fully aware of the details and are able to fulfill the obligation. Besides, each and every transaction is backed by performance bond deposits, and backed by the exchange's clearinghouse.

Hence, someone holding the underlying commodity can sell a futures contract against her cash market position, protecting it against eroding in value, because when delivery comes, she knows that the price movement in the futures market will very closely track that of the change in price of the underlying commodity market. This is done by initiating a *short hedge position.*

> ## def•i•ni•tion
>
> A **short hedge position** is selling a futures contract when you have a need in the future to sell a commodity. A short hedge is protection against falling prices. A **long hedge position** is buying a futures contract when you have a need to purchase the commodity in the future. A long hedge is protection against rising prices.

Individuals with a future obligation to purchase a physical commodity can protect themselves from rising prices by buying a futures contract, knowing that the futures contract will change in value in a fashion very similar to the underlying commodity. Thus they are able to plan ahead, without having to be exposed to changes in the underlying value of raw materials and how that will affect costs of production. This is done by initiating a *long hedge position.*

Leverage, Margin, and Bang for Your Buck

As we mentioned earlier in this book, the futures markets operate on a margining system. You do not need to put up all of the value of a contract, only post an adequate margin to control a lot of a commodity. For example, most margin requirements range from 2.5 to roughly 12.5 percent of the total cash value of the contract. As such, a small amount of money can control a large amount of a commodity.

For example, the initial margin requirement for corn as of this writing is $338 and the maintenance margin requirement is $250. With Corn trading at $2.05 per bushel, a deposit of $338 controls $10,250 worth of corn (5,000 bushel contract size × $2.05 per bushel).

Thus, a small initial deposit in the form of margin can result in a large dollar per contract move in your futures account. This relationship of deposited funds to amount of commodity controlled is leverage. A small move in the underlying market can result in a large move in the value of the account relative to funds deposited.

This is similar to buying a house. Most people put up a down payment of 10 to 20 percent on their home. Thus when the price of the home appreciates by 10 percent, they see a large return versus their initial investment. For example, assume you own a $200,000 home and you put down $20,000 on it when purchasing it. If you sell the house a couple of years later for $220,000, you have doubled your money from a small initial investment because of the leverage of your mortgage.

It works in a similar fashion in the futures market. A small move, say $0.10 in Corn, will result in a $500 profit or loss, which is more than a 100 percent return versus the initial margin requirement of $338.

However, everyone should be warned that leverage works both ways. A small move against you—buy corn and the price drops –$0.10—can result in large losses as well. In fact, because of the leverage involved in futures trading, it is possible to lose more than your initial investment. (In Chapters 18 and 20, we discuss how to avoid this, or at least lessen the risk involved.)

The leverage involved in futures also makes hedging easier. Because a hedger only has to put up a small percentage of the total value of the commodity they are trying to hedge, their funds are not unduly tied up.

Elements of a Successful Hedging Program

Hedging involves making an assessment about the future. Are you, as a potential hedger, happy with the current prices and the profit margin you would be locking in by hedging?

In order to decide if hedging is appropriate for you, you really need to understand your business. Successful hedgers understand their own costs, and are able to assess whether the target price they are attempting to hedge is beneficial to them or not.

Successful hedgers also understand how their local markets react to the national market. They know the normal basis and are constantly on the lookout for opportunities where they can lock in an attractive basis. Because local conditions can severely affect basis, sometimes a hedger will have to make or accept delivery against the futures contract. The successful hedger is aware of this and understands how to do it and how this will affect their bottom line profitability.

Successful hedgers are also willing to change their views. They are flexible as conditions change. Sometimes the risk of locking in a small profit or minimizing a loss is greater than the risk of just going unhedged and being able to benefit from price changes as well. They understand that no risk can be the riskiest position of all.

In general, successful hedgers understand their own operations and costs. They also know how their local conditions are versus the rest of the country and understand the normal behavior of their local basis.

The Least You Need to Know

- ◆ Hedgers swap unlimited price risk of a commodity rising or falling for the smaller risk that the relationship between cash and futures prices will change (basis).

- ◆ If you own the physical commodity, your risk that this asset will drop in value can be protected by selling a futures contract—a short hedge position.

- ◆ If you need to buy a physical commodity, your risk that prices will rise, increasing your obligation, can be protected by buying a futures contract—a long hedge position.

- ◆ Hedging with futures works because the cash commodity can be delivered against the futures or the futures represent an equal amount of money.

Chapter 6

Speculating in the Futures Market

In This Chapter

- ◆ Speculation is not a dirty word for futures traders
- ◆ Defining the speculators
- ◆ Profits and losses
- ◆ Leverage is a dual-edged sword
- ◆ Game plans and trading strategy

Speculators in the futures markets fulfill several vital economic functions that facilitate the marketing of basic commodities and trade in financial instruments. Most important, speculators assume risk. Speculators gladly accept the risk of loss for the opportunity to profit—risk that producers and consumers of commodities try to avoid. The risk-taking speculator allows for risk transferring, often acting as the middleman for transactions, always providing an opportunity for buying or selling, or basically adding liquidity and depth to a market.

In a market without speculators, it would be difficult—if not impossible—for hedgers to agree upon a price because the sellers (or short hedgers) want the highest price possible, while buyers (or long hedgers) want the lowest price possible. Finding offsetting hedging opportunities would be difficult and time-consuming without speculators bridging the gap.

In this chapter, we will show you how the futures markets are used by speculators for profit. This is important to understand because the goal of a speculator is to make money! And you can't make money if you don't understand how the basic system works.

Speculating

Speculators fill the gap between producers and consumers in the futures market. When speculators enter the marketplace, the number of ready buyers and sellers increases, and hedgers are no longer limited by the hedging needs of others.

def•i•ni•tion

Liquidity is a characteristic of a security or commodity market with enough units outstanding to allow large transactions without a substantial change in price. In other words, in a liquid market, buy and sell orders will not unduly change prices.

In addition to assuming the risk and providing *liquidity* and capital, speculators help to ensure the stability of the marketplace. Active speculation in futures markets tends to dampen extreme price movements. For example, by purchasing futures contracts when prices are historically low, speculators add to demand. The effect of rising demand is an increase in price. By selling futures when prices are high, speculators add to supply and decrease demand, and therefore, help to lower prices. Thus the extreme price swings, which may have otherwise occurred, are dampened by the activities of speculators.

Think about selling your car. You can run an ad in the classified section of your local paper, field phone calls about inquiries, and accept bids for it, or you can go to your local used car lot and get a bid from them. The used car lot will give you a price—you may not like it, but they will make an offer. If you have to sell the car in a hurry, this may be the best option. However, if you can afford to run the classified ad and wait, you may be able to get a better price.

The used car lot will buy your car, speculating that they can resell it at a higher price. By being in this business of car speculating, one selling a used car always knows he can sell it to someone, or he can wait, incur the expense of placing ads and the time involved in selling. Because the car dealership exists, the market for used cars is larger, or more liquid, with less differential between the price a buyer is willing to pay, and the price a seller wants.

Speculators trade futures to profit from the natural price fluctuations. There are many external factors that can affect prices of commodity futures. For example, droughts tend to cause grain prices to increase, as future supplies are feared to be more limited. Metals prices fluctuate on supply concerns regarding mining strikes, or transportation problems and political uncertainty in producing nations like South Africa, Russia, Brazil, and even Canada. Petroleum prices can spike up or down with news from the Organization of Petroleum Exporting Countries (OPEC), while changes in interest rates, inflation levels, and a whole host of other factors ranging from economic to political can affect all of these markets.

Who Are the Speculators?

There are several ways to classify speculators. The most direct is to refer to them as either long or short. If a speculator is long futures, she has bought one or more futures contracts in anticipation of higher prices. If a speculator is short futures, she has sold one or more contracts in anticipation of lower prices.

In addition to long or short, speculators may be classified by the size of their trading positions relative to the Commodity Futures Trading Commission's (CFTC) position reporting limits. Speculators' futures and options holdings must be reported to the CFTC periodically if they reach a specific number of open contracts (this is usually in the hundreds of contracts range, similar to reporting stock holdings when you own a certain percentage of a company).

If you haven't had to report to the SEC, then you probably won't have to report to the CFTC. These speculators are classified as Large Speculators. The CFTC issues a weekly report, called the Commitment of Traders, which classifies the holders of futures positions as Commercial Hedgers, Large Speculators, and others (usually referred to as Small Speculators). The Large Speculators are usually professional money managers who control millions of dollars in the futures markets, and trade in large quantities. Public speculators who carry smaller positions are not required to report their positions to the CFTC.

> ### Commodity Corn
>
> Traders who are long in anticipation of higher prices are said to be bullish. Traders who are short in anticipation of lower prices are said to be bearish. These expressions come from the old bull and bear fights. The bull would gore the bear by shifting his horns upward. The bear would attack the bull by heaving his mighty claws downward. Hence bulls became the symbol of upward movement and bears became the mascot for downward movement.

Traders can also be classified by the time period in which they trade. Traders who hold futures contracts for a series of days, weeks, or even months could be classified as position traders. Position trading is by far the most popular time frame for speculators, both large and small.

Those who enter and exit positions within the context of a day, holding positions for minutes or hours, are typically referred to as day traders. Day traders rarely hold a position after the close. For many years, day trading was strictly the venue of professionals and exchange members, but with the advent of the Internet and electronic order placement, the general public has begun day trading as well.

The shortest time frame traders are known as scalpers. Scalpers are professional traders, usually exchange members, who trade for themselves in the pits of the exchanges. Scalpers make the market in a futures market, posting bids and offers, and trying to make a small amount by buying or selling on heavy volume. The scalper's willingness to make a market and buy at the bid, and sell at the offer or ask, adds a great amount of liquidity to the market, allowing the market to more easily absorb large volumes of trades with a minimal effect on prices. Scalpers, like the day traders, usually do not carry positions over night, but try to go home with no market position, or *flat*. Having been on the trading floor myself, and tried my hand at scalping, I know that just keeping track of the total number of contracts you have bought or sold is a daunting task.

For example, assume you bought 150 contracts at $142\frac{1}{2}$, then turned around and sold 40 at $142\frac{3}{4}$, 20 at $142\frac{1}{2}$, 25 at $142\frac{1}{4}$, 30 at $142\frac{1}{2}$, and 15 more at 143. How many contracts do you have? Are you long or short? Don't go back and read this again and add it up, as a scalper has to be yelling his bids and offers and keep track of their position, and all of these transactions could have taken place in the course of less than 30 seconds! By the way, you bought 150 and sold 120, so you are net long 30 contracts still.

Speculators may also be categorized by their analysis method. Some speculators believe that in order to anticipate prices, one needs to study supply and demand trends, assess the conditions of crops, and changes to these factors to forecast prices. These speculators are known as fundamental analysts. Other speculators believe in studying price patterns and trends in pricing to forecast prices. These technical analysts believe that price itself is an indicator, which incorporates all the known fundamentals already, and believe that the action of price is the best tool to forecast pricing. Both types have their success and failure stories and are the subject of Chapters 10 and 11.

Buy Low and Sell High or Sell High and Buy Low

Speculation in the futures markets can lead to either profits or losses—just like actually owning the physical (cash) commodity. But speculators rarely have an interest in owning the cash commodity or financial instrument that underlies the futures contract. They buy futures contracts when they think prices are going to rise, hoping to later offset the position by selling a futures contract at a higher price and reaping the profit. Speculators also sell futures contracts (initiate short positions) when they anticipate falling prices, hoping to buy back the futures contract at a lower price and make a profit. What is truly unique about the futures market versus other markets (like stocks, bonds, and physical commodities) is that futures positions can be entered into either by initially buying or selling a futures contract. Speculators can initiate short positions just like the short hedgers do by selling first, and buying later. The decision to be a buyer or seller first depends upon the speculator's market expectation.

Trading Tips

When initiating a long position (buying) you hope for higher prices, as your profits are the difference between the purchase price and the sale price. When initiating a short position (selling) you hope for lower prices as profits are still calculated by the sale price less the purchase price. In other words, buy low and sell high—the order does not matter.

Profits are proportional to the speculator's skill in anticipating price movement. Potential gains and losses are as great for the short speculator (selling first, then buying) as they are for the long speculator (buying first, then selling). Whether it is a long or short position, the speculator has to post the same margin requirement and can offset the position in the futures market, without ever having to deal with the physical commodity. The only thing the speculator is interested in is if they made a profit, and they are calculated the same for either long or short positions.

Profit or Loss = Sale Price – Purchase Price

The order does not matter between buying and selling. For example, assume a speculator bought March Corn at $2.15 per bushel and sold it two weeks later at $2.30 per bushel. He would have reaped a profit of $0.15 per bushel, or $750.00 before commissions and fees (Sale Price [$2.30] – Purchase Price [$2.15] = $0.15 × 5,000 bushels = $750). A bearish speculator would initiate a position by selling March Corn at $2.30 and buying a few weeks later at $2.15 per bushel, making the same $0.15 per bushel, or $750.00 before commissions and fees.

In essence, the speculators' job and goal are very simple—buy low and sell high! This can be done by first initiating a position in the futures contract through buying (long) and later offsetting the position by selling the futures contract, or it can be done by first initiating the position by selling a futures contract (short), and later buying it back to offset the position. The order in which the position was initiated and liquidated does not matter, as long as the speculator sold his futures contract at a price greater than he purchased it for—buy low and sell high or sell high and buy low.

Leverage and Futures Trading

Most speculators are attracted to the futures market because of the leverage involved in futures trading. Leverage is an attractive feature of trading futures because it enables a speculator to control a large amount of a commodity or financial instrument with a relatively small amount of capital.

Trading Tips

Examples of trading in the grains are used throughout this book. The grain markets offer an excellent opportunity for new speculators in the futures markets. Though they are not as sexy as foreign currency futures or stock index futures, these markets are relatively inexpensive to enter from a margin standpoint, and many great books and websites are available to give up-to-date and accurate news and forecasts about current conditions. Consider trading the grains and visit www.grainguide.com.

For example, assume July Chicago Board of Trade Wheat is trading at $2.80 per bushel. Each futures contract represents 5,000 bushels of wheat, or roughly $14,000 worth of Wheat per contract. The required margin for Chicago Board of Trade Wheat at the time this is being written is $608 initial margin and $450 maintenance, or roughly 4 percent of the value of the contract. So for an initial performance bond deposit of $608, a speculator can control $14,000 worth of Wheat.

Remember that margins are determined on the basis of market risk. Because margins are adjusted to risk, they help to assure the financial soundness of futures exchanges and provide valuable price protection for hedgers with a minimum tie-up of capital. Margins are typically set at 4 to 18 percent of the value of the commodity underlying the futures contract and assessed each day depending upon the settlement of the underlying futures market. At the end of each trading day, all the outstanding futures contracts are valued based on a settlement price. The open position profits or losses are credited or debited (put in or taken out, respectively) in a process known as marking to market. For example, assume you buy Chicago Board of Trade Wheat for $2.80 per bushel. If wheat prices rise $0.10 per bushel during the trading session, your account will be marked to market by being credited $500—or the difference between your entry price and the settlement price or ($2.90 – $2.80 = $0.10 per bushel × 5,000 bushels = $500 profit).

After the account is marked to market, then each account is reviewed, and any margin deficiencies are noted. This is known as a margin call if your account is deficient, and one must either deposit additional funds or liquidate the position.

The exchanges set two types of margin requirements: initial margin and maintenance margin. The initial margin requirement is the amount of money a party must have on account with a clearing firm (your broker) at the time the order is placed. Initial margin funds must be on deposit before any trade can be accepted. Maintenance margin is a set minimum margin—per outstanding futures contract—that a party to a futures contract must maintain in their margin account to hold a futures position.

Using our wheat example, a speculator must have at least $608 in his account before he would be allowed to purchase a contract of Wheat. Each night, his profits from open positions are credited to his account, and losses are taken out (debited). If the value of the account falls below the maintenance margin level ($450), then the speculator will be required to post additional funds or have the position liquidated.

Margin is not a down payment for a futures contract, but a security deposit to ensure contract performance. If the market moves against the position, the speculator will be required to deposit additional margin or the position will be liquidated. If the market moves in favor of the position, the account will be credited.

For example, let's assume a speculator opens a trading account with $5,000. She wants to buy five contracts of July Wheat on May 1st. The initial margin requirement is $608 per contract and maintenance of $450. Our speculator is able to purchase the five Wheat contracts, because she has more than enough capital to meet the initial margin requirement of $608 per contract, or $3,040 for five contracts.

May 1st

Account Balance: $5,000

Purchased five July Wheat contacts at $2.80 per bushel

Initial Margin Required: $3,040

Maintenance Margin Required: $2,250

Available Funds: $2,750

On May 1st, our speculator buys five contracts of July Wheat. Since her account has more than the initial margin required, she is able to initiate the position. The maintenance margin requirement is $2,250, which leaves a $2,750 cushion before margin call. She could initiate other positions with this money as well, if she chooses.

May 2nd

July Futures Close at $2.70

Account Balance: $2,500 ($5,000 − [$2.70 − $2.80 = − $0.10 × 25,000 bushels] or $2,500)

Initial Margin: $3,040

Maintenance Margin: $2,250

Available Funds: $250

On May 2nd, news that China had canceled a large wheat importing deal sends Wheat prices crashing 10 cents per bushel lower. Our speculator, who is long five contracts, loses a total of $2,500, or −$500 per contract. This amount is debited from her account at the end of the day, leaving her account balance at $2,500 ($5,000 initial balance less −$2,500 open position loss).

May 3rd

July Futures Close at $2.72

Account Balance: $3,000 ($5,000 − [$2.72 − $2.80 = − $0.08 × 25,000 bushels] or $2,000)

Initial Margin: $3,040

Maintenance Margin: $2,250

Available Funds: $750

On May 3rd, Wheat futures gain +2 cents, adding $500 to our speculator's account balance, or lessening her loss by $500 from a −$2,500 loss to a −$2,000 loss. The 2-cent gain, or $500, is credited to her account that evening, leaving his account balance at $3,000 based on her open position loss of −$0.08 per contract (−$2,000).

May 6th

July Futures Close at $2.65

Account Balance: $1,250

Initial Margin: $3,040

Maintenance Margin: $2,250

Available Funds: Margin Call!

Rains over the weekend ease concerns that crop conditions may deteriorate, and Wheat futures lose 7 cents per bushel on this Monday. Our speculator has an open position loss of –$0.15 per contract, or –$3,750.

She is experiencing a margin call! She has two choices at this point: either bring her available funds (or the difference between his account balance and maintenance margin requirement) back above the initial margin requirement, or liquidate her position. In order to hold her position, she would have to deposit $1,790 with her broker, bringing her available funds back above both the initial and maintenance margin levels. Though it is often more prudent to liquidate a position that is showing this kind of loss, our speculator decides to hold on to the position for a few more days, and wire transfers $1,800 to her broker the following morning.

May 7th

July Futures Close at $2.71

Account Balance: $4,550 = 6,800 in deposits – $2,250 in open position losses

Initial Margin: $3,040

Maintenance Margin: $2,250

Available Funds: $2,300

News that China will be admitted to the World Trade Organization rekindles hopes for China importing U.S. Wheat. This gain of 6 cents per bushel adds $1,500 to our speculator's account, bringing her total open position loss down to –$2,250. Since she wired $1,500 into her account to satisfy her margin requirement, her account balance now stands at $4,250, or the $5,000 initial deposit plus the $1,500 just sent in less an open position loss of –$2,250. Since her maintenance margin requirement is $2,000, she has an available balance of $2,300.

May 14th

July Futures Close at $2.90

Account Balance: $9,300 = $6,800 in deposits + $2,500 in open position gains

Initial Margin: $3,040

Maintenance Margin: $2,250

Available Funds: $6,750

In the ensuing week, July Wheat rallies as speculation that China's entry into the World Trade Organization will increase its appetite for U.S. Wheat. Our speculator is very happy. She has an open position profit of $0.10 per bushel per contract, or $2,500.

She decides the next day to close out her position, when July Wheat opens at $2.92½, and instructs her broker to sell five July Wheat at the market. Her broker confirms that she sold five July Wheat contracts at $2.92½, and our speculator makes $3,125 before commissions and fees. This represents a return of 48 percent in just over two weeks! Don't you just love a happy ending?

As can be seen in the above example, the leverage in the futures market is great. By depositing just 4 to 12 percent of the underlying value of the commodity contract, a speculator in the futures markets can control a large amount of a physical commodity, magnifying their profits or losses. For example, each 1-cent move is worth $50 and the barrier to entry in this market is only $608 per contract.

It is important to note that leverage is a dual-edged sword. Profits can accrue at a tremendous speed, and losses can mount just as quickly. It is possible to take a small sum of money and turn it into a large sum of money in a short amount of time. It is also possible to take a large amount of money and turn it into a small amount of money quickly. Speculators should also be aware that, given the leverage involved in the futures market, it is possible to lose more than your initial investment, and that they will be held liable for the difference.

Speculators need to be aware of both the potential rewards and risks offered by leverage. The futures markets are known as a zero sum game, meaning that for every winner there is a loser. Study the markets hard, and learn to recognize the best trading strategies and situations and hopefully you will be on the winning side.

Trading Strategy

When speculating in futures, it is important to develop a trading strategy or plan to guide your market activity. Although such a strategy must be geared to the individual speculator, a systematic approach is helpful.

In order to make sound judgments about price movements, it is imperative to have adequate knowledge about the contract being traded and to limit the number of contracts being followed. This is true for either the speculator using fundamental analysis or the speculator using technical analysis, or someone using a combination of both. Even experienced traders have difficulty following more than three different contracts at a time.

Price forecasts must be combined with a realistic and potentially profitable trading strategy. Profit potential should far outweigh the risk involved, or perceived. When deciding whether or not to enter into a futures position, speculators should specify profit objectives as well as the maximum losses they are willing to sustain. Personal preferences determine the acceptable minimum levels for profits and maximum levels of losses.

 Trading Time Bomb

In the stock market many people advise dollar cost averaging, or buying a stock as it falls, lowering your average price. Because of the large amount of leverage involved in the futures market, this can spell disaster for traders as losses mount by adding to losing positions. The old trading saying, "Keep your losses small," has survived the test of time. Respect it!

After the profit objective and loss limit have been set, determine the amount of money to be risked. To maximize returns, experienced speculators often recommend limiting the amount of money risked on a single trade. Also, open positions should be limited to as many as can be adequately followed, and some capital should be left in reserve for additional opportunities.

Successful speculators often advise that additions to an initial position should be made only after the position has been proven correct by showing a profit. Additional investments should be in amounts less than the initial position. Liquidation of positions should be based on the original plan. Market conditions do change, however, so it is essential that speculators maintain some degree of flexibility.

The desirability of a trade—based on potential risk to reward—depends upon a speculator's experience and preferences. Determining profit objectives and loss limits, additions to the original position, and when to close a position, also depends upon personal preferences and experience. Successful price forecasting and trading are ultimately influenced by individual temperament and objectivity, as well as analysis and trading plans that were developed.

Trading System Guidelines

Many successful speculators use the following guidelines in their own trading:

- Before initiating a futures position, they carefully analyze that market, never acting on rumors or "hot tips."

- They do not speculate without having a plan or if there is doubt about the price forecast.

- Most speculators do not try to pick the exact bottom of a market nor do they try to get the exact high. Instead they settle for getting the middle of a price move, allowing the market to begin to prove their analysis correct before initiating a position.

- Most professional speculators are indifferent to initiating long positions in anticipation of rising prices or initiating short positions in anticipation of lower prices. They will trade in whatever direction they think the market is going to go.

- They speculate only where they think the potential profit is great relative to the potential risk.

- Successful speculators have learned to keep losses small and let their profits grow. Most successful speculators are willing to accept several small losses to keep losses small, but are able to maximize the profits of a few extremely profitable situations.

For example, Freddie the fundamental trader has been studying the supply to usage situation in the Soybean market. He knows that relative to supply, the current demand is running pretty high. In fact, in previous years with a similar supply and usage situation, the July Soybean futures should stay above $5.00 per bushel. With the planting season fast approaching—and with it fear that the crop might not get planted or may be susceptible to adverse weather—he decides to buy one contract of July Soybeans at $5.26¼ when the market posts a new 10-day high. His trading plan goes something like this:

Buy one contract of July Soybeans when the price reaches a new 10-day high during March. Risk the trade to $5.10 with an objective of $5.60 by the end of May, when the Soybean crop is typically fully planted in the United States.

Each of these points was picked based on how the Soybean market has reacted in the past to similar supply and demand situations. The risk to reward ratio is –$0.16¼ (–$812.50 before commissions) in risk, versus +$0.33¾ ($1,687.50 before commissions) in potential reward.

Freddie has a $5,000 account, so the initial margin on Soybeans of $1,148 and $800 Maintenance is not a problem. Risking of –$0.16¼ cents versus a potential gain of +$0.33¾ cents fits appropriately with the rule of keeping risk relative to rewards— profit potential is twice the potential risk! He obviously understands the grain markets, and reads several wonderful grain futures periodicals like the Grain Trader's Almanac available at www.grainguide.com. His decision to enter the market was through his careful analysis of the situation and not based on any "hot tips" or recommendations from friends, family, or brokers.

Freddie's carefully crafted plan came to fruition in the next several weeks as July Soybeans first dipped down to $5.20, giving Freddie an open position loss of –$312.50 based on a –$0.06¼ loss per bushel on a 5,000 bushel Soybean contract, before the Soybean market turned around and headed up to $5.66 in the next three weeks, netting Freddie a gain of +$0.33¾ per bushel, or $1,687.50 before commissions and fees. In three weeks' time, Freddie made a gain of 33.75 percent on his funds, thanks to a well-crafted plan and the leverage involved in trading.

The Least You Need to Know

◆ The basic goal of speculators is to buy low and sell high.

◆ The risk-taking speculator allows for risk transferring, often acting as the middleman for transactions, and always providing an opportunity for buying or selling, or basically adding liquidity and depth to a market.

◆ A long position is initiated by first buying with the hope of selling it at a higher price … buy low, then sell high.

◆ A short position is initiated by first selling with the hope of buying it back at a lower price … sell high, then buy low.

◆ Leverage enables you to control vast amounts of a physical asset with small amounts of money. However, leverage can cause you to lose large amounts of money in a short amount of time.

◆ Successful speculators tend to always have a well-thought-out plan, manage their risk, and never act upon rumors or "hot tips" from friends and acquaintances.

Brokers, Clearing Firms, and Orders

In This Chapter

- ◆ Government in the futures and options business
- ◆ Brokers: Who are they and who watches them?
- ◆ Guide to the National Futures Association, the Futures Police
- ◆ Picking a broker: backgrounds, services, and costs
- ◆ What to expect from a good broker
- ◆ Basic order placement

Like any industry, the futures and options industry has a governing body that enforces the rules and regulation of fair trade. The futures and options industry also has many talented individuals who help people facilitate their trading. These brokers help hedgers and speculators execute their orders and act as news resources as well.

In this chapter, you will learn about the vital functions that regulators, brokers, and other industry professionals perform to ensure a smoothly functioning system between the outside public and the exchanges and their membership who make markets. You will also learn the language that the exchanges and these professionals use to disseminate orders.

The Regulators

The U.S. futures industry has a long history of self-regulation—remember that one of the key components of standardized futures was self-regulated exchanges. Self-regulation in the futures industry predates state and federal regulation.

The rules and regulations of the exchanges are extensive and are designed to support competitive, efficient, liquid markets. Most state and federal regulations, which began shortly after futures trading developed in the United States, have been designed to enforce self-regulation by the exchanges.

Trading Tips

At first glance, the idea of self-regulation may suggest that this business is slanted toward insiders. However, industry regulators take a hard-line approach to protecting the public. If you ever have a problem that cannot be resolved by your broker, be sure to contact the National Futures Association at 1-800-621-5370 or online at www.nfa.futures.org.

U.S. futures exchanges are required by state and federal law to regulate the conduct of their members, member firms, and their employees. The obligations of the exchanges to enforce their own rules and regulations were enhanced in the 1900s with the passing of several commodity trading federal acts, including the Grain Futures Act of 1922, The Commodity Exchange Act of 1936, the Commodity Futures Trading Commission Act of 1974, and the Futures Trading Acts of 1978, 1982, and 1986.

The Commodity Futures Trading Commission

In 1974, Congress wanted to improve commodity regulation and amended the Commodity Exchange Act to create an independent Commodity Futures Trading Commission (CFTC) Existing Commodity Exchange Authority and Commodity Exchange Commission personnel, records, and appropriations were transferred to the new commission. And on April 21, 1975, the CFTC assumed federal regulatory authority over all commodity futures markets.

The amended Commodity Exchange Act gave the CFTC the authority to regulate all futures trading, giving the CFTC authority over all futures trading in existence at the time as well as any new futures contracts to be developed. Prior to 1974, several futures contracts—such as Currencies, Financial Instruments, and Metals—were not regulated by the Government.

CFTC regulation of options on Financial futures began in 1981 with the initiation of a pilot program. The success of this program led to the approval of nonagricultural options in 1982. Then, in 1984, the CFTC extended trading in options to Agricultural futures as well.

The CFTC's regulatory powers extend to exchange actions and to the review and approval of futures contracts proposed by an exchange. Before a new contract is approved for trading, the CFTC must determine that a futures contract is in the public interest. In making that assessment, the commission examines how contracts are used commercially for pricing and hedging to ensure that they serve an economic purpose.

One of the first actions taken by the commission in 1975 was to redefine the term hedge. The definition was broadened to permit anticipatory hedging and cross-hedging within certain limits:

Trading Tips _____

Redefining the term *hedging* allowed industry participants to use listed commodities as a substitute for nonlisted commodity needs. For example, both heating oil and jet fuel are distillate fuels, which tend to be affected by the same forces and have equal changes in prices. Airlines can hedge their jet fuel needs by using the Heating Oil market.

- ◆ Anticipatory hedging allows market users to buy and sell a futures contract before they actually own the cash commodity.

- ◆ Cross-hedging allows market users to hedge a commodity using a different but related commodity futures contract when there is no futures contract for the cash commodity being traded.

Exchanges must submit all proposed trading rules and contract terms to the CFTC for approval. When reviewing trading rules, the CFTC tries to assure that the rule will not restrict competition, and may require the exchange to amend its proposal. Exchange regulations of major economic significance must be made available to the public, and are published in the Federal Register.

Delivery points for commodities that underlie the futures contracts also are governed by the CFTC. The Commodity Futures Trading Commission has the right to require an exchange to add or change delivery locations when necessary as well.

The CFTC also has the right to review exchange actions, such as denying membership, access privileges, or disciplining members. In reviewing exchange actions, the CFTC may affirm, modify, or set aside an exchange's decision. The commission also is authorized to take emergency steps in the markets under certain conditions, such as actual or threatened market manipulation, or some other event that prevents the market from reflecting true supply-and-demand factors.

The CFTC also has broad regulatory power over floor brokers, Introducing Brokers (IBs), Futures Commission Merchants (FCMs) Associated Persons (APs), and other market participants. I explain their roles below.

Futures Commission Merchant (FCM)

A *futures commission merchant (FCM)* is a firm that transacts futures and options business on futures exchanges on behalf of financial and commercial institutions as well as the general public. Futures commission merchants are also called wire houses, brokerage houses, and commission houses. FCMs are a highly diversified segment of the financial world. Some conduct business in all types of financial investments while others confine their operations strictly to futures and options on futures.

def·i·ni·tion

A **futures commission merchant (FCM)** is a firm that transacts futures and options business on futures exchanges on behalf of financial and commercial institutions, as well as the general public.

FCMs become registered member firms of futures exchanges in order to trade or handle accounts in the markets conducted by those exchanges. Under the rules of most exchanges, however, membership can only be held by individuals. Usually, officers of the partnerships or corporations holding exchange memberships register their membership for the benefit of the corporations or partnerships. The individual member retains full control over the membership and full responsibility for the acts of the firm and its employees under the rules and regulations of the exchange.

Regardless of the size, scope, and name of the FCM, its basic function is to represent the interests of those in the market who do not hold membership on the futures exchanges. Some of the many services provided by FCMs include placing orders, collecting and segregating margin monies, providing basic accounting records, disseminating market information and research, and counseling and training customers in futures and options trading practices and strategies.

Introducing Brokers

An *introducing broker (IB)* is a person or firm that solicits or accepts orders to buy or sell futures contracts or commodity options but does not accept money. The job of an IB is to introduce business to the FCM. This is similar to the branch office arrangement of insurance agents. Your local insurance agent can help you find the appropriate policy and coverage, answering all the questions and setting you to be insured.

However, when you make out the check, you make it to the parent company, not the individual office you are dealing with. If the policy needs to be paid out, the main office pays, not the branch or agent's office.

def•i•ni•tion

The **introducing broker (IB)** is a person or firm that solicits or accepts orders to buy or sell futures contracts or commodity options but does not accept money. Money can only be accepted by futures clearing merchants. **Associated persons (AP)** are series three licensed employees of either Introducing Brokers or Futures Clearing Merchants who act as agents of a firm. The most common Associated Persons are brokers, or broker assistants.

When you deposit money with an IB, the funds are made payable to the FCM, not the firm you are dealing with. Your account statements come from the FCM, though you place all of your orders with the IB, and direct all the questions to the IB.

The funds are held by the FCM, not the IB, which is a good feature as FCMs are typically better capitalized. IBs provide customer service, answering questions and performing research. Usually the commission charged by an IB is no higher than the FCM would charge for similar services.

Associated Persons

Associated persons (APs) are licensed employees of an IB or FCM. Typically, prospective customers discuss their financial goals with an associated person, who explains the risks involved in futures and options. Information about the current prospectives of a market are told or sent via the AP, who also accepts the orders from the customer. APs are typically referred to as brokers, and serve as the marketing and customer service arm of an IB or FCM. All associated persons are series three registered and licensed to represent a customer's needs. The series three exam is a general licensing test given to all associated persons to ensure their basic proficiency with the concepts of futures trading and hedging (see the following section on National Futures Association Membership screening). If your prospective broker or firm is not a member of the National Futures Association (NFA), do not do business with them!

National Futures Association

Under the CFTC Act of 1974, the futures industry was authorized to create registered futures associations. One such organization is the National Futures Association (NFA).

The National Futures Association is an industry-supported, industry-wide, self-regulatory organization for the futures industry.

The NFA was formally designated a futures association by the CFTC in 1981 and became operational in 1982. The primary duties of the NFA are to enforce the ethical standards and customer protection rules of the CFTC, screen futures industry professionals for membership, audit and monitor futures professionals for financial and general ethical and compliance rule-following, provide an arbitration of futures-related disputes, and promote customer and member education concerning the NFA's role in the futures industry.

Customer Protection

To protect customers, NFA's ethical standards prohibit fraud, manipulative and deceptive acts and practices, and unfair business dealings. In addition, employees who handle discretionary accounts must follow procedures similar to the CFTC requirements.

All research from NFA members must be two-sided, providing equal opportunity of explaining the risks and rewards involved in futures and options trading. All research and statements of opinion must be based on fact.

All members—and membership is mandatory for IBs, FCMs, and APs—must conduct themselves in an ethical manner and with the customer's best interests or face revocation of membership, fines, and disciplinary actions.

Membership Screening

Membership in the NFA and CFTC registration are mandatory for futures commission merchants, introducing brokers, and associated persons.

Regulation of futures professionals begins with application screening. In addition to approving applicants for NFA membership, NFA is authorized by the CFTC to screen and approve applications for federal registration. Eligibility requirements are strict and specific, ensuring that the high standards of the profession and the industry are met, and that all members are professional and meet the highest standards of financial responsibility and ethics.

Proficiency testing is another NFA activity and is now required for CFTC registration. FCMs, IBs, and APs applying for membership must pass the National Commodity Futures Exam (series 3), which tests their knowledge of trading futures and options on futures as well as their understanding of exchanges, industry, and federal regulations.

Arbitration

Another important function of the NFA is to provide a centralized, uniform arbitration system. In most cases, when requested by the customer, arbitration is mandatory for all NFA member firms and their employees, including FCMs, IBs, and APs. Counterclaims made by members and disputes between NFA members also may be heard by the NFA arbitrators. Decisions of the arbitrators are generally final and may not be appealed to the NFA. Alternatives to NFA arbitration include the CFTC's reparation procedure, exchange arbitration, or any other arbitration system mutually agreed to by the member and the customer. After a suitable method is agreed upon, no other method may be used unless mutually agreed upon.

Under NFA rules, any NFA member or employee of a member who refuses to comply with an arbitration agreement is subject to disciplinary action.

Trading Tips

A broker must be licensed with the NFA before soliciting any business. This license is granted after the broker has passed the series 3 exam, which is a four-hour exam testing market knowledge and rules and regulations. A 70 percent passing score must be achieved on both the rules and regulation portion as well as the market knowledge section.

Education

The NFA educational efforts are directed to both members and the investing public. Members are assisted in complying with NFA rules and regulations, as well as CFTC rules and regulations. For the investing public, the NFA produces materials concerning fraud and how to avoid it, as well as the fundamentals of futures trading.

Choosing a Broker

Choosing a brokerage firm and an individual broker is an important component of any futures trading program. Though commissions are an important factor to consider in choosing a broker, we personally do not believe that it is the most important, especially for those fairly new to futures trading and/or hedging.

In choosing a brokerage firm, several factors should be considered:

- Disciplinary record
- Clearing arrangement

- Length of time in business

- Services

- Commissions

Let's look at each.

Disciplinary Record

The brokerage firm you do business with should be of the highest moral integrity. Ask any broker if their firm is of the highest moral integrity, and they will respond affirmatively. However, sometimes this isn't the case. By *moral integrity*, we mean they have resolved their customers' problems in a fair and equitable way. Making sure that the firm you are considering has a history of resolving customer complaints with moral integrity can make all the difference in trading profits and losses, as one mistake on your broker's part can cost you, the speculator, several months' (or years') worth of profits.

Trading Time Bomb

Before choosing a brokerage firm, we recommend that you check with the NFA at www.nfa.futures.org. If you can't find them in the NFA database, do not do business with them without calling them to get their NFA identification number, and confirming for yourself that they are registered. If you find the firm has a disciplinary record, avoid the firm. There are many good firms out there.

Clearing Arrangement

Clearing arrangement is the industry term for what type of firm they are. There are three major types of brokerage firms out there:

- Futures commission merchant

- Independent introducing brokers

- Guaranteed introducing brokers

A *futures commission merchant* is either an individual or an organization that solicits or accepts orders to buy or sell futures or options contracts and accepts money or other assets from customers in connection with such orders. They must be registered with the Commodity Futures Trading Commission. FCMs can solicit business directly, but most act as exchange liaisons for introducing brokers.

An *independent introducing broker* is an IB that is subject to minimum capital and financial reporting requirements. This type of IB may introduce accounts to any FCM. Independent IBs may be mom-and-pop shops, and have no backing beyond their capitalization.

A *guaranteed introducing broker* is an IB whose operations are guaranteed by an FCM. This type of IB has no minimum capital or financial reporting requirements. All of the accounts of a guaranteed introducing broker must be carried by the guaranteeing FCM. By being guaranteed, the IB has all of its accounts backed by the FCM, so your account is backed by the capitalization of the FCM, not your IB.

When choosing a brokerage firm, my preference is for the guaranteed introducing broker, first and foremost. This is because the money in your trading account is backed not only by the guaranteed introducing broker, but also by the FCM. Make sure that the brokerage firm you do business with is adequately capitalized, by checking to see that that they are either a guaranteed introducing broker or an FCM. When checking the disciplinary track record of a guaranteed introducing brokerage, weigh the disciplinary record of the brokerage on its own merits, separate from the FCM. FCMs rarely have clean disciplinary records because they usually have problems with other professionals, which are addressed in arbitration, and hence a record is kept.

> **Trading Tips**
> Consider choosing a guaranteed introducing brokerage firm to safeguard your funds. This is similar to having a bonded tradesman do work on your house. You have a good idea that their work is adequate and they do not take undue risks because someone is willing to underwrite their debts above and beyond their capitalization. Better safe than sorry—after all, futures trading accounts are not government guaranteed.

Length of Time in Business

Most firms, brokerages included, go out of business in the first five years of operation. Since you plan to do business with your brokerage for an extended period of time, make sure they have a track record of being in business at least five years. Also, be sure they've been doing business in the same name for five years, so you can examine their disciplinary record, checking to see that they deal with customer complaints with moral integrity. Also, by five years in the business, your brokerage firm should have enough experience to deal with the day-to-day problems associated with trading.

Services

Once you've established that your potential broker is a registered firm (preferably a guaranteed introducing brokerage or futures commission merchant), that has been in business at least five years, and has a clean NFA disciplinary record, then you should start looking at the firm's services.

Contact Medians

A brokerage firm should have some type of toll free phone number for customers to call their brokers. You should not have to pay for the phone call to contact your broker. Second, your broker should have a Web page, and it should be more than just a place to get account information. It should provide quotes, charts, and research.

Research

All brokerage firms should have an in-house analyst (self-serving, as I was an analyst and now sell research to brokerage firms). The in-house analyst(s) should be available to customers, so that a customer can have access to an unbiased opinion of the market. By unbiased, I mean someone who does not get paid directly by your commissions.

The research department should produce nightly reports, recapping the trading day's events and news. The purpose of a firm's research is to produce commissions (sad but true, just like the purpose of my research is to sell my books and newsletters), but trading recommendations should always have the following criteria: entry technique, profit objective, stop loss, and follow-up procedures.

def•i•ni•tion

Some participants in the futures market believe that different price patterns—which are usually given colorful names like 1-2-3s, Head and Shoulders, Triangles, and such—can be used to predict future price movement. The study of these patterns is known as Technical Analysis and is the subject of Chapter 17.

Good research and trading recommendations should be able to be followed, not just be bullish or bearish. Besides news, and recommendations, the firm's research department should be knowledgeable about classic technical trading techniques (*1-2-3s*, *Head and Shoulders*, *Triangles*, and so on) as well as have a firm grasp on the seasonal nature of the commodities markets.

Paper Trading: Practice Doesn't Make Perfect, But It Should Help

With the popularity of futures as a trading venue, a few service-oriented firms have begun to encourage *paper trading*. The act of paper trading allows the customer to interact with a representative of the firm, in an informal question-and-answer type of environment. The paper trader can get direct help from the broker or a firm representative, and learn much in the process.

Look for firms that have separate paper trading departments, for two reasons: first, so that the individual paper trading broker can spend time with you answering your questions; and second, so that when you graduate to moneyed trading, your broker can focus on your concerns without the added burden of fielding paper trading questions.

def•i•ni•tion

Paper trading is the practice of fictitious trading or mock trading, in which all the money made or lost is on paper. With a little help from someone with experience, you can get a pretty good idea of the risk and potential reward involved in market speculation through realistic paper trading.

Commissions

Commissions are typically quoted in one of two ways: per side or round turn. Round turn commissions refer to the cost charged for both entering and exiting a futures or options trade, while a per side quote refers to simply the cost of entering or exiting, or only one side of a trade. Commissions are typically negotiable, depending upon your opening account balance, prior trading experience, and trading frequency. Commissions vary from firm to firm, and client to client. The maximum any firm should charge is $85 round turn (plus exchange and floor fees).

Do not choose a firm based only on commissions. You typically get what you pay for! If you do business with a reputable firm, meeting the criteria above, and start your trading with $5,000 (the recommended minimum to trade futures), you should expect to pay commissions in the ball park of $60.00 for full-service and $35.00 for discount, round turn plus fees.

Full-service brokers are paid to keep your errors to a minimum. If you forget to cancel an order which is contingent upon an existing futures position, such as a stop loss to exit a market to minimize a loss (see order type information below in "Order Types"), a reputable full-service broker will cancel it for you when you exit your position, saving you from establishing a position you did not intend to have. I have seen many new traders go the route of discount, and due to confusion when placing an order, lose $2,000 or more (that's 50 round turn commissions before the commission discount would have paid for the mistake!). Until you have traded for more than three years, you should seriously consider using a full-service broker.

The bottom line to commissions is that brokers and brokerages get paid for what they provide. If you require a lot of services and use a lot of time, then expect to pay more. If you take up little of the broker's time, then expect to pay less.

Choosing an Individual Broker

Once you have decided upon a firm, you should then move to deciding on an individual broker. Individual brokers vary greatly in style, so choose someone you like talking to. Yes, you should enjoy your broker's voice and manner, as they will be calling with either great news or very bad news, so you had better like the messenger.

Do not look for a broker to tell you when to buy or sell. If you want someone to manage your money, turn it over to a *CPO/CTA (Commodity Pool Operator/Commodity Trading Advisor)*, not your broker, as they have a vested interest in you trading and generating commissions, while an advisor has to make money to get paid. Your broker's job is to handle and execute your orders, keep you informed of potential news, and advise you on risk management. Make sure that they are qualified to do this by determining that they have an understanding of all commodities—or at least the ones you are specifically interested in—their seasonal tendencies, and what factors will affect prices during specific times of the year.

def•i•ni•tion

A **Commodity Trading Advisor**, or **CTA**, is an official designation given by the CFTC to anyone who handles other people's money or gives personalized trading advice. Typically, the trader for a **Commodity Pool Operator (CPO)** is a licensed CTA. A Commodity Pool Operator is the organizer of a Commodity fund run for the specific purpose of professional management. These are similar to mutual funds in the stock market. Commodity Pools are also referred to as Managed Futures Portfolios.

Some people like brokers who trade and some don't. Brokers who trade do have a better understanding of risk and losses, but an actively trading broker can also worry more about their trades than yours, and they can help perpetuate your losses by instilling their bad habits in you. Think of a broker or analyst as a coach: Does a coach have to be a great player to be an effective coach?

Choosing a brokerage firm and individual broker is a very important decision. Choose wisely and you will be rewarded, not by profits but by a lack of headaches! Follow the guidelines mentioned, and though we cannot guarantee profits, we can guarantee you will have a much greater chance for profitability.

Order Types

Futures markets participants are required to post performance bond margins with an FCM before entering into a position. Performance bond margins are financial guarantees required by both the buyer and seller of a futures contract to ensure that they fulfill the obligation of the contract.

The main purpose of the performance bond margin is to provide contract integrity. It is not at all like the margin on stocks, which provides a down payment and a loan by the broker/dealer for the purchase of equities. Futures margin requirements are set by the exchanges based on the volatility of the market. The more volatile a market is, the greater the risk associated with that market and the higher the margin requirement. The lower the volatility, the less the risk and the lower the requirement. Thus, the exchanges, under the careful eye of the CFTC, set performance bond margins based on risk, increasing and decreasing them to account for risk associated with the market.

Initial margin is the amount of money a market participant must have on deposit with an FCM at the time an order is placed. The customer must always maintain a safety cushion after the position is placed and the daily change is credited or debited from their account with an FCM. If, on any day, the debits resulting from market activity (losses) reduce the funds in the account to below this maintenance level (maintenance margin), the FCM, IB, or AP calls the holder of these contracts to either deposit additional funds to bring the account back above the initial margin requirement, or liquidate the position.

The CFTC and the NFA, by enforcing these procedures, ensure that the system performs efficiently. Just as every buyer and seller must keep adequate margin funds in their account to maintain a futures position, so must each IB/FCM maintain its account with each exchange's central clearinghouse. IBs accomplish this by making sure all their customers are adequately margined with the FCM.

Handling margins and ensuring the soundness of the financial system underlying futures trading is an important role that many in the futures industry must maintain. However, responsibility for placing orders, collecting margin deposits, and overseeing accounts is generally only the responsibility of the IB and AP.

Order Placing

Understanding the customer's objectives and properly relaying orders are vital functions that are carefully scrutinized by regulators. The AP must write and enter orders without vagueness or ambiguity to ensure that they are properly handled on the trading floor. A mistake in this process can be very costly, therefore, both the customer and the AP must accurately communicate the order.

In this age of online trading, it is even more important for traders to understand order placing. Without thorough knowledge of the order-placing process and understanding what each order does, the speculators could place orders that do the opposite of their intended purposes, which may result in financial losses.

The common order types include the market order, limit order, stop order, day or good-till-canceled, and one-cancels-other (OCO).

Market Order

The *market order* is the most common type of order. With a market order, the customer states the number of contracts of a particular delivery month of a specific commodity they wish to buy or sell. The price of the order is not specified, as the market order is filled "at the market" or the current price when the order enters the trading pit. Market orders are placed when the speculator or hedger wants in or out of the market fast, as time, not price, is the most important factor.

A customer wishing to buy July Corn would state, "buy me two July Corn at the market." A seller would state "sell two July Corn at the market."

Limit Order (Price)

The *limit order*, or "or better" order, specifies a price limit at which the order can be filled. The limit order can only be filled at the specified price "or better."

A customer wishing to buy two July Corn at 210 when July Corn is trading at 211 would place the following order: "Buy two July Corn at 210, limit." Buy limit orders must be placed at the current market price or lower; this is because when buying, you want the lowest price. The lower the price, the better, and limit orders can only be filled at the specified price or lower. Hence, one can only place a buy limit order at the current price or lower.

A customer wishing to sell two July Corn at 215 when July Corn is trading at 211 would place the following order: "Sell two July Corn at 215, limit." Sell limit orders must be placed at the current market price or higher; this is because when selling, you want the highest price possible. The higher the price the better, and sell limit orders can only be filled at the specified price or higher.

An important note about limit orders is that when a buy limit is placed above the market it can turn into a market order, and get filled immediately. This is because if the current price is below the limit price, the market is in a better situation and it becomes a market order. The same principle applies to sell limits: when a sell limit is placed below the market, it becomes a market order, as the higher market price is better.

Stop Order

A *stop order* is not executed until the market reaches the specified price level. Once the stop level is hit, the stop order becomes a market order. Buy stops are always placed above the market, while sell stops are placed below the market.

A customer wishing to buy July Soybeans at 485 when the current market price is 475 would place a stop order: "Buy one July Soybean at 485, stop." If the Soybean market trades as high as 485 or is bid at 485, the order would become a market order and would be filled as quickly as possible.

A customer wishing to sell July Soybeans at 465 when the market is currently priced at 475 would place a stop order as follows: "Sell one July Soybean at 465, stop." If the Soybean market traded as low as 465 or was offered at 465, the order would become a market order and would be filled as quickly as possible.

Stop orders are usually used to liquidate earlier transactions, to cut losses, or to protect profits. For example, let's assume that speculators bought three July Corn at 210 and the market is currently trading at 225. They may wish to protect some of their 15-cent profit per contract ($2,250 profit before commissions and fees) by placing a sell stop at 220, to protect 10 cents ($1,500 of the profit before commissions and fees). This would be done by placing the following order: "Sell three July Corn at 220, stop."

If our speculators wished to take profits at 230, they would place a sell limit order as follows: "Sell three July Corn at 230, limit."

Day or Good-Till-Canceled

All orders are assumed good for the session they are placed unless specified otherwise. If you wish to have an order working until you request it to be canceled, then use the "GTC" at the end of the order (good-till-canceled).

For example, our Corn speculators with the stop at 220 above may wish to place this order good-till-canceled, as follows: "Sell three July Corn at 220, stop and good-till-canceled." By signifying good-till-canceled, the speculators are telling their brokers to place the order every day until it is either executed or canceled.

One Cancels Other (OCO)

The one-cancels-other (OCO) designation on an order links two orders together, having one order cancel the other order if it is executed.

For example, our Corn speculators have a sell stop order working at 220 to protect profits and a sell limit order at 230 to take profits. They may wish to make these orders contingent by making them OCO as follows: "Sell three July Corn at 220, stop. Sell three July Corn 230, limit, good-till-canceled." This order instructs the broker to sell three July Corn if the price reaches 220 on the downside and to sell three July Corn at 230 or better (higher) if the price reaches 230. If either order is executed, the broker has been instructed to cancel the other order. The good-till-canceled designation tells the broker to keep the order valid until either executed or canceled.

The Least You Need to Know

♦ The futures industry is federally regulated by the Commodity Futures Trading Commission (CFTC). Customers and market participants are protected by the National Futures Association (NFA), which enforces the rules and resolves disputes between customers and their brokers.

♦ Generally, new traders should strongly consider choosing to work with a full-service broker.

♦ Make sure that the individual broker and the firm you choose are registered with the NFA.

♦ The most common order placed in the futures markets is a market order, which simply means to initiate a futures transaction at the current price.

♦ Stop orders can be used for both initiating a position or for managing risk.

♦ Without thorough knowledge of the order-placing process and understanding what each order does, speculators could place orders that do the opposite of their intended purposes, which may result in financial losses.

Part 3

Options on Futures: Basics and Strategies

You can learn about the options markets and how to use put and call options on futures to either protect against unwanted price changes or profit from changing prices.

Besides futures contracts, hedgers and speculators can use the options markets to transfer or accept risk of price change. In this section, the two types of options—puts and calls—are explained in an easy-to-follow format.

Learn how to use put options to profit from or protect yourself from falling prices, and how call options can be used to protect against or profit from rising prices.

Different combinations of puts, calls, and futures are explained. You also explore how these different combinations can be tailored to create various positions that can profit from any future price outlook.

Chapter 8

Options Basics

In This Chapter

- ◆ The right to buy or sell … options
- ◆ Calling the market up with options
- ◆ Putting down the market with options
- ◆ Time, volatility, and the price of options
- ◆ Options strategies for every market condition
- ◆ Options and futures, protecting against unlimited risk

Options on futures were introduced in 1982 when the Chicago Board of Trade began trading options on Treasury Bond futures as part of a government pilot program. The success of the program led the way for options on Agricultural Products, Metals, and other Financial futures.

Trading in options is not new. Options have been used with physical commodities, securities (stocks and bonds), and real estate for decades. There was over-the-counter trading in stock options long before the creation of the Chicago Board Options Exchange (CBOE) in the mid-1970s. Typically, speculators in the stock options markets are investors seeking to profit from changes in a stock's price on a more leveraged basis. Many of the same principles that apply to options in the physical commodities markets and stock options market can be used effectively with options on futures contracts.

In this chapter, you will learn what options are and how you can use them to speculate and to minimize your risk.

What Is an Option?

An *option*, as the definition implies, provides you with a choice. The buyer of an option acquires the right—but not the obligation—to buy or sell an underlying futures contract under specific conditions in exchange for payment for that right (premium). The buyer of an option has the right to exercise the option, converting it into a futures contract if it is profitable for them to do so.

There are two basic types of options:

◆ A call option gives the buyer the right, but not the obligation, to purchase a particular futures contract at a specific price anytime during the life of the option.

◆ A put option gives the buyer the right, but not the obligation, to sell a particular futures contract at a specific price anytime during the life of the option.

def•i•ni•tion

The **strike price** is the price at which the futures contract underlying a call or put option can be purchased (if a call) or sold (if a put). Also referred to as the "exercise price." Options on futures generally expire on a specific date during the month preceding the futures contract delivery month, known as the **expiration month.** For example, an option on a March futures contract expires in February but is referred to as a March option because its exercise would result in a March futures contract position.

The price at which the buyer of a call option has the right to purchase the futures contract or the buyer of a put option has the right to sell the futures contract is known as the *strike price* (or exercise price).

The amount of time the purchaser of the option has the right to purchase (call options) or sell (put options) the underlying futures contract is known as the *expiration month.*

Just as futures contracts are standardized, so are options contracts on futures. Each option has predetermined strike prices and expiration dates. Each options contract can only be offset before expiration by selling a like option (same commodity, month, and strike price call or put). The only variable in the equation is the price paid for this right, known as premium.

For example, assume a speculator is expecting Soybean prices to rise in the next three months. First, he would look to see which options are available. Assuming it is March, he may look at July Soybean options, which can be exercised into the July CBOT Soybean contract. Soybean options trade in 20 cents per bushel strike price intervals. With July Soybeans trading at $4.37 per bushel, strike prices are available ranging from $3.40 to $8.40 for the July contract. These options expire about one week before the first notice day of the futures contract, allowing a little time for the option to be converted to a futures contract (exercised).

Our bullish speculator may wish to look at the July 460 Call Soybean options, which are trading at 9½ cents per bushel (or $475.00 per contract before commissions and fees). In exchange for the premium (9½ cents or $475.00 per contract), our speculator has the right to buy July Soybeans at the strike price ($4.60 per bushel, or 460) on or before the options expiration date in the last week of June. If July Soybean prices stay below 460, the option will expire worthless and our option speculator will be out his premium. However, if soybeans rally above the strike price, he could exercise the option and get a futures contract in exchange or sell the option (offset) on the open market for a gain.

Understanding Options Prices

The price of an option is a function of where the underlying futures market is in relation to …

♦ The strike price

♦ The amount of time left until expiration (time value)

♦ The volatility of the underlying instrument

Option prices are based on these factors, and are determined in trading pits in a fashion very similar to futures.

Strike Price

The biggest factor in determining the price of an option is where the underlying futures contract is in relation to the strike price. A call option with a strike price below the current price of the underlying futures contract has intrinsic value. For example, a July 460 call option in the Soybean market is worth at least 20 cents (intrinsic value) if the July futures are trading at $4.80 per bushel. A put option with a strike price above the current price of the underlying futures contract has intrinsic value as well. For example, if July Soybeans were trading at $4.80 per bushel, a July 500 Put would be worth at least 20 cents. Basically, an option has intrinsic value when it can be exercised profitably. For example, the right to buy Soybeans at 460 is worth at least 20 cents when the price of Soybeans is at 480. If the option traded for anything less, arbitragers would buy the call options and sell the futures, profiting from the differential until the two came back into line.

def•i•ni•tion

The **intrinsic value** of an option is the amount of money that option would be worth if it were exercised and turned into a futures contract today. For example, a 100 call option with the futures at 120 would have an intrinsic value of 20. A 100 put option with the futures at 80 would also have an intrinsic value of 20 (Call Option's Intrinsic Value = Futures − Strike and Put Option's Intrinsic Value = Strike − Futures).

A call option is considered **in-the-money** if the futures price is above the strike price. Put options are considered in-the-money if the futures are trading below the strike price of the put. If the strike price of the option equals the futures price, the option is considered **at-the-money**.

Intrinsic value is the difference, if any, between the market price of the underlying commodity and the strike price of the option. A call option has intrinsic value if its strike price is below the price of the underlying futures price. A put option has intrinsic value if the strike price is above the current underlying futures price. Any option that has intrinsic value is said to be *in-the-money*. As a general rule, the larger the amount of intrinsic value of an option, the higher the premium paid for that option will be.

If an option has no intrinsic value, it is said to be either *at-the-money* or *out-of-the-money*. An at-the-money option is one where the underlying futures price is equal to the strike price of the option. For example, with soybeans trading at 480, the 480 Calls and Puts are referred to as at-the-money options. If a call option has a strike price higher than the current underlying futures price, the option is said to be out-of-the-money. If a put option has a strike price below the current underlying futures price, the put option is said to be out-of-the-money. At-the-money and out-of-the-money options have what is known as extrinsic value or time value. You can use the Intrinsic Value table for easy reference to find futures with intrinsic value:

Trading Tip: Intrinsic Value

	Call	Put
In-The-Money	Futures > Strike	Futures < Strike
At-The-Money	Futures = Strike	Futures = Strike
Out-Of-The-Money	Futures < Strike	Futures > Strike

Time Value

The second major component of an option price—or premium—is time value. Time value is the amount of money that option buyers are willing to pay for an option in the anticipation that over time the price of the underlying futures will change in value, causing the option to increase in value. Time value also reflects the amount of money that a seller of an option requires to relinquish the right to the purchaser.

Generally speaking, the longer the amount of time until an option's expiration, the greater the time value of the option will be. This is because the right to buy or sell something is more valuable to a market participant if they have several months to decide what to do, than if they only have several days. Conversely, the option seller has more risk over time that the option will go in-the-money (or stay in-the-money), and thus demands more premium in exchange for selling the right to buy or sell over a longer period of time.

Some parallels can be made between options and insurance policies in this case. The premium charged for term causality insurance increases the longer the policy period, because obviously the likelihood of a claim being made increases with the length of the policy. The longer the time of the policy, the greater the likelihood that the policyholder will make a claim, hence the greater the risk to the policy writer (the insurance company), and thus the higher the premium paid for the policy.

The same general principle applies to the options on the futures market—the longer the time to expiration, the greater the likelihood that the option will be exercised, hence the greater the risk to the option writer, and thus the higher the premium charged for the option. In general, because of the risk and potential reward associated with time, the greater the amount of time to expiration of the option, the more expensive the premium of the option will be.

Volatility

Another component of extrinsic value—or time value—is the *volatility* of the underlying futures contract. Volatility is the amount of movement in the underlying market over a period of time. Obviously, if prices are moving up and down and changing by large amounts, the risk and potential reward associated with this market is greater, and hence the price of the option will be greater.

For example, assume that Soybean prices have traded between $4.30 and $5.30 per bushel for the last year. The risk associated with writing a $5.40 call option may seem minute, as well as the profit potential of this option. Thus, in this case, the cost of

def•i•ni•tion

Volatility is the amount of movement in the underlying market over a period of time. Options tend to be more expensive when volatility is high and tend to be cheaper when volatility is low. Options buyers should look to buy quiet markets and sell their options when prices become volatile.

this option would be relatively small, as the risk to the option should be perceived as minimal and the potential reward perceived by the buyer would be small. However, if Soybean prices were to rise from $4.30 to $5.30 in a single week, suddenly the risk associated with writing a $5.40 call option would seem large, as well as the potential reward in purchasing such an option. Thus, the price commanded by sellers in return for the right would increase and buyers would be more willing to pay this price. So, generally speaking, the greater the volatility, the greater the price of the option.

Volatility and time to expiration have tremendous impact on the price of out-of-the-money and at-the-money options. These factors affect the extrinsic value portion of an in-the-money option as well. Just because an option is in-the-money does not mean that it does not have any extrinsic value. But as an option gets deeper and deeper in-the-money, it loses time value as a component of its pricing.

Because options have extrinsic value, or time value, they are decaying assets. As time passes, the amount of time value decreases. The rate of decay of time value increases as you get closer to expiration, speeding way up close to six weeks until expiration. Hence, for the option purchaser, time is the enemy, slowly eroding the value of an option (see the following graph).

Time value vs. months to expiration.

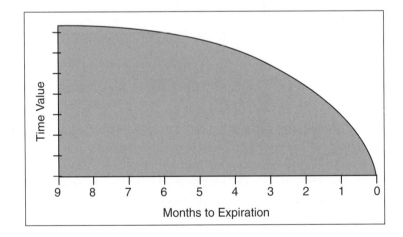

Option Pricing Models

There are many option pricing models that take these different variables—intrinsic value, time remaining to expiration, and volatility—into account (as well as other factors like short-term interest rates) to calculate the theoretical value of an option. These theoretical values may or may not correspond to the actual market values in the pit, but are used as price gauges by professional option traders.

Probably the most prominent option-pricing model is the Black-Scholes model, developed by Fisher Black and Myron Scholes in 1973 (they received a Nobel Prize in Economics for it). These models are extremely complex, and generally only give the trader a small edge in pricing options, and thus are well beyond the scope of this text. However, very serious option speculators should look into them.

The general purpose of these models is to break option prices into components. These models derive from what option traders call the Greeks: *delta*, *gamma*, *vega*, and *theta*. Understanding these concepts can help a trader understand how an option's price should change versus changes in the underlying and given changes in volatility and time.

Delta is the change of the option versus a change in the underlying futures contract. For example, if Soybean prices go up 10 cents and your call option increases in value by 4½ cents, then the option is said to have a delta of 45 percent (Delta = Change in Option Price/Change in Futures Price).

Gamma is the rate of change of delta. For example, if the next day, Soybean prices increase another 10 cents, and the option price goes up 5 cents, the gamma of this option is 5 percent, or delta today – delta yesterday ($\frac{5}{10} - 4\frac{1}{2} \div 10$ = 50% delta today – 45% delta yesterday = 5% gamma).

Generally, out-of-the-money options have a lower delta than at-the-money options. At-the-money options tend to have deltas very near 50 percent, and in-the-money

def•i•ni•tion

Delta is the change of the option versus a change in the underlying futures contract. **Gamma** is the rate of change of delta. At-the-money options tend to have deltas very near 50 percent, and in-the-money deltas approach 100 percent (equal change) when they are deep in-the-money. **Theta** is the time component of prices, or a mathematical expression of how much value is lost each day. **Vega** is the measurement of how the price of an option changes versus a change in volatility, typically expressed as a percentage of the change in volatility.

deltas approach 100 percent (equal change) when they are deep in-the-money. By understanding that an out-of-the-money option has less delta, traders can use this to create equivalent futures positions. The delta of an option is also thought of as a hedge ratio, meaning it takes four 25 percent delta options to create a long futures position. However, as time goes by and the market moves in the favor of the option holder, eventually this position could equal four futures positions if the option goes deep in-the-money.

Trading Tips

When purchasing options, it is very tempting to buy deep out-of-the-money options because they are cheap. Ask your broker for the delta on the option. Delta is considered by many to be a good judge of the odds that the option will be in-the-money at expiration. Only buy deep out-of-the-money options if you like betting on long shots!

Theta is the mathematical expression of time decay. As we mentioned earlier in this chapter, options are a decaying asset. The closer they get to expiration, the less time value they have. The rate of decay is known as theta. Vega is the effect that a change in volatility has upon the price of an option. Generally, when market volatility increases, the premium of an option will increase as well. However, vega changes are less than delta and gamma, so a large run-up in prices will not cause put prices to increase just because volatility increases. The increased volatility will be counteracted by the change in price away from the strike price (delta).

Option Strategies

Options can be used in any market environment:

- Bullish
- Slightly bullish
- Neutral
- Slightly bearish
- Extremely bearish

The combination of option purchases and sales using calls and puts is almost limitless, and as such it would be impossible to cover all the strategies in this chapter. But you will get a solid appreciation for the power of options and the flexibility they provide and gain an appreciation for why put and call options are bought and sold en masse on a daily basis. In Chapter 9, we will examine different option combinations and strategies, but first we need to understand how you can make money by buying and selling options.

Long Call Options

A call option gives the buyer the right to buy a futures contract at a predetermined price (the strike price) during a specific amount of time (expiration date). In exchange for this right, the buyer of the option pays a premium. The general logic behind buying a call option is either to hedge against higher prices or a bullish position in which the buyer hopes that the futures market will rally, increasing the premium he paid for the option.

For example, assume that a speculator is bullish about the Wheat market. She may look at buying a July CBOT Wheat call option with a 290 strike price in March, when the futures are trading at 270. In return for this right, she would pay the going price for this option, which we will assume is 10 cents. Wheat futures are based on a 5,000 bushel contract size, so the cost of the option would be $500 (or $0.10 × 5,000 bushels).

Suppose that the price of wheat rises from 270 to 280 in the next two weeks. Though this option is still out-of-the-money, the market price for the option (premium) should increase. For example, assume that two weeks later, after a 10-cent rally in July Wheat futures, the July 280 CBOT Wheat call option is being bid on the floor at 14 cents. The holder of this option can sell this option for 14 cents, and make a quick $200 (14 cents – 10 cents × 5,000 bushels = $200 before commissions and fees). The purchaser of the option has the right to resell the option at any time, or exercise it into a futures contract. Because the value of the option increased, the speculator may wish to take her profit, which represents a 40 percent return on the money invested in just two weeks.

Our speculator may wish to hold on to this option. Suppose over the next several weeks, July Wheat futures rally to $3.00 per bushel (300 cents). The option would be worth a minimum of 10 cents ($500 or the price he paid for it), as it would be 10 cents in-the-money. However, because there is still time value in the option, the 290 call option in July Wheat may be worth close to 24 cents, representing a profit of 14 cents, or $700 before commissions and fees.

Again, the purchaser of the call option has the right to exercise it, sell it on the open market, or hold it until expiration. In this example, as in most, the speculator would not exercise the option. By exercising the option, she would get a long July futures position at 290, when the market is trading at 300. However, if she decides to sell the option on the open market, the option could be sold for 24 cents, increasing her profit potential by 14 cents.

Let's suppose our speculator decides to hold the option longer. If July Wheat turns and goes south, declines from 300 to 285 at expiration, the holder of the 290 July

Wheat call option is out her initial investment only, of 10 cents, or $500 before commissions and fees. Because July Wheat was selling below the strike price at options expiration—below 290 in this case—the option expires worthless. The holder of the call option sacrifices the premium paid, and the seller of the call option gets to keep the premium without having to initiate a short position in the futures market.

In essence, the purchaser of a call option—initiating a long call position—is making a limited risk speculation that prices will rise between the purchase date and the option's expiration, or the time he decides to exit the position by offsetting it. The total risk of the position is limited to the premium paid.

The following graph illustrates the profit and loss nature of a long call position. The x-axis, or horizontal axis, represents the price of the underlying futures contract, while the y-axis, or vertical axis, represents the profit or loss of the total position at expiration. The break-even point on a call purchase at the option's expiration is equal to the strike price plus the premium paid for the option, while the maximum loss is equal to the amount paid for the option.

Long call option P&L.

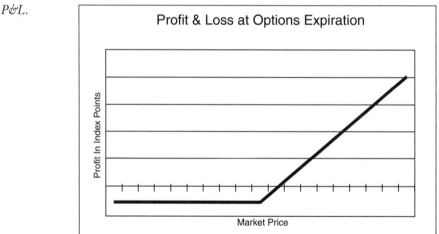

Long Put Options

A put option gives the buyer the right to sell a futures contract at a predetermined price (the strike price) during a specific amount of time (expiration date). In exchange for this right, the buyer of the option pays a premium. The general logic behind buying a put option is either to hedge against lower prices or a bearish position in which the buyer hopes that the futures market will decrease, increasing the premium he paid for the option.

Remember, because put options give the buyer of the option the right to sell the futures contract, put options increase in value when the price of the underlying futures declines in value.

For example, let's assume that a trader feels that given recent press coverage of Mad Cow Disease or BSE, that consumption of beef will decrease. With less beef being consumed, prices should decrease. As such, in late March, he decides to buy a June 7200 Live Cattle put option. With June Live Cattle futures trading at 72.475 cents per pound (or 7247), this option is selling for 1.25 cents per pound or $500 (Live Cattle futures represent 40,000 pounds, so $0.0125 × 40,000 lbs = $500 per option).

Assume that over the course of the next three weeks, June Live Cattle futures decline four cents, from 72.475 to 68.475. The price of the 7200 June Live Cattle put should increase by roughly two cents, to 3.25 from 1.25, being that it is in-the-money, for a potential profit of $800 ($0.02 × 40,000 pounds = $800).

Our speculator can either liquidate the option by offsetting it (selling the exact same put option that he sold) or hold on. Let's assume that our speculator decides to hold on to the position. After the sharp break in prices, June Live Cattle prices rally back up to 72.45 over the next four weeks. Our speculator's in-the-money put option is now out-of-the-money and bid on the exchange floor at 0.50 cents, representing a loss on the option of $300 (0.50 – 1.25 = 0.75 cent loss on the option, or 0.75 × 40,000 = $300). Because the option has roughly seven weeks of life left, the option originally worth 1.25 cents has declined to being worth only 0.50 cents, due to time decay.

With only about three weeks left to the expiration of the option, our speculator can either hold on to the option, and risk it expiring worthless but also retain the possibility that it increases in value, or offset the position (sell the put option) and take his loss.

As it happened, Live Cattle prices declined to settle at 71.90 on options expiration. If our speculator had held on, his option would have expired in-the-money by 0.10 cents. Unless instructed otherwise, the exchange would automatically convert this into a short futures position at 72.00, and our speculator would be out the premium paid for the option.

In essence, the purchaser of a put option—initiating a long put position—is making a limited risk speculation that prices will decline between the purchase date and options expiration, or the time he decides to exit the position by offsetting it. The total risk of the position is limited to the premium paid.

The following graph illustrates the profit and loss nature of a long put position. The x-axis, or horizontal axis, represents the price of the underlying futures contract, while the y-axis, or vertical axis, represents the profit or loss of the total position at expiration. The break-even point on a put purchase at the option's expiration is equal to the strike price minus the premium paid for the option, while the maximum loss is equal to the amount paid for the option.

Long put option P&L.

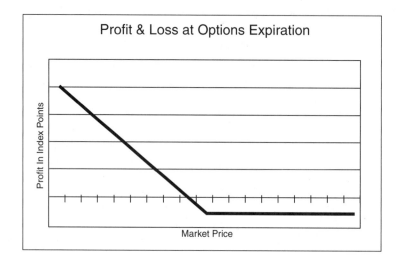

Short Call Position

Until this point we have only looked at buying options. Industry lore holds that 85 percent of all options expire worthless! Add this with the fact that options are a decaying asset, meaning that options decrease in value the closer they get to expiration, and one can see why some industry experts believe that option selling is the way to go.

However, selling options can be extremely difficult. A short options position has a limited reward to the premium collected at the time of the sale, while risk is unlimited. Second, the writer of an option has obligations, not rights. He must deliver the futures contract only if it is unprofitable for him.

Selling options, or short option positions, is slightly akin to writing an insurance policy. Think about life insurance for a minute. Life insurance companies know you will eventually die. However, they write policies because they charge enough in premiums to compensate them for the fact that you will eventually collect on the policy. Though option sellers do not know for sure whether an option will be exercised, they are always faced with the possibility. As such, option sellers demand a price for their options that they feel compensates them for the risk.

For example, let's assume that our speculator is looking at the Gold market. With the large amounts of central bank selling going on in recent years, and a weakening economy, she feels that the coming Christmas shopping season will be lackluster and that the demand for jewelry at Christmas will be less than average.

Based on this assumption, our speculator feels that December Gold futures will not go above $300 per troy ounce between Thanksgiving and Christmas. Based on this she decides to sell a December Gold 300 call option for $4.50 per ounce when December Gold is trading at $275 per ounce. Gold futures control 100 ounces of Gold, so she collects $450 for his 300 December Gold call.

Trading Tips

Unlike options purchases, where the risk is limited to the premium paid, writers of options have unlimited risk. Given this unlimited risk feature, option writers have to post margin. Generally the initial margin on a short options position is equal to three times the current value of the option. The margin requirement can change daily, so be sure to consult with your broker about this before starting an option-writing program.

Over the next two weeks, Gold prices decline from $275 to $265, and the price of the December 300 call option declines from $4.50 to $3.00, representing an unrealized profit of $150 per option ($4.50 – $3.00 = $1.50 profit per ounce based on a 100 ounce contract = $150 per option). Our speculator could take this profit by offsetting her short call position by buying a December 300 Gold call option. However, she decides to hold the option, hoping prices will decline more.

Federal Reserve interest rate cuts, and a stronger-than-expected economy, drive Gold prices up to 290 per ounce in the next two weeks. Our speculator's December 300 Gold call option is now worth $5.00 per troy ounce, representing a loss of $50 per option. This option is still out-of-the-money and could expire worthless—letting our speculator keep the $450 in premium collected from the sale of the option. However, Gold prices could go higher, and our speculator's loss potential is unlimited.

Our speculator decides to hold on, and Gold prices do indeed rally up to 302 on the December futures on options expiration. Our speculator is assigned a short December futures position at $300 per ounce. However, our speculator is able to offset her futures position at $302, and takes a $200 loss on the futures contract, but he collected $450 in premium from the sale of the option. So in total, our speculator would have made $250 before commissions and fees from the sale of the option.

If Gold futures had stayed below $300 before options expiration, the 300 December Gold call would have expired worthless, and the writer of the option would have gotten to keep the entire premium, without ever having to enter the futures market.

In essence, the writer of a call option—initiating a short call position—is making a limited profit potential, unlimited risk speculation that prices will decline between the purchase date and options expiration, or the time he decides to exit the position by offsetting it. The total risk on this position is unlimited, as futures prices can advance, while the profit potential is limited to the premium collected. However, because options are a decaying asset, meaning that their value declines the closer they get to expiration, call option writers not only benefit from declining prices, but they also benefit from stable, sideways price movement as well.

The following graph illustrates the profit and loss nature of a short call position. The x-axis, or horizontal axis, represents the price of the underlying futures contract, while the y-axis, or vertical axis, represents the profit or loss of the total position at expiration. The break-even point on a call sale at the option's expiration is equal to the strike price plus the premium paid for the option. The maximum profit potential is the premium received from the sale of the option, while the maximum loss is equal to the market price minus the strike price plus the premium received.

Short call option P&L.

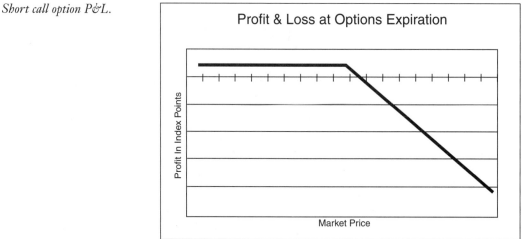

Short Put Position

The writer of a put is selling the right to sell a futures contract at a predetermined price (the strike price) during a specific period of time (expiration date). In return for granting these rights to the purchaser, the writer of an option collects the premium paid.

Selling put options is an unlimited risk, limited reward speculation that prices will rise or at least not decline below the strike price by an amount greater than the premium received for the option.

Assume that a speculator believes that oil prices will continue to go higher, based on recent grumbling from OPEC about production cuts. With June Crude Oil futures trading at $62 a barrel in late February, the June 29 Crude Oil put options are trading at $0.60 per barrel. Since he believes that Crude Oil prices will rise, he sells a June 29 Crude Oil put and collects $600 in premium for the option (Crude Oil futures represent 1,000 barrels of Crude, so $0.60 × 1,000 barrels = $600 per option).

If over the next four weeks, Crude Oil prices decline to $60 a barrel, due to a lack of consumption given a softening economy, the price of the June 29 put options should increase to $1.20 per option. This represents an unrealized loss of $600 per option ($0.60 – $1.20 × 1,000 barrels = –$600 per option).

Our speculator may decide that his assumption on Crude Oil prices was incorrect, and offset the position by buying a June 29 Crude Oil put option for $1.20 and realizing a $0.60 per option, or $600, loss. Or our speculator may still think his original assumption was correct and prices will rally, so he will continue to hold the position.

Assume for a moment that our speculator continues to hold the position and prices decline rapidly. Instead of cutting production, OPEC decides to raise production, and prices continue to fall. Over the next two weeks, Crude Oil prices fall to $57 per barrel, and the June 29 put option increases in value to $2.30 cents, representing a loss of $1,700 per option ($0.60 – $2.30 = $1.70 per barrel loss × 1,000 barrels = –$1,700 loss). At this point the option is in-the-money by $2.00 per barrel, and our speculator is facing major losses in relation to the original premium collected. He may wish to offset the position by purchasing a June 29 Crude Oil put option, and taking the loss.

Now, assume instead of prices declining, they remain basically unchanged for the next three weeks. With only about a week left to expiration of the option and June Crude Oil futures trading at $60 a barrel, the June 29 Crude Oil put options may be trading about $0.35 per barrel. Though our speculator was wrong about direction—given that Crude Oil prices fell by $2.00 per barrel over the previous six weeks—the price of the option declined in value because the "odds" that Crude Oil will decline below $59 are significantly less given the short amount of time left to expiration. In this case, our speculator could either offset his position and realize a profit of $250 before commission, or continue to hold the position for the next week, and hope that Crude Oil prices stay above $59 and get to collect the entire premium.

As it happened, Crude Oil prices rallied on the back of a solid summer driving season demand and the option expired worthless, so the writer of the option got to collect the entire $600 in premium.

In essence, the writer of a put option—initiating a short put position—is making a limited profit potential, unlimited risk speculation that prices will rise between the purchase date and options expiration, or the time he decides to exit the position by offsetting it. The total risk on this position is unlimited, as futures prices can decline to theoretically zero, while the profit potential is limited to the premium collected. However, because options are a decaying asset, meaning that their value declines the closer they get to expiration, put option writers not only benefit from rising prices, but they also benefit from stable, sideways price movement as well.

The following graph illustrates the profit and loss nature of a short put position. The x-axis, or horizontal axis, represents the price of the underlying futures contract, while the y-axis, or vertical axis, represents the profit or loss of the total position at expiration. The break-even point on a put sale at the option's expiration is equal to the strike price minus the premium paid for the option. The maximum profit potential is the premium received from the sale of the option, while the maximum loss is equal to the market price minus the strike price plus the premium received.

Short put P&L.

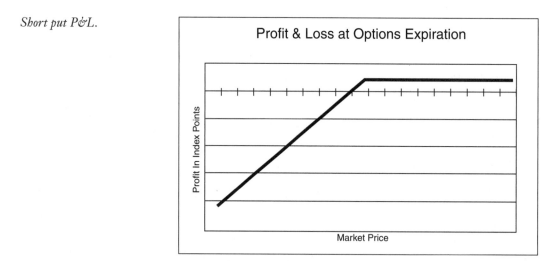

Option Buying Offers Limited Risk

It is worth restating one of the basic tenets of the options market. The purchase of a long options position (put or call) is a limited risk endeavor. The owner of an option can lose no more than the initial price—or premium—paid for the option. This is not true for short options positions or for futures contracts.

Buying options is the only limited risk, unlimited reward way to speculate in the commodities market. However, do not discount the risk of losing your premium. It has been estimated that most long option purchases expire worthless. This is especially true of the "cheap" out-of-the-money options that are popular for the retail trading public.

Option buyers also pay a time premium for the option. As the option approaches expiration, this premium is removed and can result in financial losses for the option purchaser. Because options are a decaying asset—losing time value—it is possible to correct on the direction of the market and still lose money on the purchase of an option.

Most option traders use options in conjunction with other options or with futures to establish option positions that can generate more likely profits or reduced risk in the market. These strategies are the subject of Chapter 9.

Option Market Wrap-Up

Like futures, the options market has the same basic safeguards to ensure market integrity. Option sellers are required to post performance bond margin to ensure fulfillment of the options contract. Options margins are assessed only on positions that have unlimited risk (like short call or short put positions, not covered positions like Bull call and Bear put spreads—see Chapter 9), and are subject to change at the discretion of the exchange. Option margin levels are set by the exchange at levels that ensure market integrity without unduly increasing the cost of participation by speculators and hedgers.

Following the conclusion of trade each day, just like futures, options positions are marked to market, with short option positions requiring margin to be posted. Long option positions require no margin to be posted as risk is limited to the amount paid for by the option.

Generally, options provide traders and hedgers another vehicle to either profit from or reduce the risk of price movements. Options can be used in any market environment: bullish, slightly bullish, neutral, slightly bearish, or extremely bearish. The combination of option purchases and sales using calls and puts is almost limitless, but the basic strategies explained in this chapter give the reader an idea of the trading possibilities for using options.

The Least You Need to Know

- A call option represents the right to buy a futures contract at a predetermined price during a specific time period.

- A put option represents the right to sell a futures contract at a predetermined price during a specific time period.

- The buyer of an option (long position) has risk limited to the amount paid for the option, and potentially unlimited profit potential.

- The seller of an option (short position) has potentially unlimited risk potential, and profit potential limited to the amount someone paid for the option. However, most options expire worthless and options are a decaying asset, so either strategy can be profitable if proper risk management is used.

- The buyer of an option pays for the rights associated with the option in return for the rights granted.

- The seller of an option grants those rights in return for payment. It is possible to establish both long or short positions in the options market.

Options Strategies

In This Chapter

- ◆ How to profit from up or down markets
- ◆ Using bull calls
- ◆ Finding bear puts
- ◆ Using call and put options
- ◆ Margins and option strategies

Options on futures can be used alone or in conjunction with futures contracts to establish a plethora of positions, which can profit from almost any market scenario imaginable. The most basic strategies (see Chapter 8), like long call options or long put options, offer traders a limited risk and unlimited reward way to profit from changing prices.

Slightly more complex strategies, like straddles, can be used to profit from large changes in prices in either direction (up or down), while options used in conjunction with futures can be used to hedge the unlimited risk potential inherent in the futures market.

In this chapter, we highlight some strategies you can use to speculate in the options market.

The Straddle

Wouldn't it be nice to be able to profit if prices either went up or down? Using a simple options strategy known as a straddle, you can. A straddle position involves both calls and puts.

The purchaser of a straddle, or long straddle position, buys both a call and a put option. Generally the long straddle position is a limited risk, unlimited profit potential speculation that prices will change greatly, either up or down. This position is typically initiated by purchasing an at-the-money call option and an at-the-money put option. Because the risk involved in buying options is limited to only the amount paid in premium for the option, the risk on either position (call or put) is limited, while the potential reward remains unlimited. Thus, given a large enough move, either the call or the put will expire worthless, while the other option will be deep enough in the money to offset the cost of the position.

For example, our speculator, who is familiar with the old saying "stocks will fluctuate," decides to buy a straddle in the Standards and Poor's E-mini Options market. With the June S&P E-mini futures trading at 1252.50, he buys a 1250 call option and a 1250 put option for June delivery. The June 1250 call options are trading at 28.25 points, and the June 1250 put options are trading at 31.75 points. Because the S&P E-mini represents 50 shares of the S&P, the call would be purchased for a price of $1,412.50 and the put would be purchased for a price of $1,587.50 (28.25 × 50 = $1,412.50 for the call, 31.75 × 50 = $1,587.50 for the put). The total cost of this position would be $3,000 or 60.00 S&P E-mini Index points.

Trading Tips

It is best to buy a straddle when the market is extremely quiet. In order for this strategy to be profitable at the option's expiration, the market must move enough to cover the total outlay of the position, which can be a large amount. Active traders may wish to take off the losing side of the position when a large price change looks like it is beginning.

Assume that over the next two weeks stock prices collapse, and the S&P E-mini declines from 1252.50 to 1150. At a bare minimum, the 1250 June S&P E-mini put option would increase in value from 31.75 to 100, representing a profit of 68.25 S&P E-mini index points ($3,412.50). Of course, such a collapse in share prices would make the call option relatively worthless. But because prices fell by a great enough amount, the gain in price of the put options of 68.25 points offsets the loss 28.25 points in the calls, yielding a profit of roughly $3,500.

Instead of share prices falling, let's assume that the Federal Reserve cut interest rates and stock prices soared from 1252.50 to 1350 over the next several weeks. The June 1250 S&P E-mini call options would increase in value to at least 100, representing a profit of 71.75 index points (or $3,587.50). Of course, the put options would be almost worthless, but the gain in the call options more than offsets the 31.75 index point cost of the puts, yielding a profit of 40.00 index points, or $2,000.

Now, let's assume that the S&P E-mini only advances 10 points in the next several weeks to 1262.50. With only a few days until expiration, even though the market advanced, the call options would decline in value. Assume that the 1250 call options are worth 18.50 (10.00 points of intrinsic value and 8.50 of time value or extrinsic value). The 1250 put options would now be out of the money and worth roughly 6.50 points. In total, the cost of the options was 60.00 points, but now the position is only worth 25 points, representing a loss of $1,750. Of course, if the June S&P E-mini had advanced to 1300 by option's expiration, the 1250 call options would be worth 50 points—a gain of 21.75 points, or $1,087.50—but the June 1250 put options would expire worthless, leaving our speculator with a loss of 31.75 points, or –$1,587.50. In total, if the June S&P E-mini were to rally to 1300 by option's expiration, this straddle position would lose 10 S&P Index points, or $500.

In review, the long straddle position is a limited risk speculation that prices will either advance or decline by a large amount, large enough to offset the cost of the options. As a general rule, if you take the total premium paid for the option and add and subtract it from the strike price of the straddle, you can see the *break-even* points of this position.

The following graph illustrates this. The x-axis, or horizontal axis, represents the price of the underlying futures contract, while the y-axis, or vertical axis, represents the profit or loss of the total position at expiration. The pointy part of the "V" chart is the strike price of the options purchased.

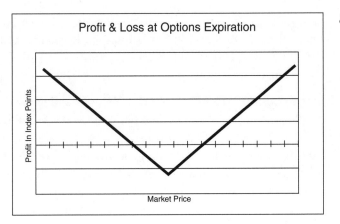

Straddle P&L.

It is also possible to sell straddles, or establish short straddle positions. This is a popular method of trading with the option-writing crowd, but can generally be very risky. Generally, traders should consider the risks very carefully before entering into short options positions, as the risk is unlimited.

Bull Call Spread

A bull call spread, like the straddle, involves two different options. This position is a limited risk, and a limited reward, strategy designed to lower the initial cost outlay. In return for a lower cost and lower risk, this strategy has limited profit potential.

Trading Tips

Bull call spreads are best implemented when a sizeable up move is expected. It is typically best to buy enough time on the options to allow the expected move to happen and to implement it with a long at-the-money call and a short call one or two strikes out-of-the-money.

This strategy involves the purchase of a call option, and the sale of a higher strike call option. Typically an at-the-money or slightly in-the-money call option is purchased and an out-of-the-money call option is sold. The advantage of this strategy is that the option strategist can set up a limited risk position for a lower initial cash outlay.

For example, assume our speculator is bullish on the U.S. Dollar, expecting the U.S. currency to appreciate in value over the next several weeks. In mid-April, our speculator thinks that the current June Dollar Index futures will appreciate from 115.00 to 118.00. Looking at the current June Dollar Index options, given the recent volatility in the market, the only call options under $800.00 in premium are the 119.00 call options, which is above his target high price.

This is a perfect example of how a bull call spread could be used. Currently, the June 115 Dollar Index calls are selling at 1.78 points (or $1,780.00 in premium based on the fact that the Dollar Index contract size is 1,000). However, the June 116 call options are trading at 1.48 points (or $1,480.00 before commissions and fees). Thus, our speculator can establish a June bull call spread by purchasing one June 115 call option and selling one June 116 call option.

The total cost, or risk, of this position is $300 before commissions and fees. This is the maximum amount he could lose, because if the market breaks below 115, and his long option expires worthless, he will lose the 1.78 points ($1,780.00) he paid for the option. But because he sold a 116 call option as well, if the market remains below 116, this short option will expire worthless as well, and our speculator will keep the premium received for writing the option. Thus, his loss of $1,780 on the long call option is partially offset by a gain on the short option position of $1,480, reducing his total loss to $300.

However, if the Dollar Index rallies—as expected—the gain in the long option position will offset the losses in the short option position and the speculator will reap a profit. For example, assume that the June Dollar Index rallies to 118, as expected. At expiration, the June 115 call option will be worth a total of $3,000, as this option is three index points in-the-money. Less the initial cost of $1,780, a speculator long in this option would gain $1,220 before commissions. At expiration, the short 116 call option will be worth $2,000 as it is also two index points in-the-money. This would represent a loss of –$620 as the option was sold for $1,480. In total the holder of the June 115/116 Dollar Index bull call spread would reap a profit of $600 before commissions and fees, or twice his/her initial outlay of $300 for the position.

Though the gain is substantially less than it would have been had a straight options purchase been made, the risk was substantially less as well.

In review, the bull call position is a limited risk and reward speculation that prices will advance. Purchasing a call option and selling a higher strike call option in the same commodity establishes this position. This position has risk limited to the total cost of the position, which is usually substantially less than an outright call option purchase. The break-even point for profitability is the cost of the position plus the long strike price. The maximum reward potential is limited to the difference between strike prices, less the cost of the position.

The following graph illustrates the profit and loss potential of the bull call spread. The x-axis, or horizontal axis, represents the price of the underlying futures contract, while the y-axis, or vertical axis, represents the profit or loss of the total position at expiration. The graph moves into positive territory at the long strike price plus the total cost of the position. The maximum loss is bounded by the cost of the position, while the maximum gain of the difference between the two strike prices, minus the cost of the position, is achieved if the market is at or above the higher (short) options strike price at expiration.

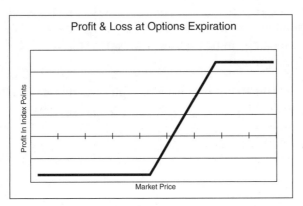

Bull call spread P&L.

Bear Put Spread

A bear put spread is similar to the bull call spread in that it is a limited risk, limited reward option strategy. As the name implies, the bear put spread is established when the speculator has a bearish bias, or thinks that prices will fall.

The bear put spread is established by buying a put option and selling a lower strike price option, on the same commodity in the same contract month, with a lower strike price. Typically, this position is established by buying an at-the-money put option and selling an out-of-the-money option to defray costs. Because this strategy involves selling an option against a long option, the initial cost of the position is reduced, and thus, so is the risk. However, by reducing risk, the potential for reward is diminished as well.

Trading Tips

Bear put spreads are best implemented when a speculator has a negative market bias using a long at-the-money put option and a short option one or two strikes out-of-the-money.

For example, assume a speculator is bearish on Pork Belly prices. Our speculator believes that the summer demand for bacon (the primary product of Pork Bellies) will be low, and thus prices will decline from the end of April through the beginning of July, when the July Pork Belly options expire.

Based on her assessment of the Pork Belly market, our speculator establishes a July Pork Belly bear put spread by buying a July 90 put option for 6.50 cents ($2,600 = $0.0650 × 40,000 lbs) and selling a July 86 put option for 5.25 cents ($2,100 = $0.0525 × 40,000 lbs), when the futures are trading at 89.50. This position is established at a total cost of 1.25 cents per contract (6.50 cents paid for the July 90 put − 5.25 received for the sale of the July 86 put = 1.25 cents, or $500).

The maximum risk on this position is the cost of the spread −1.25 cents, or $500 before commissions and fees. If July Pork Bellies are at or above 88.75 cents on option's expiration, then this position will result in a loss. The maximum profit potential on this position is the difference between the strike prices, less the cost of the position −2.75 cents, or $1,100 before commissions and fees.

For example, assume that July Pork Bellies move from 89.50 to 92.00 over the next several weeks. The long July 90 put options will expire worthless for a loss of 6.50 cents per contract ($2,600). However, the short July 86 put options will also expire worthless, and our speculator will get to keep the proceeds from the option sale of 5.25 cents per contract ($2,100). Thus, in total our speculator will suffer a loss of −1.25 cents, or $500.

However, if prices drop substantially, our speculator is positioned to make money. For example, assume that prices drop from 89.50 to 80.00 between the time the position was initiated and option's expiration. The July 90 put option would be worth 10 cents at option's expiration, thus earning him a profit of 3.50 cents beyond the cost of the option (10 – 6.50 = 3.50 profit). However, the July 86 put option would be six cents in-the-money, resulting in a loss of 0.75 cents. Thus in total the bear put spread would have resulted in a profit of 2.75 cents or $1,100 dollars before commissions and fees (long July 90 put worth 10 cents – short July 86 put worth 6 cents = 4 cents less the cost of the spread of 1.25 cents equals a profit of 2.75 cents per contract; each contract represents 40,000 pounds for a profit of $1,100 per spread).

In review, the bear put position is a limited risk and reward speculation that prices will decline. This position is established by purchasing a put option and selling a lower strike price put option. This position has risk limited to the total cost of the position, which is usually substantially less than an outright put option purchase. The break-even point for profitability is the cost of the position minus the long strike price. The maximum reward potential is limited to the difference between strike prices, less the cost of the position.

The following graph illustrates the profit and loss potential of the bear put spread. The x-axis, or horizontal axis, represents the price of the underlying futures contract, while the y-axis, or vertical axis, represents the profit or loss of the total position at expiration. The graph moves into positive territory at the long strike price minus the total cost of the position. The maximum loss is bounded by the cost of the position, while the maximum gain of the difference between the two strike prices, minus the cost of the position, is achieved if the market is at or below the lower (short) options strike price at expiration.

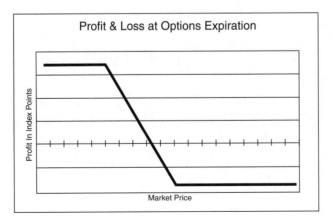

Bear put spread P&L.

Options in Conjunction with Futures: Married Positions

Options offer a myriad of choices and possible positions, though we have only touched on a few. Option buyers (long option holders) are usually attracted to the options market because of the limited risk feature it offers. Remember that the purchaser of an option can never lose more than their initial investment. Option writers (short option holders) are typically drawn to this type of position because of the fact that most options expire worthless, and the fact that option values decline with the passage of time (time decay or theta—refer to Chapter 8 for a review). Thus, option writers are willing to risk unlimited losses for a high probability of limited returns.

Trading Tips

Generally, married options, or the purchase of an option in conjunction with a futures position, is best used in extremely volatile markets, or markets in which the fundamental picture may be changing, and thus a stop loss order on the futures position may not be suitable.

In between these extremes are option position traders. They look for limited risk/limited reward positions, such as bull call and bear put spreads. In exchange for lowering their initial risk, these options traders give up the unlimited potential reward in establishing positions.

In some circumstances, through a combination of futures and options, you can set up limited risk and theoretically almost unlimited reward positions.

Married Put Position

If you think of a put option as an insurance policy, like casualty insurance, that pays off when prices drop, this position makes perfect sense. The risk in a long futures position is that prices will decline. The risk involved in a futures contract is unlimited, but so is the potential reward. A long put option position, on the other hand, increases in value when the price of the underlying futures contract decreases in value. The risk involved in purchasing a put option is limited to the premium paid, while the potential reward is unlimited.

Thus, if these two positions (long futures, long put option) were combined, a limited risk and potentially unlimited reward position could be established (actually reward is unlimited, less the cost of the option). This position is known in trading circles as a married put or covered long position. A married put position is established simply by purchasing a futures contract and buying a put option to hedge against the downside. The amount of risk associated with this position is limited to the cost of the option and the difference between the purchase price of the futures contract and the strike price of the option.

If prices rise during the holding of this position, then the long put option will decrease in value. However, the long futures contract will increase in value, offsetting the loss in the option if it is great enough. However, if prices decline, the losses in the futures contract will be partially offset by the increase in the long put options value.

For example, assume a trader is looking at buying July Corn at $2.02 per bushel, or 202 cents. The July 200 put options are trading at 8½ cents and the July 190 put options are trading at 4¼ cents.

The maximum risk involved in purchasing July Corn at 202 and buying a July 200 put option is 10½ cents, or $525 before commissions and fees. This is figured by cost of the option, 8½ cents, and the difference in the purchase price of the futures, 202, and the strike price of the option, –200. Thus July Corn would have to decline by –2.00 cents before the put option offers any protection.

The maximum risk involved in purchasing July Corn in combination with the 190 put option would be –16¼ cents (or $812.50 before commissions and fees). There is 12 cents of risk before the put option would start providing a hedge (202 – 190 strike price) plus the cost of the option (4¼ cents).

In order for a married put position to be profitable, the price of the futures contract must increase in value at least as much as the initial cost of the option. Thus, the more expensive the "insurance" provided by the put option, the higher the price that the futures contract must rise to be profitable.

For example, assume the same criteria as above: Buying July Corn futures at 202 when the July 200 puts are trading at 8½ cents and the July 190 puts are trading at 4¼ cents.

Combining the July 200 put for a cost of 8½ cents with a long futures position at 202, the upside break-even at the end of June (when the options expire) would be 210½ (or Futures Entry Price + Option Premium = Married Put Position Break-Even at expiration, or 202 + 8½ = 210½).

Combining the July 190 put for a cost of 4¼ cents with a long futures position at 202 would yield an upside break-even of 206¼ on options expiration (or Futures Entry Price + Option Premium = Married Put Position Break-Even at expiration, or 202 + 4¼ = 206¼).

So when considering a married put position, it is important to look at the cost of the insurance in relation to the break-even. Ideally, you would want to look for situations where the detrimental costs are outweighed by the protection provided by the option.

Sticking with our Corn example, the 200 put bought in combination with the long futures position at 202 provides a better risk to reward. Though the cost of the option is twice as much (8½ cents vs. 4¼ cents), the risk is half as great because the 200 put option is closer to the futures position.

In review, the married put position is a limited risk speculation that prices will rise. This position is established by purchasing a put option in conjunction with a long futures position. This position has risk limited to the cost of the option plus the difference between the futures purchase price and the strike price of the put option. The break-even point for profitability is the cost of the option. The maximum reward potential is theoretically unlimited, less the cost of the option.

The following graph illustrates the profit and loss potential of the married put position. The x-axis, or horizontal axis, represents the price of the underlying futures contract, while the y-axis, or vertical axis, represents the profit or loss of the total position at expiration. The graph moves into positive territory at the purchase price of the futures contract plus the cost of the option. The maximum loss is bounded by the cost of the difference between the purchase price and the strike price of the put option plus the premium paid for the option. The maximum reward is only limited by how high the market can go, less the cost of the put option.

Married put P&L.

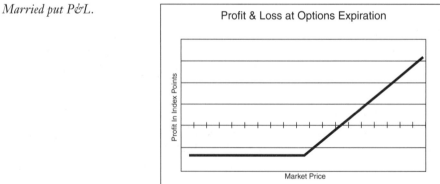

Married Call Option

Just as a put option can be thought of as insurance against lower futures prices, a call option can be thought of as insurance against higher prices. Thus, the combination of a long call option and a short futures position creates a limited risk and theoretically unlimited profit potential position—less the cost of the option.

The risk associated with a short futures position is higher prices. Call options increase in value when the price of the underlying futures contract increases in value, but the risk associated with the call option is limited to the price paid for the option. So combining these two positions, a short futures position and a long call option, creates a limited risk and theoretically unlimited reward speculative position.

For example, assume that a speculator is bearish in the CBOT Wheat market. He feels that Wheat is overvalued at 275 per bushel, but fears that spring weather could cause prices to go up as well. Thus, fearing higher prices, our speculator looks to establish a married call position by selling July Wheat at 275 and buying a July 280 Wheat call option for 7 cents.

Trading Tips

Like married put positions, a married call position can have a reduced margin requirement because of the hedged nature of this position. Be sure to ask your broker about a commission break when using this strategy, as the limited risk nature of it reduces their risk as well.

If prices rise, as feared, to 300, the short futures position will have a loss of 25 cents, or $1,250 before commissions and fees ($0.25 × 5,000 bushels per contract = $1,250). However, the July 280 call option would be worth 20 cents at options expiration, for a profit of 13 cents (Call Option Value at Expiration = Futures Price – Strike Price of Option; Call Option profit equals Option Value less cost of the option; or 300 – 280 = 20 cents Value at Expiration less 7-cent option cost = 13 cents profit). Thus, the call option reduced the loss on the position from 25 cents ($1,250) to 12 cents ($600).

However, if the analysis had proven correct and July Wheat declined to 250 by option's expiration, our speculator would have made a profit of 18 cents, or $900. The short futures position would have reaped a profit of 25 cents ($1,250), but the 280 call option would have expired worthless for a loss of 7 cents ($350). Thus in total, the position would have had a profit of 18 cents, or $900 before commissions and fees.

In review, the married call position is a limited risk speculation that prices will fall. This position is established by purchasing a call option in conjunction with a short futures position. This position has risk limited to the cost of the option plus the difference between the futures sales price and the strike price of the call option. The break-even point for profitability is the sale price of the futures contract less the cost of the option. The maximum reward potential is theoretically unlimited, less the cost of the option.

The following graph illustrates the profit and loss potential of a married call position. The x-axis, or horizontal axis, represents the price of the underlying futures contract, while the y-axis, or vertical axis, represents the profit or loss of the total position at expiration. The graph moves into positive territory as futures prices go below the entry price of the futures position less the cost of the call option. The maximum loss is bounded by the combination of the difference between the entry price of the short futures contract and the strike price of the long call option and the cost of the call option, while the maximum is limited to how low the futures market can go, less the cost of the option.

Married call P&L.

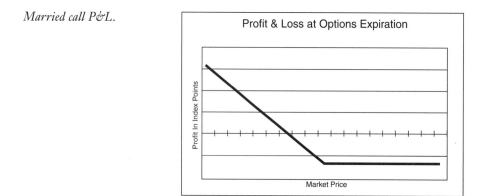

Options Wrap-Up

Options on futures can be used alone or in conjunction with futures contracts to establish a plethora of positions, which can profit from almost any market scenario imaginable. Simple combinations of puts and calls—like a straddle—allow speculators to profit from changes in prices with limited risk. Options can also be used in conjunction with futures positions to limit the risk in this usually risky trading arena. Options are the pinnacle of risk transference vehicles.

Covered options positions—limited risk option positions like bull call and bear put spreads—do not require margins to be posted as the position has risk limited to the amount paid for by the position. The short option is hedged versus the long option position.

The Least You Need to Know

♦ A straddle involves buying both a put and call option in the same commodity. A long straddle position is a speculation on a large move in the underlying market.

♦ Buying a call option and selling a higher strike call option is known as a bull call spread. This strategy involves less risk than the outright purchase of calls, but also limits rewards.

♦ Buying a put option and selling a lower strike price put option is known as a bear put spread. This is a hedged position with a limited risk and limited reward potential.

♦ One can guard against the unlimited loss feature of futures by taking an opposite position in the options market. This is known as having a married option.

♦ A married call option will limit risk involved in a short futures position to a finite amount.

♦ A married put option will limit the downside exposure of a long futures position to a specific amount.

Part 4

Fundamentals: What Makes Markets Tick

You can explore the forces that cause prices to change. General supply and demand themes are laid out for the Grain, Food, Livestock, Metals, Petroleum, and Financial markets. This part is designed to help you not only understand prices and their direction, but to anticipate them.

For example, we show you how different weather during different stages of development of a crop can affect the price of grains. Or how Petroleum prices tend to be driven by changes in wholesale demand much more than retail demand.

This part is intended as a primer for those seriously interested in speculation in the futures market, with an introduction to the various supply and demand forces that cause prices to fluctuate over the long term.

Chapter 10

Price Analysis: The Fundamental Approach

In This Chapter

- Learn how prices reflect supply and demand
- Understand field crops
- Livestock supply and demand
- Metals, a demand-driven market
- Petroleum, OPEC, and prices
- Financial markets—it's the economy, stupid

Speculating in the futures markets is a serious business. If you approach this like going to the track, you will probably have the same results! Though many of the concepts presented in the next several chapters may seem tedious, by understanding what forces drive supply and demand, you may be able to understand and correctly interpret this information to turn it into profitable trading decisions.

In this chapter, we'll show you how to find and use the basic economic and government reports to anticipate price movement and hopefully how to synthesize this information to make informed decisions in the futures markets.

Introduction to Market Fundamentals

The basic goal of speculating in the futures market is to buy low and sell high. The basic goal of hedging in the futures market is to lock in prices that are at advantageous levels. The common theme through both of these functions—risk acceptance and risk avoidance—is making an assumption about the future level of prices.

A speculator buys a futures contract—enters a long position—in the hopes that prices will rise and he can sell it at a profit. A hedger sells his production forward by entering a short position to avoid falling prices. By entering into positions in the futures markets, both are making assumptions about the future course of prices.

def•i•ni•tion

Fundamental analysis is the study of how changes in supply and demand affect prices. Traders and analysts look at the production and consumption patterns of commodities and markets, note how the picture is changing, and use this information to attempt to ascertain the future course of prices.

One of the major methods for ascertaining the future direction of prices is *fundamental analysis.* Fundamental analysis is the study of the factors that affect supply and demand. The key to fundamental analysis is to gather and interpret this information and then to act before this information is incorporated into the futures price.

What Is Price?

Price represents the point at which a producer is willing to part with her product and a buyer is willing to purchase it.

All current factual information regarding supply and demand plus the mood of the masses, hopes, fears, estimates, and "guesstimates" of everyone in the market is crystallized in a commodity's current price. As perceptions of future supply and demand change, then prices change as buyers and sellers absorb this new information and react in the marketplace accordingly.

In essence, price is simply a point at which the perceived economic advantage of bringing goods to market is equal to the perceived economic benefit received from purchasing them. Price represents a brief equilibrium between buyers and sellers.

The sellers of a commodity control the supply of that commodity. For example, it is not possible to buy corn unless a farmer is willing to sell it. Stock is not issued for sale unless the holders of the certificates—be they individuals or corporations—are willing to relinquish their rights to it in exchange for payment.

The buyers of a commodity are in control of the demand for that commodity. As the old saying goes …

"Something is only worth what someone is willing to pay for it."

The demand for a product, service, or commodity only exists if someone is willing to buy it.

For example, I am a frequent singer in the shower. I have a large supply of available songs waiting to be sung. However, because I cannot carry a tune, no one (including my loving wife) would be willing to pay to hear me sing. Hence, though there is available supply, there is no demand and the resulting price of my song styling is currently zero.

Because a buyer and a seller agree upon a price, price represents the point at which supply equals demand, at least temporarily.

The futures markets are a direct product of the economics of price theory, an embodiment of the laws of supply and demand.

The Laws of Supply and Demand

Supply is the quantity of a product available at a given price. Demand is the quantity of a product that is willingly purchased at a given price.

The Law of Supply dictates that the price of a given product is a direct function of the availability of the product. Under the Law of Supply, as price increases, sellers are more willing to provide large quantities of their product to the marketplace; when prices are low, sellers are less willing to provide product to the market.

> **Trading Tips**
>
> The Law of Supply says that prices move in the opposite direction of supply—increases in supply equal lower prices, while decreasing supply should result in higher prices. The Law of Demand says that demand moves opposite to price as well. Higher prices lead to lower demand and lower prices lead to more demand.

The Law of Demand dictates that the price of a given product is a direct function of the demand for it. Under the Law of Demand, as price decreases, the demand for the product increases as buyers are more willing to purchase it; as the price of a product increases, buyers are less willing to purchase it according to the Law of Demand.

The price of a product or commodity depends on the relationship between supply and demand. Because both supply and demand are dependent upon the current price of the product, changes in price can cause changes in supply and demand. Neither supply nor demand is static, and both change as new information is filtered throughout the economy. Changes in supply or demand cause changes in price, which cause further changes in supply and demand.

The trader who uses fundamental analysis watches the economic factors which affect supply and demand in an attempt to forecast prices and develop profitable trading strategies.

Using Fundamental Analysis to Forecast Prices

Fundamental analysis—or the study of supply and demand and how they affect prices—rests on the assumption that any economic factor that decreases supply or increases the use of a commodity (demand) will tend to cause an increase in prices. Conversely, any factor that increases the supply of a commodity or decreases its use (demand) tends to cause prices to fall.

The key to fundamental analysis is to gather and interpret supply and demand information and then to act before this information is incorporated into the futures price. Many practitioners of this style of analysis concentrate on the current supply and demand situations, not taking into account possible changes. The purpose of any analysis of the futures markets is to anticipate price movement, not just explain it.

Trading Tips

The USDA gathers information from around the world on growing conditions, acres planted, crop conditions, and such. This information is so important and closely watched by the futures markets that the USDA compiles all this information in Washington, D.C. When the reports are prepared, the collators of the summary information are kept under lock and key in a room with no windows and no telephones so the information cannot be leaked. These safeguards are taken to ensure that the information is released at precisely the same time for everyone, and no one has advance notice of them.

Agricultural Markets

The agricultural markets are an excellent market segment for the fundamental trader, as the United States Department of Agriculture (USDA) releases crop supply and demand estimates monthly on a range of crops: corn, wheat, oats, soybeans, soybean meal, soybean oil, sugar, and cotton. Outside of their standard monthly crop report, the USDA and its various agencies track supply and usage statistics for a wide range of commodities including orange juice, coffee, and cocoa.

The basic supply and demand factors that a fundamental analyst considers in the agricultural markets are production, consumption (usage), exports, and politics.

The uncertainty of weather can cause more anxiety in the marketplace than all other fundamental factors combined. Traders constantly monitor the amount of moisture, the time of frost, and temperatures during the growing season and its impact on world growing conditions to gauge how crop production is affected around the world.

Trading Tips _____

China is a major consumer of U.S. grains and agricultural products. In recent years, China has become a major producer and in years when their crop production is good, China has even exported some grains. Because they are both a major consumer and producer, China can be a pivotal player in the world markets. Chinese selling of agricultural commodities not only increases competition for the U.S. but also spells lower demand for U.S. products. Watch China, as they are a major force to be reckoned with in the markets.

Normally during the growing season in the grains, volatility in the market increases precipitously as weather is an important factor in assessing future grain market production. Traders typically refer to the summer months as "weather markets." Generally, you should remember the old battle cry of grain traders on the Chicago Board of Trade: *Rain makes grain.* Rainfall in the growing areas of the country, or forecasts for rainfall, generally weigh on prices, while dry weather tends to support prices.

Worldwide competition is another important factor affecting the demand for agricultural commodities. The United States is a major agricultural product producer. Most other countries in the world also grow crops, and, at times, some countries compete with the United States for export business; at other times they buy U.S. production to supplement their own needs. Many key countries to watch are China, Russia, European Union, Australia, Japan, and Canada.

Agricultural commodity traders watch all of these factors to help them make educated decisions as to how these markets are priced. Generally each aspect is looked at by how it affects supply or demand. Items that lower supply (or future production) or increase demand are taken as being indicative of higher prices. Items that would likely increase supply (or future production) or lower demand are usually construed as being an indication that prices may be going lower.

The futures markets that would fall under this category and this type of analysis are Corn, Soybeans, Soybean Meal, Soybean Oil, Wheat (Hard Red Winter [KCBT], Soft Red Winter [CBOT], Soft Red Spring [MPLS], and White Wheat [MPLS]), Oats, Rice, Cotton, Sugar, Cocoa, Coffee, and Orange Juice. For more information about the field crop markets, see Chapters 11 and 12.

Livestock Markets

Unlike the agricultural markets, which are mainly field crops and storable, the Livestock futures represent commodities that are neither grown specifically nor storable over an extended period of time.

A key characteristic to analyzing Livestock markets, which is different than other agricultural commodities, is the fact that all meat production is consumed within a relatively short period of time. Following slaughter, meat must be refrigerated. Cold storage facilities are expensive to build and operate; therefore, the capacity to store meat is limited.

Trading Tips

The demand for meat can be highly seasonal in nature. We are all familiar with the summer driving season, but many analysts call the summer months' barbeque season or BLT season as the demand for meat typically increases during the warm summer months.

Because meat is basically a nonstorable commodity, stock levels are considered an insignificant factor in determining future price direction by most analysts.

The United States has the ability to store roughly nine days' worth of red meat consumption on the wholesale level. A minimum of five days of supply must be maintained by meat packers to function smoothly with retail distribution. So, unlike the grain markets, meat production is sold at prevailing prices as producers and packers do not have the ability to withhold supply from the market during times of unfavorable pricing.

Thus, the important factors to look at affecting the price of Livestock markets are herd sizes and consumer tastes.

Consumers are the ultimate price setters in the Livestock market. When consumer tastes are running toward meat or particular types of meat, prices should increase. However, trends toward lower cholesterol alternatives and other meats can seriously diminish demand and reduce price. Competition between different types of meat plays a major role in consumers' decisions. For example, if pork chops are on special, a family may eat pork instead of London broil.

Consumer tastes are also affected by the normal broad economic conditions. Income levels, job security, and such have a direct bearing on consumer buying habits. Government programs, trade relations, and such also have a direct bearing on meat consumption and production.

The futures markets that fall under the heading Livestock and would benefit from this type of analysis are …

- ◆ Live Cattle
- ◆ Feeder Cattle
- ◆ Lean Hogs
- ◆ Pork Bellies

For more information specifically about the Livestock markets, see Chapter 13.

Metals Markets

The Metals markets tend to be more demand-driven than the agricultural markets. Because metals are mined, production can be turned on and off given changes in prices, so it is difficult to gauge supply. This is especially true for gold, which many hoard as an investment and could be sold on the open market if prices rise by a significant amount.

Commodity Corn
From 1816 until 1971, most of the major currencies of the world were backed by gold. The most famous of these was the Bretton Woods Gold Standard for the U.S. Dollar. Under Bretton Woods, the United States Dollar, and other global currencies, were tied to a value of gold. From 1934 to 1968, this amount was $35/oz of gold. To protect the amount of gold held in reserve for protecting the dollar, it was illegal for United States citizens to own gold prior to President Nixon's revocation of the Gold Standard.

The demand or usage side of the equation is a little more rational in the metals market. More and more as we enter into the electronics age, the demand for metals is becoming more closely tied to this form of demand.

So when examining the Metals markets, it is important to look at the overall economy for signs of strength and weakness, as this is probably the most reliable and best long-term indicator of future strength or weakness.

The Metals markets include futures in Gold, Silver, Copper, Platinum, and Palladium. For more information on the Metals markets, see Chapter 14.

Petroleum Markets

Like the Metals markets, the Petroleum markets are a constant supply market, in which demand is probably one of the most major features in understanding market movement. However, the Petroleum markets have one hitch on the supply side—the Organization of Petroleum Exporting Countries (OPEC). OPEC's key tool is collective limitation of production by a quota system.

Trading Tips

An old trader's saying is "the best cure for low prices is low prices" and "the best cure for high prices is high prices." When prices are low, supply is cut back as producers don't like to work for less. However, when prices are low, consumers tend to buy more and are less efficient in using the product. Just look at the boom in gas-guzzling SUVs in the late 1990s, when gas prices were relatively low. When prices are high, producers try to maximize production to boost their profits. Hence, high prices tend to increase supply, while usage drops as consumers can't afford to buy as much and look for more efficient ways to use the commodity. Consider the popularity of gas-efficient vehicles in the mid-1970s, when the world energy crisis emerged, or look at how automobile manufacturers advertise great gas mileage when gas prices are over $2.00.

The following countries are OPEC members: Algeria, Indonesia, Iran, Iraq, Kuwait, Libya, Nigeria, Qatar, Saudi Arabia, the United Arab Emirates, and Venezuela. According to recent American Petroleum Institute statistics, OPEC countries account for roughly 40 percent of the world's daily crude oil production.

The supply of oil, like metals, is a direct function of price. When prices are high, supply can increase as previously unprofitable wells can now be run, increasing supply. This is especially true for U.S. production and deep-sea rigs.

The demand for oil and petroleum products is a direct function of the economy. Generally, a strong economy equates to more usage of petroleum as more factories and businesses consume more energy. Also, during strong economic times, people tend to drive more and are less worried about the fuel efficiency of their vehicles.

Thus, when looking at the Petroleum markets, it is important to have a solid grasp on the state of the world economy and its expected growth, as this will set the stage for consumption.

The Petroleum markets include futures on the following: Crude Oil, Unleaded Gasoline, Heating Oil, and Natural Gas. For more information on the Petroleum markets, see Chapter 15.

Financial Markets and the Economy

One of the fundamental keys to any market is judging demand for that commodity. Demand is a measure of usage by consumers and is a direct function of the health of the economy.

The broadest and most useful indicator of the health of the economy is interest rates. Interest rate policy by the Federal Reserve is key to understanding the current economy and possibly any future changes in economic activity.

U.S. monetary policy is formed through the Federal Reserve Bank Board and is administered through the Federal Reserve System. Because the Federal Reserve controls the circulation of money, its policies and actions have a great impact on interest rate levels. In a slow economy, the Federal Reserve can lower the *discount rate* in an effort to increase spending and increase the level of economic growth. During inflationary times, the Federal Reserve can raise the discount rate to reduce borrowing and slow the overheating economy.

The task of the fundamental analyst is to sort through the volumes of financial information available daily, pinpoint the significant factors, and accurately weigh their effect on the supply and demand for credit. For it is credit and the cost of money (interest rates) that probably have the greatest effect on all the financial markets (stocks and currencies) as well as other commodities.

def•i•ni•tion

The interest rate at which banks can borrow money from the Federal Reserve is called the **discount rate**. This widely watched interest rate is set by the Federal Reserve Board. Changes in this interest rate have a broad impact on the economy, causing financial markets to rally on lower interest rates and decline on higher rates, generally. Usually, changes in the discount rate make front-page news.

Economic reports are released by the U.S. government on almost a daily basis and are excellent sources of financial information. The elements that make up these reports can be categorized as follows:

- Leading Indicators
- Concurrent Indicators
- Lagging Indicators

Leading economic indicators signal the state of the economy for the coming months. They imply possible changes in the business cycle and, as a result, provide the analyst with an early indication of the possible changes to the economy. Concurrent and lagging indicators showable for the short-term volatility they often cause in the interest rate, stock, and foreign exchange markets. One of the best places to find all the key economic data is the website of the Federal Reserve Bank of St. Louis (http://research.stlouisfed.org/fred2/), which is the keeper of the database FRED (Federal Reserve Economic Data).

Trading Tips

Think of the economy as a big circle. When people have jobs, they get paychecks. We all spend our paychecks, creating more jobs. Eventually, everyone has a job and is still buying things. Because the supply of labor is diminishing, the cost of workers increases. As labor costs increase, the price of goods increases. When things cost more, workers demand more money, further driving prices higher, or causing inflation. Because each dollar now buys less stuff, due to rising prices (inflation), lenders of money demand higher returns (higher interest rates). Thus, during economic expansion, though sales can be increasing, the cost to finance those sales could become so high that companies lose money. This is why signs of a strong economy often cause stock prices to decrease, even though logic says a strong economy should mean more sales.

No one indicator permanently dominates the financial markets. During particular stages in the business cycle, the stock market may find falling interest rates to be bullish as it lowers the cost of borrowing. However, during another stage of the economic cycle, stock prices may react negatively to falling interest rates, as low interest rates usually coincide with a weak economy, which may translate into poor earnings and sales.

Thus, it is important to understand the various influences each factor has. The most important factor to keep in mind is simple logic. Think about what factors most analysts and traders are expecting, and learn to spot when these themes are playing themselves out or not.

The Financial markets include futures on the following: Interest Rate (Treasury Bonds, Notes, Bills), Eurodollar Deposits, Foreign Currencies (Eurocurrency, Swiss Franc, British Pound, Japanese Yen, Australian Dollar, and Canadian Dollar), Stock Indexes (S&P 500, E-mini S&P, NASDAQ Index, NSDAQ E-mini), and single stocks. For more information on the financial markets, see Chapter 16.

Using Fundamental Analysis

According to the laws of supply and demand, the market price of a commodity should reflect a point where the quantity being sold is equal to the demand. The purpose of fundamental analysis is to pinpoint and recognize the major factors in the market and to predict how changes in these forces will affect prices. Profit opportunities exist when a fundamentalist can project how these factors will affect both the short-term and long-term market prices.

Using fundamental analysis involves formulating an economic model—a systematic description of the various supply and demand factors that interact to determine prices. The sophistication of these economic models can vary greatly—from complex models with thousands of inputs to simple two- or three-input models—but the key to all of them is understanding the basic elements of supply and demand for a specific market.

It is often said in trading circles to "buy the rumor and sell the fact." Many analysts are employed simply to estimate government reports. If the consensus forecast for the Consumer Price Index (CPI) is an average rate of 2.8 to 3.2 percent, and the monthly report comes in at 3.1 percent, the markets may break, even though a 3.1 percent rate may be historically very benign in terms of inflation. Because markets tend to act before the data is released, markets tend to react in the short term in a fashion which is quite opposite of what logic would dictate. Consider how much of the news has been factored into prices before you buy or sell.

It is important for the fundamental analyst to remember that even though supply and demand can vary greatly from commodity to commodity, the general process and the laws, which dictate prices, are similar for all.

The Least You Need to Know

- Price represents the point at which a producer is willing to part with his product and a buyer is willing to purchase it.

- Under the Law of Supply, as price increases, sellers are more willing to provide large quantities of their product to the marketplace, and when prices are low sellers are less willing to provide product to the market.

- Under the Law of Demand, as price decreases, the demand for the product increases, as buyers are more willing to purchase it; as the price of a product increases, buyers are less willing to purchase it.

◆ Any factor that tends to decrease supply and/or increase demand should have a positive effect on prices.

◆ Any factor that tends to increase supply and/or decrease demand should have a negative effect on prices.

◆ The purpose of fundamental analysis is to pinpoint and recognize the major factors in the market and to predict how changes in these forces will affect prices.

Chapter 11

Grain Futures Overview

In This Chapter

- Discover how the annual production markets work
- Understand risk premiums and price rationing
- Find out what affects Corn futures
- Learn about the different types of Wheat futures
- Distinguish Soybean futures by bean, oil, and meal

Field crops operate on an annual supply schedule and a variable demand schedule. Field crops include the following commodity futures markets: Corn, Wheat, Soybeans (Soybean Meal and Soybean Oil), Cotton, Sugar, Cocoa, Orange Juice, and Coffee. The first three are covered in this chapter. The rest are covered in Chapter 12.

The main reason you need to understand the supply and demand schedules of corn, wheat, and soybean crops is because it greatly affects the prices in their futures markets. For example, if the coming year's wheat crop is in jeopardy at any given point between planting and harvesting, the prices can rise and fall dramatically. Each of the crops mentioned in this chapter will be described as to their production and consumption considerations, which can be translated into dollars for you in their respective futures market (hopefully on the positive side).

Production: Supply vs. Demand

Though the production of field crop commodities has become a world operation during the last 10 to 20 years, the bulk of the supply is usually available at the time of harvest for the major producing regions. Demand, on the other hand, is fairly evenly spread throughout the year, though certain periods, such as the spring and early summer, tend to see increased grain demand. This sets up a unique feature in the market, where price acts as a rationing device for annually produced commodities, as consumers and producers cycle through being gripped by the forces of fear and greed.

When a market has annual production, or supply is replenished once a year, this supply must be rationed or spread out over the rest of the year. The market mechanism for rationing supply is price. When prices are high, consumers are discouraged from consumption to some degree and the supply will last longer. When prices are low, consumers are encouraged to use the product to a certain extent and the supply is used up.

But price also acts as a stimulus for supply. When prices are high, producers are encouraged to increase production to increase profits. However, when prices are low, producers tend to decrease production since profit margins are not as great. This type of market behavior sets up a paradox, in which low prices discourage production, and high prices encourage production, but producer reactions to prices cannot occur until the following year. As such, swings in annually produced commodities—especially when supplies are currently tight—tend to be exaggerated when the crop is vulnerable to damage.

Risk Premiums and Commodity Futures

The exaggerations of price are often referred to as building a *risk premium* into the crop. When future supply is feared to be limited, prices tend to rise, which should slow down consumption and ration supply until the new smaller supply is available at harvest. Annually produced commodities tend to go through cycles of building risk premium and destroying risk premium as the crop goes through its various stages of production. Risk premiums are built when consumers fear limited supply and producers have an economic motive to withhold supply from the marketplace. So during potentially tight supply times, consumers tend to pay higher prices for fear of not being able to secure supply, while producers must be encouraged to sell at these higher prices to satisfy their profit motive, or greed.

However, as the consumers meet their current demand needs, they tend to be motivated to find alternate sources of supply or will use other products in substitution (greed) while producers fear missing the higher prices and tend to open the floodgates of supply. As such, when the crop is in danger of potential damage, fear grips the consumer and greed the producer. Prices then rise as the marketplace builds the risk premium into the crop to ensure supply at a later date.

As the crop matures and supply looks more probable in the future, the producer now

def•i•ni•tion

A **risk premium** is when prices rise in anticipation of lower future demand. Markets often build risk premiums ahead of the actual fact. For example, grain prices may rise in the early spring following a dry winter, as the market is worried that low subsoil moisture may reduce future supply. However, as the crop is planted and rain falls, prices tend to fall, undoing the risk premium built in.

removes the risk premium from the market. There is fear of missing the attractive higher prices of selling their product to consumers who have now met their demand with alternate sources and supplies. Hence, as a crop goes through its natural planting, maturating, and harvesting cycle, the risk premium is built and destroyed depending upon the forces of nature as well as the emotional forces of fear and greed.

This process of building and removing of risk premiums is key to understanding the rationality of grain prices. Because fear and greed are important in building and removing of risk premiums, markets tend to move much farther than would be thought, and can stay at emotional levels longer than most people would anticipate. It is this factor which makes the markets, especially the grains and field crops, difficult to analyze since they are constantly being buoyed by this "irrational exuberance," to quote the former Chairman of the Federal Reserve, Alan Greenspan.

Corn Futures

During the last decade, corn has been the leading crop in terms of production and acreage grown. The major producing nation for corn in the world is the United States of America. Over 80 percent of the production of corn is centered in the Midwestern states known as the Corn Belt: Iowa, Illinois, Nebraska, Minnesota, and Indiana.

Corn Production Considerations

Planting in the Corn Belt states tends to start in mid-April and run through mid-May (refer to the corn timeline that follows). In recent years, the majority of planting in the Corn Belt has started by April 20th and been completed by June 8th. Ideally, planting should be done when the temperature is moderate and conditions are dry. If the fields are either too wet or a late snow hits, then planting will have to be put off. Late-planted crops tend to produce lower yields. Historically, the probability of delay is quite large, so very often during planting the Corn market begins to build a risk premium into the crop at this time.

Several days after the corn crop has been planted, sprouts begin to emerge from the soil. These sprouts grow into the tall lanky plant we all recognize as corn. As the corn plant matures, ears grow. The kernel that grows inside the ear of corn is a seed, and before seeds can be produced, the plant must be pollinated. In order for pollination to occur, the corn ear produces a tassel, which is used to capture pollen. Tasseling usually occurs 10 days before the corn plant begins to silk, and is indicated by the emergence of a silklike strand from the end of the ears.

A typical corn crop timeline.

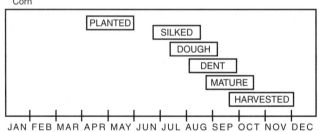

Silking, or pollination, is the most crucial stage of development of the corn plant. Pollination only occurs when the crop receives an adequate amount of moisture and temperatures are semi-moderate. If pollination does not go well, crop production will drop substantially. However, once pollination has occurred, the corn crop is almost impervious to damage, and is often referred to as a *made crop*. The median date for pollination is the fourth of July, and hence the Corn market tends to reach its maximum price by the first week of July. On average, from 1981 to 2000, September Corn futures have lost –16¾ (–$837.50 per contract) per bushel on a monthly settlement basis in July.

In several years, the high of the calendar year or seasonal top is put in by late May as the last of the new corn crop is planted. In most years after planting, corn prices tend to be weighed down by progress of the crop. Only in years when severe droughts have interfered with pollination have corn prices continued to rise.

After pollination, in late June and early July, the corn kernels begin to form. The kernels are said to have *doughed* when they are showing a thick or doughlike substance. The doughlike substance is filled with a milk, or protein. It is the high protein content of corn that makes it an attractive feed, which accounts for the bulk of the demand for corn grown in the United States.

As the corn crop is doughing, the plant needs only minimal precipitation to survive as long as pollination has occurred properly. However, extreme heat, with little or no precipitation, can speed up denting (the drying and concentration of the protein), lessening the protein content of the corn grown and, hence, its usefulness as a feed (this situation is extremely rare). Normally, the U.S. corn crop completes doughing by late September.

As the corn plant concentrates its resources on making kernels, the stalk of the plant begins to die. This causes the entire corn plant to die, and the kernels begin to dry up. As the kernels dry out, the rounded end of the kernel not attached to the cob begins to get a small impression in it, or a *dent*. When roughly half of the kernels are showing dents, doughing is considered completed.

Denting of corn in the kernels usually occurs from mid-August through September. Denting is said to be completed when all kernels are showing the tell-tale dent and the ear is firm and solid. There is no milk present in most kernels. During the final stages of denting, the crop is susceptible to early autumn frost damage. It is not uncommon to see a *retracement rally* within the context of a greater bear market during either the doughing or denting stages of development, due to an extreme heat wave or an early frost.

def•i•ni•tion

A **retracement rally** is when prices retrace part of a previous down move. For example, if prices were to decline from $2.50 to $2.00 per bushel and then rally back up to $2.25 per bushel, this would be coined a retracement rally. Typically, technical analysts (see Chapter 17) classify retracement moves as counter-trend moves. During a period of generally falling prices long term, the shorter-term price increases are classified as retracement rallies. During periods of generally increasing prices longer term, short-term price drops are referred to as retracement breaks, or corrections.

The corn plant is considered mature when the plant is about ready to be harvested, with shucks opening and no green foliage present. When the corn plant is mature, it is considered safe from frost. Corn typically matures from early September, for early planted crops, to early November for late planted and replanted crops.

After the corn crop has matured, it is harvested. The bulk of harvesting takes place in late September through mid-October. Ideally, after the corn plant has matured, farmers like to see cold weather, and little or no precipitation, so the ground is firm for the harvesting equipment. When too much precipitation is present and the weather is unseasonably warm, the ground can be too muddy for the heavy equipment used in the harvest effort, and there is a potential for mold-based diseases and insect problems in extreme cases. Harvest delays are typical, but very rarely do they result in any real widespread loss of supply.

Corn Consumption Considerations

Livestock feed accounts for roughly 60 to 65 percent of the total use of the cash corn crop. In recent years, corn has accounted for a quarter of all livestock feed used. Corn is attractive as a livestock feed for two major reasons:

◆ Corn is good grain for fattening livestock and poultry because of its high starch content. In addition, it contains more oil than other cereal grains, making it an excellent source of nutrients and a very high-energy feed.

◆ Acre for acre, corn yields more animal feed in both grain and forage than any other crop, although the cost to produce corn, in terms of labor and equipment, is no more expensive than other cereal grains (and most other crops).

There are two main processes used to mill corn into end products:

◆ Wet milling is when the corn kernel is soaked in diluted sulfuric acid for roughly 60 hours. The hulls are then separated from the kernels and used for corn oil, starches, dextrin, syrup, adhesives, glues, textile fibers, soaps, sizing, paints, varnishes, explosives, and a host of other industrial and human consumption products.

◆ Dry milling is when the cornhusks are sprayed with steam to soften the cob and the kernels are removed. The kernels are then ground to make cereals, flour, hominy, grits, feeds, and various industrial products.

In addition to wet and dry milling, the entire plant is also heavily used for industrial purposes. Paper and wallboard are made from the stalks, while husks are used as fillers. Cobs are used to make charcoal, as fuel in burning, or processed into industrial solvents. However, the kernel is still the most valued part of the plant for industry.

With the plethora of uses for corn, it is no wonder that it is the most widely exported commodity in the United States. The United States is the world's largest producer of corn and the world's largest exporter. The largest users of U.S. corn are China, the former Soviet Union, South Korea, Mexico, and Japan. Sales to Eastern Europe have been expanding rapidly in recent years, as well.

Wheat Futures

A rose by any other name may be a rose; however, wheat by any other name is not wheat. There are three main types of wheat with active, liquid futures contracts traded on them:

- Soft Red Winter Wheat (Chicago Board of Trade)

- Hard Red Winter Wheat (Kansas City Board of Trade)

- Hard Red Spring Wheat (Minneapolis Board of Trade)

In futures vernacular, each type of wheat is typically referred to by the city in which it is traded.

Though there are many different varieties of wheat grown throughout the world, such as Soft/Hard/White/Red, there are two main classifications: Winter and Spring. Winter Wheat is planted in the winter and Spring Wheat is planted in the spring, hence the names. Each particular type of wheat—Hard Red, Soft Red, Durum, and White—requires slightly different climatic conditions for growth and is best suited for each type.

- **Hard Red Winter (Kansas City).** Grown predominantly in Kansas, Nebraska, Oklahoma, and the Texas panhandle. The cold, subzero winters and the general lack of precipitation make these regions of the country ideal. The primary use of Hard Red Winter Wheat flour is for bread-making.

- **Soft Red Winter Wheat futures (Chicago).** The most actively traded Wheat futures contract is grown in diverse areas of the country, in central Texas, toward the northeastern Great Lakes, and east to the Atlantic. The flour from Soft Red Winter Wheat is used to make cakes, cookies, snack foods, crackers, and pastries.

- **Hard Red Spring Wheat (Minneapolis).** Grown in the Northern Plains states where the rich black soil and the dry, hot summers make it ideal for this type of wheat. This high-grade wheat is suitable for milling and is used primarily in breads.

Each of the exchanges specifies a type and grade of wheat for delivery against its contract; however, most of the exchanges allow for delivery of different types of wheat at variable price differentials (premiums or discounts). This is why not all of the different types of wheat have active futures contracts on them, as some types of wheat can be delivered against other futures contracts at premiums or discounts, so there is no need for a specific wheat contract covering that. Because of the major differences in the production cycle and uses of Spring and Winter Wheat, we have broken them down separately in the following sections.

Winter Wheat Futures

Because the most prevalent variety of wheat grown in the United States is Hard Red Winter Wheat, the type of wheat that underlies the Kansas City Board of Trade (KCBT) Wheat Futures, we will highlight this futures contract. Generally, many of the same conclusions drawn about Kansas City Wheat futures can be extrapolated to the Chicago Board of Trade contract as well.

Winter Wheat Production Considerations

Winter Wheat is planted in the fall, goes dormant during the winter, and is harvested for grain during the following spring (refer to the Winter Wheat timeline that follows). During ideal weather conditions for early fall growth, much of the Winter Wheat (KCBT) grown in the southern plains is grazed by cattle prior to the wheat entering the dormant stage for the winter.

Wheat is usually planted in September or early October when the soil is sufficiently moist to germinate the seed. Late season warm spells are a potential problem during planting, as the warmth allows insects to survive long enough to eat the seeds. After planting, freezing temperatures and a blanket of snow protect the seeds while they lay dormant awaiting the spring thaw.

Trading Tips

Winter Wheat futures face the greatest risk during planting in late fall/early winter as well as during the heading stage in spring. It is typically during these times that prices have gained the most. Following these developmental stages, prices tend to decline. For example, Winter Wheat tends to head during May. From 1981 to 2000, May has been the worst month on average for CBOT Wheat prices, declining an average of −10¼ cents per bushel ($512.50) on a monthly settlement basis as the Wheat market passes this critical stage of development. Understanding when the wheat crop is susceptible to risk can help you anticipate major changes in supply and price.

Early warm weather is another hazard seeds face. Early thaws followed by a frost can cause the soil to heave, severing the stem from the root system. Wheat traders watch the weather closely in mid-February for signs of early thaws followed by frosts. As Winter Wheat's protective blanket of snow disappears, the small wheat shoots, which look like grass, begin to grow taller and begin to form a head. The head of the wheat stalk consists of small seeds or kernels, which are milled into flour.

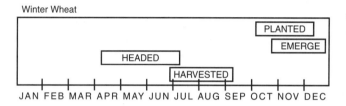

A typical Winter Wheat crop timeline.

The wheat crop is most vulnerable to damage during the heading stage. In order for wheat to head, it must pollinate, which requires adequate precipitation and seasonable temperatures. In normal years, Winter Wheat pollinates in early May. Typically, the wheat crop becomes visible as the snows melt and prices decline. The risk premium from heading built into prices usually erodes quickly during February. During March and April the crop is developing, fear grips the trading pits of Kansas City and Chicago, and the price of wheat tends to rally on pollination concerns. After pollination, the crop completes its heading and is left to dry in the heat of summer.

Like other crops, wheat uses most of its available resources in building the head. Now, the root system tends to die and the grasslike wheat begins to dry in the fields. Excessive rains, and below-normal temperatures after heading is complete, have produced minor rallies in June on fears that the wheat crop is too wet and, therefore, will not have adequate protein content.

The Winter Wheat harvest usually takes place from late May through early September, with the bulk of the crop being harvested between early June and mid-July. Excessive rains during harvest can slow down the harvest process, though very rarely does yield suffer much in years with a protracted harvest. The greatest damage to Winter Wheat during the spring and summer is from disease. Hot, humid conditions create ideal growing for mold-based diseases, which have commonly afflicted wheat in recent years.

Winter Wheat Consumption Considerations

Winter Wheat is used primarily for making flour for bread, and is the type of wheat most of us think of when we think of wheat.

Approximately two-thirds of U.S. wheat production is exported. The U.S. accounts for roughly 15 percent of the world's wheat production. The bulk of U.S. Wheat production is exported to such countries as Japan, India, and China. Eastern Europe and Australia can have major effects on export levels since poor crops in these countries increase the demand for Winter Wheat.

Government export programs are also a major component of wheat demand. In recent years, the U.S. government has used wheat as an extremely useful and effective bargaining tool in trade and political negotiations. Rumors of foreign buyers not getting government guarantees for wheat purchases have caused extreme price movements in recent years. Unlike most other grains, wheat is primarily an export product, and can be drastically affected by export programs.

Trading Tips

Though China is a major wheat producer, its large population necessitates that they buy additional wheat from the world. Japan is a minor producer, whose large population demands importation of wheat; the growing masses in India eat more than their own production, necessitating imports as well. It is important for traders and hedgers to pay attention to relations and growing conditions in these countries. Embargoes, changes in tariffs, or droughts and other weather problems can severely affect global demand and prices of wheat.

The relative price of the U.S. Dollar versus other major wheat-producing nations is also a major factor in the export markets. Severe changes in the exchange rates between Canada, Australia, India, and Eastern Europe with the United States will also severely affect the export attractiveness of U.S. Wheat.

Trading Tips

Winter Wheat is covered in this chapter because Winter Wheat futures are the only ones actively traded on the exchanges. Spring Wheat is very thinly traded, and though it may be okay for a little bit of hedging, it is difficult to get into and out of that market; the basis relationship makes it a poor hedging vehicle as well. In total, Spring Wheat futures trade about 3 percent as much as Winter Wheat futures.

Soybean Futures

Soybeans are relatively new to the agricultural scene. The importance of soybeans did not begin to show itself until after the Second World War. However, since then beans have become a major crop in the agricultural world.

Soybeans are grown primarily for the beans, which are processed into oil and meal. Grown primarily in the Corn Belt states of Illinois, Iowa, Minnesota, Indiana, and Ohio, soybeans are a short bush-like plant.

Whole soybeans have very limited uses. They can be held for seed for the coming crop, baked, puffed, steamed, or roasted for animal feed. The greatest demand for soybeans is its products, soybean oil and soybean meal.

Soybean oil and soybean meal are extracted from soybeans in a process known as *The Crush*. Originally, oil and meal were extracted from soybeans using large mechanical devices, which would crush the beans to extract the oil, and the leftover product was cleaned to make meal. Today, the common method of extraction is chemical, though the process is still referred to as *The Crush*.

Soybean Production Considerations

The bulk of soybean planting in the United States is started by May 10th, with planting usually completed by June 23rd (refer to the soybean timeline that follows). Ideally, planting should be done during mild temperatures with moderate precipitation, so the ground is soft and easily manipulated, but firm enough to support heavy farming equipment. If the temperature is too hot or cold and too much or too little precipitation is present, soybean planting can be delayed. Late-planted crops or replanted crops tend to produce lower yields. Planting delays have been a frequent problem over the years and, therefore, the marketplace is usually justified in building a risk premium this time of year. For example, March has historically been the strongest month of the year for July Soybean futures. Worries about planting and uncertainty regarding future supply prospects have caused July Soybean futures to gain an average of +13½ cents per bushel ($675 per contract) on a monthly settlement basis in March.

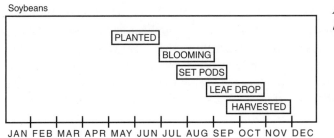

A typical soybean crop time-line.

Several days after planting, the soybean plant begins to emerge from the ground. Though the soybean plant is considered one of the most drought- and foul-weather-resistant of crops, until its extensive root system develops, it is vulnerable. The soybean plant is periodic in nature, so maturity can be tracked on a calendar with accuracy of a few days for each stage of development. After several weeks, the soybean plant begins to form buds, which will eventually bloom, setting the stage for pollination.

Soybeans are considered to have bloomed as soon as one bloom appears on the plant, which will end up with several blooms. The blooming/pollination process is the most critical stage of development. Good pollination almost assures a strong plant and good yields. Soybeans usually pollinate in the second or third week of July. After pollination, the plant begins to form bean pods, which are roughly one to two inches long and contain four to six beans. The blooming phase of development typically lasts from the beginning to the end of August, with pollination occurring roughly a third of the way through the process.

Trading Time Bomb

Because soybeans are planted in the same region of the country as corn, delays in corn plantings can be bearish for soybeans as fields are switched from corn to soybeans. This can pressure soybean prices. The two main risks to the soybean crop occur during planting and pollination (setting pods). After pollination, soybean prices usually collapse, so be warned and consider shorting the soybeans during this stage.

The soybean plant is considered to be setting pods when pods are developing on the lower nodes with some blooming still occurring on the upper nodes. Normally, during this stage of development, which lasts from late July through late September, prices drop precipitously as risk of damage to the crop is minimal.

As the pods develop fully, the lower leaves begin to die as nutrients are used for pod development. Soybeans are considered to be dropping leaves when the leaves near the bottom are yellow and dropping. At the later stages of leaf dropping, the plant is susceptible to freezes, which can split the pods and damage the crop.

The soybean harvest usually begins by September 21st, with the most active period being October 1st through October 25th. The soybean harvest is normally completed by November 10th. Ideal climatic conditions for harvest of the soybean crop are moderate to slightly above freezing temperatures with little precipitation. Warm and wet weather can make fieldwork messy, while early, heavy snowfall or severe rains can make harvest next to impossible.

Soybean Consumption Considerations

As mentioned, whole soybeans have very limited uses. The demand for soybeans rests upon the demand for the products: soybean meal and soybean oil. Each bushel of soybeans produces 11 pounds of soybean oil and 48 pounds of soybean meal.

Soybean Meal Consumption Considerations

The main demand for soybean meal is from the livestock industry, where it is used predominantly as feed. Almost 90 percent of the meal produced is used to satisfy the basic protein and amino acid requirements of livestock such as poultry, hogs, and cattle. Demand for soybean meal has a direct correlation to the demand for animal feed. Also, since animal feeds are a very *elastic market*, meaning one feed can be substituted for another, the relative pricing of other feeds and meal products such as corn, fish meal, and rapeseed meals have a great deal of impact on soybean meal prices.

def•i•ni•tion

An **elastic market** is one in which one product can be substituted for another. Flour is a classic example, in which brand (or even type) is indistinguishable. Markets that have elastic demand have many competing products that are substitutable.

The poultry industry consumes almost half of the world's soybean meal. The hog or swine industry consumes almost a quarter of the world's soybean meal, with the cattle industry consuming almost 14 percent between beef cattle and dairy cows. The remaining demand comes from pet food and aquamarine and other industries.

The largest seasonal change in demand comes from the cattle industry, which tends to use soybean meal as winter feed due to its high oil content compared to other alternative feeds. Feeds high in oil content are also high in fat, making them ideal for winter feeding since the higher fat content helps to offset the additional calories animals must burn to keep an even body temperature.

Soybean meal tends to outperform both soybeans and soybean oil from early August through mid-September, as the United States soybean crop is being prepared for harvest. Not only is demand running brisk for winter feed in South America, U.S. cattlemen tend to stock up in early September for their winter feed needs. Soybean oil, however, is being flooded with South American supply, as well as supply from competing products, such as rapeseed oil and palm oil, which have also been recently harvested.

Because animal feeds can be substituted for one another, the relative pricing of other feeds and meal products have a great deal of impact on soybean meal prices. Major macroeconomic factors such as income levels, consumer tastes, and economic growth rates have a great deal of impact on the demand for soybean meal.

Soybean Oil Consumption Considerations

The major demand for soybean oil is from the food industry. Soy oil is in a lot of products that you use every day. Margarine, shortening, salad oils, and cooking oils usually contain some soy oil content. As mentioned in the preceding "Soybean Meal Consumption Considerations" section, the edible oil market has very elastic demand, meaning that consumers are flexible in their oil consumption and many products are excellent substitutions for soy oil.

As a result, the relative pricing of animal oil substitutes and oil seed substitutes also play a major role in the demand for soy oil. Because of the elastic nature of demand for soy oil, this type of oil accounts for approximately 20 percent of world oil consumption.

Major forces in the economy, such as income levels and consumer preferences, are the basic components for soy oil consumption. As a result, the demand for soy oil is very difficult to predict.

The Least You Need to Know

- ◆ Field crops operate on an annual supply schedule, meaning supply is only available once a year, at harvest.

- ◆ Price tends to act as a rationing mechanism. High prices tend to slow down consumption, allowing supply to be spread out over the entire year, between harvests.

- ◆ When future supply is uncertain, prices tend to rise. Planting and pollination are the two biggest threats to future supply and have historically been the strongest times of the year for Grain futures.

- ◆ During times when future supply is less certain, prices tend to rise. However, as critical stages of crop development pass, prices tend to decline as the market begins to anticipate future production.

- ◆ It is important to watch major consumers and understand when their needs are great or slight to ascertain the future direction of prices.

- ◆ Each commodity market has its own unique features, and it is best to study each individually to learn its nuances before speculating.

Chapter 12

Food and Fiber (Softs) Market Overview

In This Chapter

◆ Cotton: not only breathable, but tradable

◆ Sugar: a sweet market

◆ Opportunity in Aztec money—Cocoa futures

◆ Orange futures and trading places

Softs is the name given to the group of mainly New York–based commodities, also referred to as the Food and Fiber group. These commodities trade in New York and Chicago, and range from exotic cocoa to the U.S.–dominated Orange Juice market. Primarily made up of foods, like cocoa, sugar, coffee, and OJ, it also includes the hybrid food/fiber cotton.

These markets tend to see wild price volatility and are heavily affected by ecological and political concerns. The amount of rain or frost in Brazil, or the latest coup in Côte d'Ivoire (Ivory Coast), can mean the swing of thousands of dollars in a matter of days. In this chapter, we will explain how the production and consumption of these commodities affects prices and how to use this information in your pursuit of speculative gains.

Cotton Futures

Cotton is a crop grown in more than 100 countries throughout the world. The two largest producers of cotton are the People's Republic of China and the United States. Three-fourths of the entire world's cotton crop is grown in six countries. In addition to the United States, the other four key producers are India, Pakistan, Uzbekistan, and Egypt.

def•i•ni•tion

Staple length refers to the average length of the fiber pulled from the boll of the cotton plant. It is generally thought that the longer the staple length, the higher the quality of the crop and the higher price it will fetch.

Upland cotton, with *staple lengths* of 1 to 1¼ inches, is the most common form of cotton grown, though American Pima is gaining in popularity in recent years due to its longer staple length of 1½ or more. Pima cotton is more commonly found in California and Arizona.

Cotton Production Considerations

In the United States, cotton is grown primarily south of the thirty-sixth parallel in Texas and the irrigated valleys of California and Arizona. Most cotton in the United States is grown on an annual basis from seed, as opposed to the foreign tropical producers who grow cotton on a perennial basis.

The bulk of the cotton crop is typically planted in late April and May, though planting in Texas has been known to start as early as March, given ideal weather and soil conditions. Like other crops, the ideal planting conditions for cotton are moist soil and warm temperatures. Too much rain can cause the fields to be too muddy to plant, while too little precipitation or heat can cause damage to the crop while it is still a seedling. Cotton planting is typically completed by the end of May, though in some years it can be dragged out through June. This is sometimes the case in Texas, especially if corn and/or soybean planting has been delayed.

Normally, the crop is most susceptible to damage during planting and early maturing; therefore, prices tend to rise based on the greatest potential for damage. Typically, in late May, seasonal highs are reached based upon this great potential for damage.

With the completion of planting, the cotton plant begins to grow. When a small triangular leaf-like structure begins to appear on the main growing stem of the plant, the cotton crop is considered "squaring."

After the crop has gone through the *squaring* process, it begins to flower, or set bolls. Bolls are the blooms that eventually open into the white fluffy balls we all recognize. During the boll-setting phase of development, the cotton plant is almost impervious to damage, with the exception of flooding or severe drought. Therefore, cotton prices tend to decline from the early stages of growth in late June through squaring and setting bolls, to the beginning of bolls opening in late August and early September.

The cotton crop is typically harvested in late September through early December, depending upon where and when the crop was planted. Texas, the largest cotton-producing state, typically harvests its crop from October 1st through December 2nd, though in years where planting was done very early, like in the beginning of March, Texans have been known to begin harvest as early as August. Normally, the bulk of the cotton crop is harvested from early October to mid-November. Excessive rain or snow can slow the cotton harvest down precipitously. Though harvest delays seldom affect yields much, delay scares have usually been labeled as the cause of many a late September or early October rally in cotton.

Another problem that can occur with cotton is reserving ginning space after the harvest. Shortages of gin capacity in a local area often delay harvest, as cotton farmers prefer to have little lag time between harvest and ginning. This usually comes at a time when domestic cotton supplies tend to be tight, and therefore can be a major contributing factor to the firmer bias. Higher cotton prices tend to occur from late September through December.

For a timetable of the stages of cotton production, refer to the following figure.

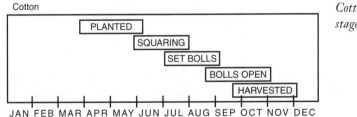

Cotton crop development stages.

Cotton Consumption Considerations

Cotton represents approximately 30 percent of the United States fiber market. The bulk of the cotton produced in the world is used in the manufacturing of clothing, followed by household goods such as linen, upholstery, drapery, and carpeting. The demand for cotton is greatly influenced by consumer taste. The general public's attitude toward competing fibers, such as polyester and rayon, greatly affect the demand for cotton.

Worldwide Cotton Considerations

China, though a major producer of cotton, tends to consume most of its crop domestically. In fact, in most years China is a net importer of cotton due to its blossoming textile industry. China's true effect on cotton prices tends more toward its importing than its production, though its own production is probably the single greatest factor in the amount of Cotton it imports or exports.

> **Trading Tips**
>
> The United States government introduced procedures in the 1985 Farm Bill to make U.S. cotton more competitive worldwide by allowing cotton farmers to borrow against crops and repay the loans at a discount to the average world price at the time they market their product. Changes to this legislation could have dramatic effects on the available supply as well as the demand for worldwide cotton.

India, too, is a major importer and exporter of cotton. With India venturing into more manufacturing and high tech businesses, look for that country to export more cotton over the next decade, as it uses its agricultural prowess to generate hard currency. Pakistan and Uzbekistan tend more toward export.

World Sugar Futures

Refined sugar comes from two sources: sugar beets and sugarcane. Although the nature and location of production as well as the processing techniques for sugarcane and sugar beets are very different, the refined sugar from each is indistinguishable.

Sugarcane is a bamboolike grass that grows in tropical and semitropical climates. Sugar beets are tubular plants, with a white, tapering root that grows to be about 12 inches long and weighs about 2 pounds. The bulk of the sugar produced throughout the world, remaining after domestic consumption, is sold internationally under special protective agreements. Of the available supply after domestic consumption, roughly 20 percent is available to be sold on the free market. It is this *free-market* sugar which is referred to as World Sugar #11.

The International Sugar Organization (ISO), a voluntary alliance of sugar importing and exporting nations, monitors the trade in World Sugar. The number 11 denoted on the end refers to the grade that is accepted at par value for the contract. Less and more refined grades of sugar are deliverable at discounts and premiums to the futures' final settlement price.

Sugar Production Considerations

The major producers of sugarcane are Brazil, India, and Cuba. The United States is the only country that grows both sugarcane and sugar beets, with cane production centered in Hawaii, Louisiana, and Florida, while beet production is centered in California and Minnesota. Sugarcane typically yields several crops, which are normally harvested fall through spring. This type of sugar source accounts for about 60 percent of the world's production of sugar.

Sugar beets are typically planted in early spring, and harvested before the first winter freeze. The major beet-growing region is in the European Union, followed by China, Thailand, and Australia. The United States only accounts for roughly 10 percent of the world's sugar production (5.7 percent of the free market), with most of that in cane form.

You should always know where a specific commodity is produced. Sugar is grown throughout the world. The top four sugar-producing nations include Brazil, India, China, and the United States. Other major producers are Australia, Cuba, Indonesia, Mexico, Thailand, and Ukraine.

By knowing where sugar is grown, the trader can be alert to changes in the political and economic situations of the major growing regions and the effects they may have on future supply and prices.

Trading Tips

One of the best places to find details about the current marketplace for Sugar, as well as other key agricultural commodities, is the United States Department of Agriculture's Foreign Agricultural Service (www.fas.usda.gov/commodities.asp). You can find import and export data and market reports on each of the major commodities.

Sugar Consumption Considerations

The demand for world sugar is tied to many long-term, macro population and political trends. Per capita income levels and population growth rates are two very important influences on the price of world sugar. Politics also play an important role in determining the price of world sugar. For example, the United States imports sugar on a USDA import quota system, typically paying domestic sugar prices (usually higher than World Sugar prices). Changes to import and export quotas can have enormous effect on the demand for imported sugar. Changes to the method of payment for sugar from importer to exporter can also have dramatic effects on sugar demand.

An increase in income levels of developing nations, such as in the Far East and South America, has increased the demand for sugar. The availability of alternative sweeteners, such as aspartame and corn syrup, has slightly dampened the demand for sugar. The major sugar-importing nations are the United States, Great Britain, Germany, and the former Soviet states.

Cocoa Futures

The cocoa tree is found only in tropical climates, typically not ranging more than 20 degrees from the equator. The fruit of the cocoa tree appears as pods, primarily on the tree's trunk and lower main branches. When ripe, these pods are cut down and opened and the beans are removed, fermented, and dried. Cocoa was originally cultivated by the Aztec Indians in North and South America, but is now widely cultivated in the tropical nations.

Cocoa Production Considerations

The cocoa tree thrives in the lower growth of the evergreen rainforest where the climate meets the following conditions:

◆ Temperature is relatively high (average temperature between 66° F to 92° F)

◆ Rainfall must be plentiful and well distributed, with average monthly rainfalls in excess of 1500mm (rainfall below 100mm per month for three months will damage Cocoa trees)

◆ Shade and humidity are preferable

The top seven cocoa-producing countries are Côte d'Ivoire (Ivory Coast), Ghana, Indonesia, Brazil, Nigeria, Cameroon, and Malaysia.

Cocoa trees take roughly three to five years to produce a cocoa crop. The average cocoa tree is productive for up to 25 years, so the long lag time between the original planting and production is not a major issue. Cocoa trees do not reach full production capacity until they are roughly 10 years of age.

The cocoa tree typically produces two crops each year. In Côte d'Ivoire, the largest cocoa-producing nation in the world, the main cocoa harvest runs from October to March, which is roughly five to six months after the wet season. The mid-crop harvest runs from May through August. The main crop accounts for roughly 75 to 80 percent of the total cocoa produced in Africa, while the mid-crop accounts for roughly 15 to 20 percent of production. The main crop and mid-crop seasons for the rest of the major producing countries is as follows:

- Ghana (main: Sep/Mar, mid: May/Aug)

- Indonesia (main: Sep/Dec, mid: Mar/Jul)

- Brazil (main: Oct/Mar, mid: Jun/Sep)

- Nigeria (main: Sep/Mar, mid: Jun/Aug)

- Cameroon (main: Sep/Feb, mid: May/Aug)

- Malaysia (main: Oct/Dec, mid: Apr/May)

Trading Tips

Cocoa production is centered along the equator, mainly in developing nations. Many of these nations are volatile politically. Political unrest can stop production and slow down the export of cocoa, or even cause shortages to the world's cocoa supply. Also, many of the major cocoa-producing nations are run by military governments, which increases the risk of trade sanctions.

Because cocoa has such a long production cycle, and because production tends to be centered in less developed countries, disease is a constant threat to the Cocoa market. Common cocoa tree diseases are Witches' Broom and Black Pod, which are devastating to a cocoa orchard. The International Cocoa Organization (ICCO), which is a cartel established to ensure fair international trade in cocoa and to steady supply and support prices, has been fighting these two common diseases for the past several years with moderate success.

Cocoa Consumption Considerations

The main demand for cocoa beans is from processors who either ferment or grind the bean for use in a variety of products ranging from chocolate to cosmetics.

The cocoa butter extracted from beans is used in a number of products, ranging from cosmetics to pharmaceuticals, but its main use is in the manufacture of chocolate candy. Once the cocoa bean is fermented and dried, the wastewater and shells are removed and the remaining *nib* is roasted. The roasted nib can then be ground into liquor for chocolate or for processing. Liquor for chocolate can be combined with sugar and milk (optional) and then blended and refined, producing a liquid chocolate (covertures), which can be molded or stored as a liquid. Liquor for processing can be refined into either cocoa cake or cocoa butter, which are used by confectioners and other industries.

The major consumers and processors of cocoa are Netherlands, United States, Germany, Côte d'Ivoire, Brazil, United Kingdom, and France. Most consumption of cocoa and cocoa by-products is done in Europe and the United States. The demand estimates show that world cocoa consumption was around 0.68 kilo per head (or 1.02 kilo per head, excluding China, whose large population has a disproportionate affect on world per capita consumption). There are, however, wide variations in consumption levels between the regions. Countries in Western Europe consume on average around 2.42 kilos per head, Eastern Europe 0.85 kilos, the Americas 1.33 kilos, Asia 0.15 kilos (0.68 kilos, including China), and Africa 0.13 kilos.

Orange Juice Futures

Almost all of the orange juice sold at the retail level is a processed, pasteurized product. The three principle forms of juice are reconstituted single-strength juice, juice not from concentrate, and frozen concentrated juice.

- Reconstituted single-strength juice is typically reconstituted by the packager and sold as a ready-to-serve product either in chilled form or in aseptic form sold in bottles or cartons without the need of refrigeration.

- Not-from-concentrate juice has been processed and pasteurized without the removal of the water content from the juice.

- Frozen concentrated juice has been partially reconstituted by the packager and must be defrosted and fully reconstituted by the consumer.

It is the frozen concentrated orange juice that is traded as a commodity.

Orange Production

Oranges are grown throughout the world, though Sao Paulo, Brazil, and Florida in the United States are the only regions that have major processing facilities. Together, Sao Paulo and Florida account for over 90 percent of the worldwide production of orange juice, and more than 50 percent of the worldwide production of oranges.

Orange trees take three to four years from the date of planting to begin bearing fruit. Production of fruit increases until they reach full maturity at approximately eight years of age. The average production life of a tree is roughly twenty years for trees in Sao Paulo, while Florida trees are productive for much greater periods (up to a total of 40 years) as irrigation and tree management are superior in Florida. The production life of a tree can be cut short if they are damaged by a hard frost.

The two major threats to the Florida orange crop are freezes and hurricanes. Both of these factors damage the tree and reduce production capacity for the next several years. There are soft and hard frosts, each having drastically different effects on the Orange Juice market. Soft frosts damage the exterior of the orange, making the oranges unappealing for retail consumption. Soft frosts reduce yields slightly, but create more orange juice supply because the damaged retail oranges are sold for juice. This is especially true of soft frosts hitting the California growing region.

Hard frosts kill orange trees, severely reducing yields for years in the future, and damage the pack, or sugary meat of the orange, so that the damaged fruit is unsuitable for squeezing. Hard frosts are probably the most bullish event that can happen to the orange crop because the damage takes roughly five years to be undone.

Hurricanes also damage the fruit or the tree, usually by battering the fruit with gale-force winds or actually uprooting and/or severely stressing the tree, thus reducing production.

The growing season in Florida lasts from January through mid-June or July, with a break in late February and early March. The bulk of Florida's crop is turned into juice because of the sweetness content and the type of oranges grown. California's orange-growing season usually runs from April through August, but the Californian oranges are mainly produced for whole consumption. In recent years, Brazil has also become a major producer of oranges.

Orange Juice Consumption Considerations

The demand for orange juice on a large scale did not begin until after World War II, following the development of the industrial process of producing concentrate. From the late 1940s until the mid-1960s, Florida was the only major producer of orange juice and the United States was the only major consumer. However, following the Florida freeze of 1962, production in Sao Paulo began. Because Brazil had historically been the provider of fresh oranges to Europe since the 1920s, the advent of juice production in Brazil led to increasing exports of orange juice. A world market for it soon followed.

The United States is still the largest consumer of orange juice, accounting for half of the world's consumption. Future demand in the United States is not expected to grow much, as this is a relatively mature market. U.S. demand should vary along traditional macroeconomic factors, such as income, population, and consumer tastes.

European demand is very segmented. Germany is the largest consumer within Europe, followed by Britain and France. These countries, too, are relatively mature markets. However, Eastern Europe and Russia have been experiencing increasing orange juice consumption in recent years, a trend which should be greatly affected by the state of their economies, since orange juice is considered a luxury item in many of these locales. Any increase in income levels should be matched by increases in orange juice consumption on a relative basis.

Japan, South Korea, and Australia are significant sources of demand for orange juice. Australia is considered an almost mature market with a relatively high per capita consumption. Other countries in Asia, including Hong Kong, Thailand, and Taiwan, have relatively low per capita consumption.

Like other agricultural products, the demand for frozen concentrated orange juice is affected by large macro trends such as income levels, consumer tastes, and population growth rates. The major consuming countries of frozen concentrated orange juice are the United States, England, Canada, and the European Union. The growing affluence of South American and other developing countries will also be major forces affecting the demand for oranges and frozen concentrated orange juice.

Using the Softs Fundamentals

It's important to understand the production and consumption cycles of the commodity futures markets you wish to speculate in. You need to understand when a crop is vulnerable to changes in supply and where the likely risk will occur. Also by understanding how the commodity is produced, you can ascertain how the market is pricing that commodity and hopefully anticipate changes in supply before they are reflected in price.

Consumption tends to be more stable than supply over the long haul. However, changes in the consumption cycle can greatly influence prices as well. Understanding the current uses and the reasons behind those uses is paramount before trying to ascertain changes to the consumption of a commodity.

Hence, by first understanding the production and consumption cycle of the markets in question, you can then look for changes in these cycles that will affect price. Without understanding the current market, you cannot notice change. Without spotting change, you cannot hope to profit from changes in the pricing of commodities.

The Least You Need to Know

♦ The Softs (also known as the "Food and Fiber" group) are a collection of commodities ranging from Cocoa to Cotton, Sugar, and Orange Juice. These markets are varied, but tend to be grouped together by analysts.

♦ Like most grown commodities, planting can be a time when future production is uncertain. During uncertainty, prices tend to rally.

♦ During the reproductive stage of development, crops are vulnerable to damage. This uncertainty regarding future supply tends to support prices.

♦ As harvest approaches, the dearth of supply expected on the market tends to drive prices lower. Often in the markets prices react before the event, anticipating the future supply.

♦ Many crops, such as cocoa and sugar, are produced in politically volatile regions of the world. Political risk can cause tremendous price volatility.

♦ Speculators and hedgers should understand the stage of development that a crop is in to judge the future course of prices. Understanding if a crop is at severe risk or not can help the speculator to judge the current price of a market more realistically.

Chapter 13

Livestock Market Overview

In This Chapter

- ◆ Understanding the process of cattle production
- ◆ Learn how times of the year affect beef prices
- ◆ Understanding pig production can help you in the Hog market
- ◆ Changes in seasons affect pork consumption and prices
- ◆ Spotting Livestock market opportunities

The Livestock markets—beef and pork—are unique markets in and of themselves. Both are annually produced by region. When you consider all regions in total, there is continual production in these markets. Unlike grains and Softs, they cannot be stored for a major period of time. Hence, the Livestock markets are truly unique.

In this chapter, we walk you through the livestock production process and highlight key factors that effect prices. This knowledge will help you make more informed decisions in the wild and wooly world of Livestock futures.

Herd Sizes, Profitability, and the Livestock Markets

Unlike the field crops or annually produced commodity markets discussed in the previous chapters, the Livestock market has year-round production and consumption, though some periods tend to see more available supply and usage than others. This creates a different type of trading environment for Livestock futures.

In the Livestock industry, supply is a function of the number of animals bred and fed. Breeding decisions can play an important function in the supply of meat. For example, if a cow/calf operation decides to increase the number of animals it raises—a process known as herd expansion—it will retain a higher percentage of female animals for breeding purposes. Typically females are withheld from slaughter and bred to produce more calves. Herd expansion usually takes between five and seven years to run its course. Hence, though the long-term supply potential of the cattle increases by this decision, in the short term the number of animals that can be slaughtered for the steaks we enjoy diminishes.

The opposite occurs when livestock producers decide to decrease herd sizes, known as herd contraction. The immediately available supply of animals for slaughter increases, though in the long term, the number of animals that can be slaughtered decreases. Herd contraction typically takes between two and four years to complete.

This cycle of herd expansion and herd contraction is a key factor in understanding livestock prices. The market price of Livestock futures reflects not only the readily available supply of slaughter weight animals, but also the future capacity of supply. The decisions regarding herd expansion and contraction are based on the producer's long-term outlook for profitability. During periods of expected future profitability they will try to expand production, to maximize profits—the goal of any business. During periods of diminishing returns, operations will be curtailed to cut losses or return to profitability.

This herd expansion and contraction is most prevalent in the Cattle industry. Indoor production and large scale "hog factories" have shifted the cycle in the Hog industry. But, nevertheless, understanding this cycle is of great benefit to participants in the Livestock futures market.

Cattle Production Process

Cattle production begins with the cow/calf operator. These traditional ranchers are in the business of breeding cows and producing calves. Cows are typically bred in the late summer or early fall to time birthing with the onset of spring, since Cattle require range to graze and the pasture conditions can support larger herd sizes more easily. Because Cattle production tends to be centered in states with harsh winters, like Texas, Kansas, Nebraska, Colorado, Oklahoma, Iowa, South Dakota, Minnesota, and Montana, spring birthing is important since the weather is more hospitable to the calves.

Roughly one to three months after a calf is born, the male calves are castrated, producing a steer. Calves are typically weaned from their mothers at 6 to 10 months of age, when they weigh between 300 to 600 pounds. Commercial cow/calf operators then usually sell the weaned calves to a stocker operation, which grazes the animals until they reach *feeder* weight of 600 to 800 pounds. There are two basic futures contracts covering the Cattle market:

◆ *Feeder cattle* represent weaned cattle, which weigh between 600 and 800 pounds and are suitable to enter into a feedlot.

◆ *Live cattle* weigh 900 to 1,400 pounds, which is an appropriate slaughter weight.

The feedlot is in the business of putting weight on cattle. Feedlots buy feeder-weight cattle and through a combination of hot and cold feeds they bring them to slaughter weight of 900 to 1,400 pounds over the course of the next three to six months.

A *cold feed* is an industry term meaning the cattle are grazed, while *hot feed* is typically corn, meal, or mash fed to cattle. Most feedlots prefer to split the time on hot and cold feeds, as cold feed is more cost effective, but hot feed produces a better animal and more choice meat cuts.

def•i•ni•tion

Cattle weighing between 600 and 800 pounds are referred to as **feeder cattle** because they are thin cows ready to be fattened up. When the feeder cattle weigh more than 800 pounds, they are referred to as **live cattle**, despite the fact that their lifespan is relatively short as the feedlots sell these fattened animals for slaughter.

So, roughly between a year and a year and a half after birth, the typical calf has been brought up to market weight and is ready for slaughter. In recent times, with consumer taste leaning toward leaner cuts of beef, larger-weight animals are being produced, so production time has been longer.

Since each stage of the production cycle is dependent upon the previous and next stage for supply and demand, any disruptions in supply or changes in demand have great effects upon the whole cattle production cycle. For example, when grain prices are high, hot feed costs are high and feedlots have to either increase the price of the finished product or decrease production, since profits are falling. If the market will not support higher beef prices, then a lack of demand for feeder cattle will develop and prices will wane.

Demand Considerations

Fattening cattle is a business requiring two main raw materials: feeder cattle and grains to feed the cattle. The demand for feeder cattle is usually proportional to the demand for live cattle and the profit margin generated from fattening cattle.

When profit margins are high, feedlot operators increase the number of head of cattle on feed, increasing demand for feeder cattle. When profits are small, or nonexistent, feedlots decrease the number of head on feed until profitability increases again. The major cost associated with fattening cattle is the price of feed.

Corn is the most commonly used livestock feed in the United States, so feeder cattle prices are negatively correlated to corn prices (when corn prices are rising, feeder cattle prices are declining and vice versa). Also, demand for beef or live cattle prices has a great deal of effect on the price of feeder cattle. The Cattle industry, especially the feedlots, is composed of small independent operators. As a result, cattle prices and feeder cattle demand are subject to radical movements.

Live cattle prices tend to be strongest in the winter (November through March) when supply is tight and during the early summer (June and July) when barbeque demand is high. They tend to be weakest in the spring (March through May) when supply is highest. Feeder cattle prices are typically strongest when live cattle prices are strong (June and July) and tend toward weakness in the spring as well, when grain prices tend to increase and the supply of feeder weight cattle is the highest.

The major demand for live cattle is as beef. Beef is what's for dinner (at least, that's what the American Beef Council would like you to think). The Cattle industry, through boards and councils (like the American Beef Council), has taken to marketing in recent years to increase public awareness of beef, as well as educate people on the nutritional aspects of beef. This type of target marketing, with an emphasis on advertising on radio, television, and print, has turned around the consumer's viewpoint of beef. After declining since 1986, average per capita beef consumption has stabilized at approximately 67 pounds per capita retail weight based on an October 2005 report from the USDA. Annual beef consumption is highest in the Midwest, where the average is 73 pounds per capita. Northeasterners eat the least amount of beef; their average is 63 pounds per capita.

The bulk of United States–produced beef is used domestically, though the export market for United States beef is increasing. Demand for beef tends to increase when population and income levels increase. Demand for the better cuts of meat, referred to as *choice beef*, has kept pace with population increases, though rarely exceeding it. Beef demand is somewhat elastic. When beef prices increase, people tend to eat more pork, poultry, and pastas. Shifts in public tastes play an important role in the cattle population cycle.

The major trends in meat consumption are set by slow-moving, macroeconomic factors, such as consumer tastes, population levels, income levels, and the like.

A big question for the future of beef production relates to the controversy about mad cow disease. On March 3, 2006, the USDA reported a possible third case of mad cow disease, which sets back efforts to reopen beef trade with Japan and South Korea. This trade has been shut off since the first case was reported in 2003. Prior to the ban, Japan imported $1.7 billion worth of U.S. beef, which was the most lucrative foreign market for the U.S. Cattle industry.

Pork Prices and the Changing Pig Market

Hog production in the United States has undergone a dramatic change in the last decade and a half. In 1988, hog farms with less than 1,000 head accounted for 32 percent of the market share of all hog producers, while large 50,000 plus-head operations accounted for roughly 7 percent of total hog production.

According to a 2003 Pork industry Structure Study done by the University of Missouri, large 50,000 plus-animal operations now account for 59 percent of the total Pork industry, while small 1,000 head or less operations only account for 1 percent of total U.S. market share. This transformation from small operators to large-scale operations has changed the nature of the Pork industry as well as Pork futures trading.

The transformation from small producers to big producers had a major impact on prices. Lean Hog futures prices went from 83.55 cents per pound in April 1997 to 20.70 cents per pound in January 1999, as new big producers dumped massive production on the market during the battle for market share. Lean Hog futures are now heading back up after that market restructuring. Futures prices as of the market close on March 15, 2006, for April 2006 Lean Hog futures was $58.10. Most smaller producers have been driven out of the hog business.

The change from small to large hog producers dominating the Pork industry has changed the nature of the hog supply. Today, systems producers, who typically use large controlled-environment buildings known as *hog factories*, dominate hog production.

def•i•ni•tion

Indoor, environmentally controlled, large-scale hog production facilities have been nicknamed **hog factories.** Known professionally as systems producers, due to the feeding and breeding systems they employ, these production facilities produce larger animals and higher meat grades at lower prices. I toured one several years ago, and they made me wear a surgical mask and hospital-type scrubs, for fear I would spread disease to the hogs. It was truly amazing.

These facilities make handling hogs easier by providing for more direct observation of animals, allowing greater control over the production process, and protecting both the animals and the workers from heat, cold, rain, and snow. Because of the close supervision of the production process and the complete control of the environment, swine production system facilities generally are able to produce a market-weight hog faster and cheaper since feed efficiency is better than at small-scale outdoor facilities.

Feed and labor are the two largest variable costs faced by Hog producers. So even though the hog factories require a larger initial investment, the cost savings over time definitely give these operations a distinct cost advantage compared to the small-scale old-fashioned pen-based method.

Hog Production

Hog production is centered in the Corn Belt states mainly, with the top five producing states being Iowa, Minnesota, Illinois, Indiana, and Ohio.

No matter what production system is used to raise hogs, the timetable is typically the same. The gestation (pregnancy) time for a sow is 114 days. The average litter size is 9 to 10 piglets, with a practical range of 6 to 13 per litter. Roughly three to four weeks after pigs are farrowing (birthing), the litter is weaned from their mother and moved to the nursery or grower stage. Each farrowing is referred to in the industry as a pig crop, which usually takes about nine months from birth to fatten the animals for slaughter.

During the growing stage, pigs are fattened from 10 to 15 pounds up to between 40 and 60 pounds on a highly concentrated diet of grain, plant proteins, and milk products. Once the pigs reach *growing weight* of 40 to 60 pounds, they are separated by sex.

Both barrows (males) and gilts (females) are fed up to nine different diets consisting mainly of corn, barley, milo (grain sorghum), oats, and sometimes wheat for dietary carbohydrates and fat, while oilseed meal (mainly soybean meal) is used as the primary source of protein to build the leaner and more muscular hogs of today. It typically takes between 38 and 42 weeks for the barrows and gilts to reach market weight of 250 pounds from their starting weights of 40 to 60 pounds.

Spring usually marks the beginning of the breeding season for hog operations. The supply of grain is plentiful from last fall's harvest and the weather is suitable for the outdoor producers. These spring pigs are usually ready for slaughter in five to seven months, so August through October tend to be characterized by high numbers of slaughters.

The number of hogs being slaughtered is the direct result of business conditions affecting the feeding of hogs. When feed prices are high, hog farmers have a tendency to slaughter more hogs because their feed costs are rising. The added supply of lean hogs and pork bellies then has a tendency to depress prices. Depressed prices tend to cause producers to lower production, which eventually will raise prices back up.

This cycle from profitability to unprofitability in the Pork industry is similar to that in the Cattle industry, but faster. The hog cycle typically lasts three to four years. As supplies increase, hog and pork belly prices tend to fall and hog operations curtail production. This limits the supply until eventually the price rises. As prices rise, production is increased until once again the supply is great, driving prices lower, and the whole cycle starts again.

The most important factors affecting the supply and price of Hog futures are feed costs and profitability considerations, the number of hogs and pigs on farms, and the birth rate of new pigs. Other important supply considerations are daily slaughter rates (marketings), Hogs and Pigs reports from the USDA, and Cold Storage reports (www.usda.gov/nass/aggraphs/coldstorage.htm).

Hog Market Consumption Factors

The Pork futures market is segmented into two main categories: Lean Hogs and Pork Bellies. Lean Hog futures represent the ham, pork chops, butts, and luncheon meat consumption of pork. Pork Bellies are mainly consumed as bacon, with some of the fatty meat used in the production of cold cuts.

The consumption of pork in the United States is increasing as producers are making leaner, less fatty hogs for slaughter. The industry has slimmed down their pigs, with today's pork containing 50 percent less fat than the pig of the 1950s. Around World War II, pigs averaged 2.86 inches of back fat, compared to today's leaner, slimmed-down hog, which contains an average of less than an inch of back fat. This trend toward leaner pork, coupled with the Pork Council's "Pork, the Other White Meat" television and print commercials, has increased the American public awareness of pork.

American eating habits concerning pork are very seasonal, with demand for pork increasing from Memorial Day and turning back down by Labor Day. Pork demand tends to be strongest during the summer in the United States when barbecuing is more prevalent, and Americans consume more processed meats, which typically contain a high amount of pork products.

Trading Time Bomb

Pork Belly futures are extremely volatile! Most futures markets have large commercial trading activity on both the buying and selling side, which tends to cancel each other out. However, in the Pork Belly market, speculators and small bacon manufacturers do the bulk of the trading. As such, this market can have dramatic price swings. This is not a market for beginning speculators, as the risk is extremely high!

Trading Tips

If you are interested in the Livestock markets and are on the Internet, you may wish to visit the following Web sites: The Chicago Mercantile Exchange (www.cme.com); The Livestock Almanac (www.livestock-futures.comfutures.com); U.S. Department of Agriculture (www.usda.gov); Great Pacific Trading (www.gptc.com).

The fast-food industry has become an ever-increasing consumer of bacon and pork bellies. Behemoths such as McDonald's, Burger King, and Wendy's feature bacon on sandwiches and have added breakfast menus in recent years. Since the busiest time of the year for the fast-food industry is summer, it is no surprise that this period sees the largest number of bellies moving out of cold storage for slicing.

Bacon and pork consumption is becoming more popular worldwide. As Americans are watching their cholesterol, Asia and South America are consuming more of these traditionally American fares, such as bacon cheeseburgers and BLTs.

The United States is the largest pork exporter in the world, followed by Denmark. The United States exports more pork to Japan than any other nation, as Japan also has a strong appetite for pork. Canada, Mexico, Russia, Hong Kong, Korea, Italy, China, the Philippines, and Britain are important markets for U.S. pork exports.

Pork has seen gains in its popularity worldwide as fears of mad cow disease have decreased beef consumption. Exports through October 2005 ran 24 percent ahead of 2004, which also set export records. Mad cow is not the only factor in this rise in pork popularity. The weaker U.S. dollar helped U.S. pork exporters gain market share in Japan, Russia, South Korea, and China according to the December 2005 USDA Hogs and Pigs report. However, the USDA did warn there was downside potential to the Hogs and Pigs market and that prices may slip lower.

Though export demand for U.S. pork is probably the most volatile component affecting the price of pork and hogs, consumer taste and competition from competing meat products have more influence. Generations of fear of trichinosis from undercooked pork had Americans overcooking pork, reducing its taste and appeal. Recent marketing campaigns from the pork industry have reversed the tide and are showing an increase in America's appetite for pork. However, pork faces strict competition from beef and poultry products for America's appetite. Though the majority of the demand components for pork are long-term macroeconomic factors, the seasonal summer increase in the consumption of pork has a strong tendency to support prices.

Trading Tips _____

You can read the most recent Hogs and Pigs report online at http://usda.mannlib.cornell.edu/reports/nassr/livestock/php-bb/. You'll also find reports dating back to 1995.

The Least You Need to Know

- ◆ During herd expansion, slaughter rates decline in the short term as females are withheld to breed. Eventually this phase ends when increased supply (production capacity) overtakes supply.

- ◆ During herd contraction, supply increases in the short term as breeding stock is sold for slaughter. However, longer-term prices go higher as less supply is eventually produced.

- ◆ Feeder cattle refers to cattle going onto feedlots (thin cattle) while live cattle refers to fattened cattle ready for slaughter.

- ◆ Lean hogs refers to post-slaughter hanging weight, and pork bellies are basically raw, unsliced bacon.

- ◆ The demand for meat is fairly static in any year, but certain periods—like holidays and summer—tend to see increased demand.

- ◆ By understanding how and when livestock are produced and when and where meat is consumed, the trader can understand why prices move and hopefully spot profitable trading opportunities.

Chapter 14

Metals Market Overview

In This Chapter

- ◆ Learn about the changing nature of the Gold market
- ◆ See how gold is more closely tied today to the economy
- ◆ Understand how the industrial usage and scrap supply nature of the Silver market affect prices
- ◆ Learn why platinum prices are tied to the fate of the automobile industry
- ◆ See how copper is a good indicator for the general economy
- ◆ Learn to think about the price of metals as a function of supply and demand

Metals have a long history of being a store of value. Gold, silver, and copper as a medium of exchange predates the Roman Empire—and their use as a basis for currency was not limited to Western societies. The Chinese and Hindu cultures used gold and silver as the basis for their coinage.

In 1816, Great Britain adopted a gold-backed paper currency and the rest of the industrialized world shortly followed suit. Prior to 1934, the United States Dollar was equal to one-twentieth of an ounce of gold, redeemable upon request. Except for a brief halt of conversions from dollars for Gold during World War II, the United States Dollar was backed by Gold under an agreement known as the Bretton Woods Agreement or the Gold Standard.

In this chapter, we present the major supply and demand factors which affect the prices of the major metals futures contracts: Gold, Silver, Platinum, and Copper.

Understanding the Gold Standard

The Gold Standard was a formal agreement to back the United States Dollar with gold. This agreement, which was signed in 1943 in Bretton Woods, New Jersey, is also known as the Bretton Woods Agreement or Standard. Under Bretton Woods, each nation's currency would have a par value in relation to the gold content of the U.S. Dollar. Every currency was convertible to U.S. Dollars, which were backed by gold. In essence, the world's money was fixed to gold. This system endured until 1972, when U.S. foreign purchases exceeded its exports for the first time. By December 31, 1974, the U.S. Dollar was no longer fixed to gold and Gold futures began trading.

Trading Tips _____

Under Bretton Woods, the United States Dollar, and other global currencies, were tied to a value of gold. From 1934 to 1968, this amount was $35/oz of gold. To protect the amount of gold held in reserve to support the dollar, it was illegal for United States citizens to own gold prior to President Nixon's revocation of the Gold Standard.

Upon revocation of the Gold Standard, gold became a popular investment medium, and the price rose from roughly $35/ounce to $800/ounce during the turbulent 1970s. During these times, gold took on the aura of being a safe haven of value against inflation and world turmoil.

However, as currencies were taken off the Gold standard and financial markets became more intertwined, gold and the rest of the precious metals began to be used less and less as a method of payment. As governments and the private sector began to have more faith in fiat currencies—paper money—the metals' role as a monetary vehicle slowly diminished.

Adding to the demise of the metals as a store of value has been the trend (which has been in effect since 1974) of central banks throughout the world selling off gold reserves previously held to back their currencies. This added supply has weighed heavily on metals prices, causing them to lose some of their luster as a financial vehicle because of the added supply, as well as the fact that gold has to be stored, and pays no dividends.

Though some people believe gold and other metals represent the only real store of value in a world of paper money, it is our belief that due to the demise of the Bretton

Woods Agreement, traders should treat the metals not as a monetary instrument, but as a commodity whose price is dictated more by supply and demand than investment value.

The Gold Fix

One of the most widely quoted prices for metals is the *London Fix*, which is held at N. M. Rothchild's at 10:30 A.M. (Morning) and at 3:00 P.M. (Afternoon). You can check the fix online at www.goldfixing.com.

The Fix is a single price for gold where the members, or Fixing Seat Holders, match up their entire buy and sell orders. The price at which the most buy and sell orders match, or balance, is known as the Fix. The strength of the Fix is that a large volume of physical gold can be bought or sold at

def•i•ni•tion

The **London Fix** is a single price set for physical metals—gold, silver, platinum, palladium, and copper—set in the morning (A.M. Fix) and evening (P.M. Fix) by major metals brokers in London. The Fix is arrived at by finding the price where the most buy and sell orders match in the physical market.

a single, clearly posted price. The Fix is a benchmark price for many transactions worldwide, whether for mines, fabricators, or central banks, because it is undisputed prices at which all six of the largest gold trading houses are willing do business.

Because of the importance of the London Fix, traders involved in the metals markets should watch the Fix as a base price for metals. It is widely quoted in the financial press, and many local papers even carry it.

Trading Tips

Because of its softness, gold for use in jewelry is mixed with other alloys. The pureness of gold is measured in terms of carats, with 24 carats being 99.99 percent pure. The most popular carat rankings of gold are 18 and 14 carat pure, representing 75 and 58.3 percent pure, respectively. The most popular carat for jewelry in Europe is 18 and 14, as it is in the United States. In the Middle East, India, and Southeast Asia, where jewelry is used as much as an investment as it is for decoration, 22 carat is more popular. In these countries, 22 carat items usually sell at a marginal markup to the metal value (usually 10 to 20 percent). These items can be traded in or sold back to distributors at any time.

The Gold Market

South Africa is the world's largest producer of gold, accounting for almost 14 percent of the world's bullion (another name for refined gold), according to the World Gold Council. The United States is the second largest producer of gold, accounting for an estimated 11 percent of the world's Gold supply. Australia is the world's third largest producer of Gold at 10 percent. The top three producing nations produced roughly 35 percent of the world Gold supply in 2001. Latin America (Mexico, Peru, Chile, and Brazil) and the Far East are growing in importance as producers, as low labor costs and expanded exploration have opened up several new mines.

Gold Supply

The total supply of gold is very difficult to measure, as it includes not only mine production and recycling, but also gold held in coin form, as well as central bank holdings.

Measuring the amount of mine production is difficult, simply because mine production can fluctuate with price. The law of supply dictates that as prices rise, more supply will become available. This is true for mine production as well. For example, if a mine has a fixed cost of production of $280/ounce of gold—the cost to get one ounce out of the ground—and prices are well below this level, the mine may be shut down. Miners do not mine gold to lose money. But if prices stay above the cost of production for a while, this mine may be brought back into production. Hence, though supply is not as variable in the metals as it is in grains or meat markets, measuring mine production can be difficult.

Russia is a major producer of several metals, including gold. Throughout Russian history, they have sought a warm-water port, one that does not freeze during the winter. The fact that many ports freeze in the winter causes many producers to dump metals and supplies in the fall (October/November) ahead of ports freezing and the increased shipping costs associated with ice breaking. Hence, be on the lookout for selling opportunities in the late fall, as a Russian Gold bear may be prowling.

Old gold scrap can also be recycled and used. This can include older jewelry, as well as old electronic components and such. Obviously, if the price of gold were high, more of this supply would find its way onto the market. For example, I had a ring made for my wife several years ago. At the time, we thought about having her old engagement ring melted down to be used in the new ring—for cost and sentimental purposes. However, because gold was only about $265 an ounce, the cost savings in gold were less than the extra labor involved in the process (note: we did it anyway for sentimental purposes).

The supply of gold coins and such is also very difficult to measure. Rising gold prices can attract some of these to the market, increasing supply. But some will never be available for consumption, because they are collectors' items and have added value as such in addition to the gold content.

Obviously many of the supply components are affected by price, but they tend to lag by several months or even years. Because of this, many analysts tend to concentrate more on gold usage than supply. Of course, radical changes in supply, like central bank-selling and mine strikes, are taken into account, but generally these issues are rare, and should be considered on a case-by-case basis.

Gold Usage

Jewelry fabrication is the crucial cornerstone of demand for this yellow metal. Gold for use in the jewelry industry accounts for roughly 54 percent of the total demand. Given that gold demand is so closely tied to the jewelry industry, the fortunes of both industries tend to rise and fall in tandem.

Gold futures are based on bullion prices, not rings. Bullion must be melted and crafted into jewelry. Hence it is the buying of manufacturers and wholesellers that drive prices. Based on this, traders should look for increases in gold prices in August and September, as jewelers begin ordering for the Christmas shopping season.

Like all of the other metals, which have underlying futures contracts, gold is becoming more and more of an industrial metal. Due to its virtues of malleability, ductility, reflectivity, resistibility to corrosion, and unparalleled ability as a thermal and electric conductor, gold is used in a wide variety of industrial applications.

The largest industrial user is the electronics industry. In the Electronics Age, gold is used in everything from microprocessors, pocket calculators, washing machines, and televisions, to missiles and spacecraft. Contacts are electroplated with a very thin layer of gold, using potassium cyanide, referred to in the industry as plating salts. The production of plating salts accounts for roughly 70 percent of the demand for gold in the electronics industry.

Gold's other major role in the electronics industry is in semi-conductors. A fine gold wire or strip is used to connect parts such as transistors and integrated circuits, and in printed circuit boards to link components. This bonding wire is one of the most specialized uses of gold, requiring it to be 99.999 percent pure with a wire diameter of one $\frac{1}{100}$ of a millimeter. Japan and the United States are the largest industrial users of gold, accounting for 45 and 30 percent of its industrial use, respectively.

Gold as an investment or *hoarding* vehicle is the third largest component of demand. The attraction of gold coins as an investment soared with the introduction of the South African Krugerrand in the mid-1970s. The success of the Krugerrand spawned most major nations to produce their own bullion coins: Australia's Nugget and Kangaroo, Austria's Philharmonkier, Britain's Britannia, Canada's Maple Leaf, and the United States' Eagle, to name a few.

The concept of a bullion coin made by a government and sold at a low premium (usually five to seven percent) to the base bullion amount (as opposed to the old numismatic coins, which had more value as a collector's item than their metal value) has endeared gold as an investment vehicle for small investors. This enables them to buy very near the spot price of gold. (The spot price of any commodity is the price at which the commodity can be bought at a specific time and place. For gold, the key spot price is the Fix in London at 10:30 A.M. and 3 P.M., discussed above.) Small bars of gold are the preferable investment vehicles of the Middle East. Together, the small bar and coin demand accounts for between 100 and 200 tons of gold on an annual basis. The hoarding demand is directly related to the level of inflation as well as political uncertainty in the Middle East and throughout India and Southeast Asia.

By understanding the uses of gold, a trader can anticipate changes in the usage picture more rapidly. Because the demand side of the Gold market is more volatile than supply, changes in demand are much easier to anticipate than changes in price. By anticipating changes in demand, traders may be able to ascertain changes in the price of gold.

The Silver Market

Until the demise of the Bretton Woods Gold Standard in the early 1970s, most countries used a bimetal platform (gold and silver) to back their currencies. Silver, being more abundant than Gold and thus costing less, has always been the metal of everyday business. Its lower cost makes it more practical for conducting transactions on a daily basis.

Commodity Corn

Silver has also played an important role throughout history in silverware and communications. The expression "born with a silver spoon in his mouth" is not a reference to wealth, but to the early eighteenth-century discovery of the fact that babies fed with a silver spoon were apt to be healthier due to silver's antibacterial properties. (Thus, silver eating utensils have become the norm.) Silver has a long and critical role in industry as well, as the first telegraph message ever sent, "What hath God wrought?" was typed out by Samuel Morse on his telegraph made with silver contact points.

Though silver has its roots as a precious metal, core demand today comes more from the industrial sector than the investment and "hoarding" segment.

Silver Supply

The supply of silver is based on two factors: mine production and recycled silver scraps. Fifteen countries produce roughly 95 percent of the world's silver from mines. The most notable producers are Mexico, Peru, Australia, China, Poland, Chile, Canada, and the United States. Mexico is the largest producer of silver from mines, Peru is the world's second largest producer, and Australia is the third largest according to The Silver Institute.

Silver is often mined as a by-product of other base metal operations, which accounts for roughly four-fifths of the mined silver supply produced annually. Known reserves, or actual mine capacity, is fairly evenly split along the lines of production.

The other major source from silver is from refining, or scrap recycling. Because silver is used in the photography industry, as well as by the chemical industry, the silver used in solvents and the like can be removed from the waste and recycled. The total supply of silver from scrap has increased dramatically in the last decade as more advanced methods of recycling have been developed.

The United States recycles the most silver in the world, with Japan being the second largest recycler. In the United States and Japan, three-quarters of all the recycled silver comes from photographic scrap, mainly in the form of spent fixer solutions and old x-ray films.

Trading Tips

Silver being an industrial metal, prices tend to be strongest ahead of consumer demand for finished products. Summer marks the height of picture-taking, building, and other activities requiring silver. As such, manufacturers tend to purchase silver in the first two quarters of the year to use in production of film, switches for new construction, and electronics to be sold in the latter part of the year. Many old traders say that silver leads the metals higher from January through May.

Silver Demand

Though silver has a long and distinguished history as being the metal of commerce, it has shifted roles in recent years to be more of an industrial metal than a precious metal. The single largest use of silver is for industrial purposes, with the electronics industry making up the lion's share of this demand. Jewelry and silverware is the second largest component, with more demand from the flatware industry than from the jewelry industry in recent years.

The photography industry is a large user of silver. Silver is an important ingredient in both the manufacturing and processing of film. The use of silver for this purpose is declining, as more and more people shift to digital cameras and away from film. Silver coinage accounts for only a small portion of the demand for silver in recent years.

Silver components are found in everything from light switches and circuit breakers, to personal computers, stereos, telephones, microwave ovens, and automobiles. Silver is also used in the production of bearings, as electroplated silver bearings have greater fatigue strength and load-carrying capacity than any other type. Silver also facilitates the joining of materials (called brazing), producing a leak-proof, smooth, corrosion-resistant joint in manufactured goods.

Silver is the best electrical conductor of all metals and hence is used in conductors, switches, contacts, and fuses. Silver, unlike most other metals, does not allow electricity to arc, which is a common cause of fires; hence, electrical switches using silver are the norm.

Silver is also used extensively in the electronics industry. Silver membrane switches, silk-screened circuit paths, and other electronics-related uses of silver accounted for more than 40 percent of the demand for silver in 2004, according to the Silver Institute.

Jewelry and silverware demand has been steadily decreasing as a percentage of total use of silver for many years, as manufacturing and electronics industrial uses of silver increase. The Silver Institute stated that 29.5 percent of silver demand was for jewelry in 2004.

Though silver has its roots in the precious metals markets, in recent years the fastest growing segment of demand and use for silver has been from industry, hence traders should view silver as more of an industrial metal than as a precious metal.

The Platinum Market

Though platinum is a relative newcomer to the metals scene, this mineral is very important to industry today. Platinum has more industrial uses than both gold and silver combined, when considering the volume of platinum that is mined on an annual basis. The industrial and materialistic uses of platinum have grown over the years. In the nineteenth century when jewelers were able to melt platinum, "white gold" began to replace silver in jewelry. The lustrous white color of platinum better accentuates diamonds, and the bands can be much smaller as it is over 100 times stronger than silver.

Trading Tips

Often referred to as *white gold*, platinum is 16 times more rare than gold and 100 times more rare than silver. I have a friend who is a jeweler, and he says some retailers pass off an alloy mix as white gold, but to a jeweler, white gold is platinum. A popular trading idea is to buy platinum futures and sell gold futures when they are trading at very close even amounts on a per ounce basis. Because platinum is traded in 50-ounce increments and gold in 100-ounce increments, this trade usually involves buying two platinum futures and selling one gold future. The general idea is that because platinum is extremely rare, it should trade at a premium to gold, and it usually does. Watch for this scenario. At the end of 1996, platinum traded at a small discount to gold, before jumping to a $50 premium, which would have resulted in a $5,000 gain using the strategy above.

Platinum Supply

The annual supply of platinum is 118 tons, which is equivalent to only 6 percent (by weight) of the Western world's annual gold production and less than 1 percent (by weight) of the world's annual silver production. To put the supply of platinum in perspective, more than twice as much steel is poured each day in the United States, than platinum is produced in the world each year!

The world's supply of platinum is highly concentrated. Platinum occurs as a native alloy in placer deposits or, more commonly, in lode deposits associated with nickel and copper. Nearly all of the world's supplies of platinum are extracted from four countries:

- The Republic of South Africa (77.9 percent)
- Russia (12.3 percent)
- Canada (4.1 percent)
- United States (1.9 percent)

Because platinum is located in only a few countries, political problems in these countries can have a major impact on prices. During the 1980s when Apartheid was being ended in South Africa, platinum prices rose dramatically as strikes and other civil unrest restricted supply. In the late 1990s and into 2006, concerns over political and economic stability in Russia have caused platinum prices to soar, from $350 an ounce to over $1,070 as of the close of the market on March 15, 2006.

Platinum Demand

It is estimated that 20 percent of all the goods manufactured today either contain platinum or are produced using platinum-containing equipment. The major industrial users of platinum are the automotive, electronic, chemical, jewelry, dental, and glass industries. Platinum is used in fuel cells, gasoline, hard disk drives, anti-cancer drugs, fiver-optic cables, LCD displays, eyeglasses, fertilizers, explosives, paints, and pacemakers. Because of platinum's catalytic qualities, it is used in catalytic converters by the automotive industry. Catalytic converters are used to turn toxic gasses produced using unleaded gasoline into carbon dioxide and water. The automotive industry accounts for roughly 80 percent of platinum demand each year.

Trading Tips

The fortunes of platinum are closely tied to the automotive industry, the largest consumer of platinum. It seems that every couple of years, rumors circulate that someone has invented a new catalytic converter that doesn't use platinum. These rumors have caused platinum prices to plummet very quickly in the past, so do not disregard them.

The automotive industry is also the fastest growing user of platinum. This trend is expected to increase, as platinum is an integral part of the emissions system of an automobile and stricter pollution controls are being put on auto manufacturers every year.

Platinum faces some competition from palladium in the automobile industry, but palladium-based catalytic converters are more effective only on diesel fuel engines. Because the demand for diesel fuel automobiles is growing in Europe, the demand for platinum from European automobile manufacturers has been slowly decreasing in recent years. In fact, according to *Panorama 2005* (published by IFP, a French scientific research and industrial development, training, and information services center), European consumption of diesel fuel more than doubled in the last 20 years because of the increase in diesel vehicles.

The second largest consumer of platinum is the chemical industry. Platinum is used in the manufacturing of paints, acids, and fertilizers, as well as explosives. Large platinum vats are constructed for the manufacturing of acids, as no other metal has platinum's resistance to corrosion. Platinum is also used in oil refining, since it is able to reduce levels of aromatics and sulfur in heavy oil products like diesel and heating oil.

The electronics industry is an increasingly important player in the Platinum market. Probably the fastest growing consumer of platinum recently, this segment uses platinum in everything from electrical components to computer chips and semiconductors.

Though platinum's use in jewelry has decreased dramatically in the last decade, platinum-based jewelry is still more popular in Japan than gold. Platinum strength and luster makes it the ideal setting for diamonds because its rich white color tends to increase the sparkle and the appeal of precious stones.

Because platinum is an industrial metal and also a jewelry metal, platinum prices tend to outperform gold prices during the first quarter of the year as industry gears up. In years when jewelry demand is high, platinum tends to benefit as well. Platinum is 16 times more rare than gold, so most factors which send gold higher tend to be more beneficial to platinum.

The Copper Market

A nonferrous metal, copper is a highly versatile substance valued for its excellent conductivity, noncorrosiveness, and heat resistance. Humans have used copper for weapons, tools, and personal adornment since prehistoric times.

Copper Supply

The United States and Chile are the two largest producers of copper in the world; each country accounts for roughly 18 percent of the total world production. U.S. mines are located in Arizona, Utah, New Mexico, Montana, and Nevada. China, the former Soviet Union, Canada, Poland, Peru, Zaire, and Zambia also are key copper producers.

Scrap copper is also an important source of supply. Roughly 40 percent of the copper consumed in the United States each year is from recycled supply.

Copper Demand

Copper has a wide range of uses in a vast variety of products. The electrical and electronics industries are the primary users of copper in the United States, accounting for roughly 70 percent of the total usage in a given year.

Construction accounts for roughly 15 percent of the copper consumed in a year. Copper is used in roofs, plumbing fixtures and pipes, hardware, and decorative products.

Look for copper prices to be the strongest during the summer months of June through September. Strong demand ahead of the consumer electronics-buying season, coupled with brisk demand from housing, generally supports prices during this time of the year. Copper is also extremely sensitive to changes in the economy. A weak economy means diminishing usage, while strong economic growth means strong demand.

Because mine production and scrap supplies are hard to ascertain and can change with prices more readily than demand, traders should pay close attention to the state of the economy and the general trends in electronics and construction for clues to the fundamental picture in copper.

Metals Review

Generally, thinking of the metals not as a monetary vehicle but as commodities whose price is dictated by supply and demand can help the trader ascertain trends in prices.

Because the various metals are raw materials for the overall economy, general levels of economic growth have great effects on demand. Generally during periods of extreme economic growth, demand will run ahead of supply, as mines and recyclers need time to adjust output to meet demand. During these growth spurts, metals prices tend to be strongest, lacking other outside influences (such as central bank-selling).

During times when the general economy is slowing, cutbacks in mine production will lag behind slowing demand and prices should generally decline. During normal economic times of moderate growth, production tends to adjust to demand and prices remain fairly steady, rising and falling with expectations of future demand.

By understanding the uses of metals, traders can ascertain much more information about future prices, because the demand component is much more variable than supply.

The Least You Need to Know

- Gold no longer backs the U.S. Dollar. As such, the Metals markets are much more industrial commodities today.

- The London Fix is the most widely quoted price for metals and is an important factor to watch when trading Metals futures.

- The price of gold is closely tied to the jewelry industry. Physical demand for gold tends to run several months ahead of retail demand for gold.

◆ Silver is closely tied to the health of the electronics industry. Silver recycling is an important and growing source of supply, which fluctuates with price.

◆ Platinum is an extremely rare metal used in catalytic converters by the automotive industry. Car sales are a good reflection of the demand for platinum.

◆ Copper is a very broad-based metal in terms of both supply and demand. Copper prices tend to ebb and flow with the general economy, as do the other metals.

Chapter 15

Petroleum Market Overview

In This Chapter

- ◆ Learn about the Petroleum markets and the economy
- ◆ See how OPEC affects prices
- ◆ Understand the dual nature of crude oil demand
- ◆ Learn unleaded gasoline demand patterns
- ◆ Discover heating oil demand patterns and how they affect prices
- ◆ Learn the geopolitical nature of petroleum prices

Oil provides about 40.2 percent of the energy Americans consume and roughly 97 percent of our transportation fuels. Oil is at the crux of the modern economic system, and its importance should not be discounted.

This chapter will give you an overview of the Petroleum market and help you understand that oil is really much more than what you have changed in your car every few thousand miles.

Black Gold, Texas Tea

Besides meeting almost half of our total energy needs and the lion's share of America's transportation fuel needs, the Oil industry employs almost one and a half million people in the United States. Not only is oil, in one form or another, used to heat our homes and fuel our vehicles, petroleum-based products can be found in a variety of everyday household items, including deodorant, toothpaste, paints, balloons, perfumes, and cosmetics.

Crude oil—oil in its raw form—has to be refined to be used. Distillation is the primary method of refining crude oil into its resulting products. The crude oil is heated at the bottom of a tall metal tower. As crude gets hotter, it turns to a gaseous state and the vapors rise. When the vapors rise, they cool. Each crude oil byproduct, in its gaseous state, has a specific cooling temperature, corresponding with a height of the tower. At these predetermined heights in the tower, pipes lead off to separate the various petroleum products. Heavier fractions, like fuel oils and diesel fuel, are taken from the bottom part of the heating tower. Lighter fractions, like butane, gasoline, and kerosene, are taken from the top of the tower. The heating tower produces the rough materials for the six basic categories of petroleum products, which are jet fuel, kerosene, motor gasoline, diesel fuel, residual fuel, and distillate fuels. The major use of crude oil is for refining into its various products, such as gasoline and heating oil.

Crude Oil Supply Considerations

One of the major influences on the supply of crude oil is the Organization of Petroleum Exporting Countries, or OPEC. In the early 1970s, the ownership of oil production in the Middle East transferred from the operating companies to the governments of the oil-producing nations, or their national oil companies. The following countries are OPEC members: Algeria, Indonesia, Iran, Iraq, Kuwait, Libya, Nigeria, Qatar, Saudi Arabia, the United Arab Emirates, and Venezuela.

It was in 1973 that OPEC began to have a major influence on the price of crude oil. Through limitation of production by a quota system, OPEC was able to curtail production and drive prices up. From the 1973 price level of $7 a barrel, prices rose roughly 400 percent in less than a decade, to $34 a barrel.

OPEC's dramatic success in increasing oil prices also has cost it a lot of influence in recent years. Higher crude oil prices have allowed new sources of supply to be brought online. For example, in the mid-1970s, OPEC production of crude oil accounted for roughly two-thirds of the world oil supply. According to recent American Petroleum Institute statistics, OPEC countries account for roughly 40.2 percent of the world's daily crude oil production.

In early 1999, OPEC regained much of its political power by effectively slashing production, coordinating its efforts with non-OPEC countries. The effectiveness of OPEC's new quota system can be seen by the fact that crude oil prices more than doubled in 1999. Though this was not the first introduction of a quota system from OPEC in the last decade, the 1999 quota system is the first in several years that has been honored by OPEC and non-OPEC members alike. As long as OPEC countries continue to honor these quotas, the price of crude oil should reflect the ever-changing OPEC price targets. Since the war in Iraq, OPEC has pushed prices higher and higher. In March 2006, OPEC made statements indicating its intentions to keep oil prices in the range of $60 per barrel by manipulating the market using its quota system.

If you decide to trade Crude Oil or the Petroleum markets, be sure to keep an ear to the ground for news concerning OPEC. You can visit their official website at www. opec.org for meeting schedules and more information.

Traders need to read between the lines when dealing with OPEC. Keep in mind that its goal is to maximize the profitability of its members' oil operations. Also watch production levels, as many OPEC members have been known to skirt the quota system and pump excess oil.

Relations have been strained in recent years between the United States and NATO countries with several OPEC member countries. These political influences have a major effect on the price of oil. Trade embargoes on oil-producing countries can have major ramifications on the price of crude oil. Political factors in non-OPEC countries are also important. The former Soviet states are major producers of crude oil, making that political climate weigh heavily on the supply of oil and its price.

The United States is a major producer and importer of oil. In recent years, the United States has become quite aggressive in using its political clout and muscle to impose trade sanctions, which can greatly affect the price of oil.

Though OPEC is losing world market share, it has greatly increased its cooperation and influence on several major non-OPEC producers. This trend toward greater cooperation between major oil-exporting countries is likely to continue, and tends to mask OPEC's influence.

Crude Oil Consumption Considerations

Crude oil has very few uses, its main use being for refining into other products. A normal barrel is 42 gallons and is usually refined into 19.5 gallons of gasoline, 9.2 gallons of distillate fuels (such as heating oil), 4.1 gallons of kerosene jet fuel, and 2.3 gallons of residual fuels, with the remainder (6.9 gallons) going into the production of lubricants and chemicals.

Several macroeconomic elements affect the demand for crude oil, gasoline, and heating oil such as income levels, economic growth levels, populations, and consumer habits. Because the demand for crude oil is directly tied to the demand for its products, we will examine each of these directly.

> **Trading Tips** _____
>
> Because the main demand for crude oil is for refining, traders and hedgers should pay close attention to two things: supplies of crude oil held by refineries, and the production capacity of refineries. Generally, accidents and scheduled shutdowns of major refining facilities—such as those in New Orleans or Northern California—can often cause short-term price increases as supplies become scarce. After the hurricanes of 2005, 16 refineries were shut down as a precaution before the storms and three of these refineries still had not reopened at the beginning of 2006. Gas prices at the pump remained well over $2 per gallon in 2006. One of the best places to find details about oil pricing and production is the U.S. Energy Information Administration (www.eia.doe.gov), which produces a daily report on the oil marketplace.

Unleaded Gasoline Usage

The demand for gasoline is dependent on two main factors: weather and consumer habits. Demand for gasoline is heavily influenced by the driving habits of the population, which are greatly influenced by the weather. As such, gasoline demand tends to rise during the summer driving season. When the weather is nice, people tend to drive more.

Couple this propensity for more driving with warm weather and more use of automobile air conditioners, which greatly diminish fuel efficiency, and the market experiences more demand and less efficient use of the available supply. The demand for gasoline is also greatly influenced by government fuel-efficiency standards and pollution-control standards.

The strongest period of demand for unleaded gasoline is the summer driving season, which is said to begin on Memorial Day and end on Labor Day. However, prices usually respond to this uptick in demand well ahead of the increased demand because gasoline wholesalers must buy supply ahead of time. Thus, crude oil and unleaded gasoline prices tend to be strong going into the driving season, or March through May.

Generally, by the time the summer driving season officially begins, prices typically steady out or decline as wholesale demand slackens.

Trading Tips _____

The supply of heating oil and unleaded gasoline are closely tied to each other. When crude oil is refined (or cracked), it turns into unleaded gasoline and heating oil. Hence, when the supply of heating oil is really big, so, too, should be the supply of unleaded gasoline. When heating oil prices are really low, gasoline prices can increase as the refineries care about total profits from processing, not the individual profits from the product.

Heating Oil Usage

Like unleaded gasoline, the demand for heating oil is dependent on two main factors: weather and consumer habits.

Extremely cold winters cause demand for heating oil to increase dramatically, resulting in sharp and powerful rallies in the futures market. Mild winters, of course, lead to lower demand for heating oil and sharp price declines.

Since heating oil is primarily used for residential heating, consumers' buying habits are an important component of the demand side of the equation. Consumers tend to stock up on heating oil during the mid-summer to prepare for the impending winter months and cold weather. In the short run, consumers do not change their heating habits in reaction to rising or falling prices; but, over longer periods of time, they will switch to alternative forms of heating such as kerosene, wood, and natural gas.

The cold-weather months of January, February, October, November, and December tend to be seasonally weak price periods for heating oil. Because the primary use for heating oil is to heat residences and it must be purchased in bulk (by the tankful), an entire season's heating oil needs are typically purchased before the cold season begins. Thus, July, August, and September are typically strong months.

Trading Tips _____

Extended cold winters can wreak havoc in the market, as above-average consumption can lead to panic buying during the cold weather. As with buying umbrellas during a rainstorm from a street vendor, you pay!

Petroleum Market Demand Picture

In general, the Petroleum markets move from an emphasis on one product to another. During the spring and summer, unleaded gasoline usage is the major force behind demand. During the fall and winter, heating oil takes center stage.

Refineries have about a 3 percent leeway in refining mix, meaning they can change their output of gasoline or heating oil by about 3 percent per barrel. During the spring and summer, refineries tend to increase their production of gasoline to meet summer driving season demand. During the winter, the output mixture is changed to favor the more heavily demanded heating oil.

Refineries cannot change their output percentages on a whim, as the retooling necessary will typically idle a refinery for a week or so. Thus, the refineries usually have one fairly fixed retooling a year—though exact dates vary by refinery—but changes in the relative pricing of heating oil and unleaded gasoline can induce them to more. Thus, it is important to watch the whole sector for clues, as price changes in unleaded gasoline affect heating prices, and vice versa.

Petroleum as a Barometer of World Tensions

Generally, Petroleum markets move due to changes in the demand picture. These moves tend to be long, drawn-out affairs with prices gradually moving in one direction. However, the Petroleum markets can be extremely volatile, and it is usually "scares" on the supply side of the equation that cause prices to jump radically.

You will notice that many of the world's major oil-producing nations, especially the exporting nations, are in the most politically unstable regions of the world: the Middle East and the former Soviet Union. Wars, or even the potential for armed conflicts, can cause petroleum prices to change radically overnight. Bombings can restrict supply by making shipping impossible, and can damage pipelines, drilling facilities, and refineries, which can interrupt oil supply to the world market for several months, if not years. Such an event would make the gas rationing of the 1970s look mild in comparison.

During the escalating tensions that led to Operation Desert Storm in 1991, Crude Oil prices increased from roughly $18.00/barrel to almost $40.00/barrel from July to October. With Crude Oil traded in 1,000 barrels per contract, this represents a change of $22,000 per contract. On January 9th, 1991, Crude Oil had an intra-day move of $8.00 per barrel (just to give you an idea of the type of volatility that tensions and war can cause in the Petroleum markets). We're seeing a similar scenario in 2006. The average price for a barrel of Crude Oil in 2002 was $22.81. In February 2003, just before the Iraq war started, Crude Oil jumped to $32.13. As the war rages on, the price of oil continues upward. The average price in 2004 for a barrel of Crude was $37.41; in 2005 it was $50.04. At the beginning of 2006, the price for a barrel of oil was over $60 and OPEC promised to keep it there.

Will consumption drop if the price stays there? If so, will the price start to drop? Based on historical trends, the price could eventually take a nosedive as the public begins greater efforts to conserve. Between 1979 and 1981, when oil hovered in the high $30s range, conservation took a stronghold as people bought more fuel-efficient cars. The price of a barrel of Crude Oil finally bottomed out in 1986 with the lowest price at $11 per barrel in July. Prices did not top $20 a barrel again until the fear of war in 1990, when Iraq invaded Kuwait.

As such, the Petroleum markets tend to rise in value in anticipation of conflict in the world's oil-producing regions, and tend to fall in price as peace becomes more likely.

So generally, by understanding not only the normal day-to-day uses and usage patterns of crude oil, unleaded gasoline, and heating oil, but also how these markets are affected by potential conflicts in oil-producing and -exporting nations, the informed speculator should have a better idea how prices will react in the future.

Trading Tips

Because of the geopolitical nature of the Petroleum markets and the general tendency for increased tensions to be reflected in higher Petroleum prices, new speculators in the Petroleum markets may wish to consider using options in conjunction with futures. For example, the Married Call strategy—short futures and long call position—is an excellent way for a speculator to limit her risk of loss to a specific amount, and not be subject to the wild price swings that can happen in this segment.

The Least You Need to Know

- ◆ The main demand for crude oil is for refining it into unleaded gasoline and heating oil.

- ◆ The supply of crude oil is dictated by long-term production cycles as well as actions by the Organization of Petroleum Exporting Countries (OPEC).

- ◆ The main demand for unleaded gasoline is for transportation purposes. Generally, prices tend to rise ahead of increased consumer driving, as wholesalers must buy inventory ahead of consumer use.

- ◆ The main demand for heating oil is from residential heating. Demand tends to run ahead of consumer usage, peaking in August or September, ahead of winter heating needs.

◆ Generally, in the Petroleum markets, as in most markets, the action of wholesalers ahead of retail demand tend to cause movements in prices.

◆ Because so much of the production of exportable oil is done in the Middle East, tensions in that region tend to cause prices of Petroleum products to rise as future supply looks less certain.

Chapter 16

Financial Market Overview

In This Chapter

- Learn why financial instruments are commodities
- See how interest rates drive the economy and markets
- Learn why Federal Reserve policy is important to understanding the economy
- See how stock prices reflect the economy and the economy reflects stock prices
- Understand how the value of the dollar changes
- Learn the relationship between interest rates, stocks, and currency prices

The economy and its vast intertwining relationships have baffled traders, politicians, and scientists for centuries. Forecasting the economy is like forecasting the weather—frustrating at best. But the major benefit of forecasting either is that one can prepare for possible outcomes.

In this chapter, we give you a brief overview of the economy, how different segments are related, and how to spot the impending storm fronts using the interest rate, stock market, and foreign currency segments of the futures markets.

Stocks, Bonds, and Currencies as Commodities

Though the term commodity is typically associated with products of mining or agriculture, financial instruments are also commodities by definition.

A commodity is a mass-produced, unspecialized product. For example, gold is a commodity because one ounce of gold is exactly the same as another ounce of gold of the same purity. There is no difference in origin—they are indistinguishable from each other. This is a key feature of commodities, and by this definition, many things are commodities, including stocks, bonds, and currencies.

Stocks are commodities in that each share in a company is the same as the rest of the shares of that company, assuming the same class. For example, say you and I both bought 100 shares of XYZ Company, but I bought mine six years earlier than you. We used different brokers, and bought them at different times, but they are both worth exactly the same. The only thing that will differentiate them when we sell them is the price we ask. Bonds or interest rate vehicles work the same way, in that they are the same as long as the maturity, coupon, and issuer are the same.

Money is also a commodity. For example, if I lend you a dollar, do you have to give me back the exact same dollar? No, any dollar will do, because they are interchangeable and nonunique. All money is interchangeable. The dollar I lent you can be repaid in 4 quarters, 10 dimes, 20 nickels, or 100 pennies—it all spends the same and is interchangeable (ignoring weight and inconvenience).

Because these instruments are commodities, they have the same risks attached to them that all commodities have, which is price risk. Financial futures have gained widespread acceptance as a hedging vehicle and have experienced tremendous growth in volume since the first contracts were introduced in the early 1970s, after the fall of the Gold Standard. Holders of financial instruments have price risk, which they wish to neutralize or diminish using futures. Speculators also find the ease of getting in and out of the futures markets attractive, along with the margin possibilities. Hence a marketplace was born for these Financial futures.

Financial futures cover three main classifications: Interest Rate Futures, Stock Futures, and Currency Futures.

Interest Rate Futures

An interest rate is the amount of money you pay to borrow money. For example, if you wish to buy a home and need to borrow $200,000, a bank may charge you 7 percent interest, meaning you have to pay 7 percent of the loan value each year in return for getting the money. Interest rates in their simplest form are the price of money.

When interest rates are low, either the supply of money (available for lending) is large or the demand for money (to be borrowed) is low. If either the supply of money available for lending diminishes or the demand for money to be borrowed increases, so does the cost associated with that money—the interest rate.

Just as the price of corn is a reflection of the market's thoughts of future supply and demand, the price of money is simply a reflection of the marketplace's thoughts on future supply and demand of money.

Interest Rates and the Economy

Interest rates are key to the current economy. The cost of money can affect all sorts of purchasing decisions, both directly and indirectly.

Assume for a moment that an automobile company is building a plant in your town. Think of all the jobs that will be created in both building the plant (carpenters, laborers, electricians, architects, engineers) and staffing the plant (shipping and receiving clerks, assembly line workers, managers, accountants, secretaries). Building the plant and staffing it would result in a boom for your town.

Restaurants near the plant would need more cooks and waitresses to serve the lunch crowds. Roads may have to be expanded to handle the traffic generated by the people employed at the plant. Doughnut shops would expand, as well as other service industries to service all those who work at the plant. The expansion of the plant would create many more jobs than people on the payroll at the auto company. The employees of the plant would buy more clothes from the local department store, and buy houses in the area. Thus, these added jobs would create more jobs and more spending.

This concept, known as a *Keynesian Multiplier*, stipulates, in essence, that economic expansion will lead to increased economic expansion beyond the initial investment.

Because the decisions to build plants and buy equipment are partially dictated by the cost of money, the level of interest rates can have a dramatic effect on the economy as a whole.

def•i•ni•tion

The **Keynesian Multiplier** is an economic hypothesis that states that money going into the economy will create more return than the initial investment. This was developed by the renowned economist John Maynard Keynes, who went on to found the International Monetary Fund, or IMF.

Generally speaking, lower interest rates tend to prompt economic activity, while higher interest rates tend to slow it down.

The Federal Reserve and Rates

Following the collapse of the Gold Standard and the rampant inflation of the 1970s, Federal Reserve Chairman Paul Volker moved from a policy of controlling the nation's money supply to a policy of controlling interest rates. Instead of the Federal Reserve shooting for target money supply levels, the Federal Reserve began adjusting the money supply to obtain a given level of interest rates.

The Federal Reserve is the central bank of the United States. Through a collection of 12 regional Federal Reserve Banks, the Federal Reserve's goal is to ensure a smooth economy and control inflation. The Federal Reserve also holds bank reserves, thus allowing the Federal Depository Insurance Corporation (FDIC) to guarantee bank deposits of member banks. The Federal Reserve also supervises banks, establishes and administers protective regulations in consumer financial matters, and handles all U.S. government debt and cash balances. In essence, the Federal Reserve is the bankers' and government's bank.

Now accepted as the normal policy in the central banking world, this shift radically changed the financial landscape, and truly broadened the scope of the financial futures markets.

The tools the Federal Reserve uses to control the supply of money are reserve requirements, changes in the discount rate, and open market operations.

Reserve requirements are the amount of money a bank must set aside to ensure smooth operations and safety of deposits. Banks are in the business of taking money in (deposits) and lending that money out (loans) at a higher interest rate than they paid for the deposit. The amount of money that they must keep to ensure that you can take your money out when you want to is the reserve requirement set by the Federal Reserve.

def•i•ni•tion

Reserve requirements are the required minimum amount of reserves (cash plus liquid assets), expressed as a percentage of deposits that a bank must maintain as mandated by the Federal Reserve. In theory, the lower the reserve requirement, the lower interest rates will be because more money is available for lending. Higher reserve requirements are generally associated with higher rates, as less money is available for lending.

The Federal Reserve sets the reserve requirement in conjunction with its monetary policy. If the Federal Reserve wishes to lower interest rates, they will decrease the reserve requirement, thus increasing the supply of money available for lending, and thus lowering the cost of money, or interest rates. Lower interest rates should increase economic activity as production of plants and equipment, and consumer purchases, become cheaper. If the economy is growing too fast, or inflation is feared, the Federal Reserve can increase the reserve requirement, thus diminishing the supply of money and increasing interest rates.

The second, and most widely reported, tool the Federal Reserve uses is changes in the discount rate. The discount rate is the rate the Federal Reserve charges member banks for loans. By lowering the discount rate, borrowing by banks becomes less expensive and banks tend to make more loans to their customers. When the Federal Reserve increases the discount rate, borrowing by banks becomes more expensive and banks tend to make fewer loans to customers. Hence, changes in the discount rate have a great effect on the supply of loanable funds and the cost associated with them (interest rates).

The last and most flexible tool the Federal Reserve has at its disposal is *open market operations.* Most member banks hold part of their reserves in the form of government debt securities (treasury bonds, notes, and bills). When the Federal Reserve wishes to increase the amount of loanable funds in the banking system, they will buy government securities from member banks, exchanging cash for treasury obligations, increasing the amount of cash the banks have available to lend. If the Federal Reserve wishes to decrease the amount of money available for lending then they sell member banks treasury debt, withdrawing cash from the system.

def•i•ni•tion

Open market operations involve the purchase or sale of government securities—bonds, bills, and notes. When the Federal Reserve wants to increase the supply of money, they buy securities. The Federal Reserve sells securities when they wish to reduce the money supply.

Armed with these three tools, the Federal Reserve attempts to control the supply of money to influence interest rates, and the U.S. and World economy. Changes in the monetary policy of the Federal Reserve can have dramatic effects on the financial markets, and the economy as a whole.

Generally, you can think of the Federal Reserve as the steward of the U.S. economy. By trying to stimulate the economy when growth is slow, and slowing it down when growth is strong, the Federal Reserve attempts to guide the economy to a sustainable level of growth over the long term.

It is important for participants in the financial markets to pay attention to the Federal Reserve, and the possible effect their actions may have on the economy, because it is the economy, both the current state and perceived future changes, which guide prices of financial futures.

Looking At Interest Rate Futures

All debt instruments can be described with the words *term* and *coupon*. Term is the time between when a debt instrument is issued and the time it matures and the debt must be repaid. Coupon is the rate of interest (paid and/or earned) on a debt instrument, expressed as an annualized percentage. For example, a U.S. Treasury Note could be described as a 6 percent 10-year note, meaning that this note matures in 10 years and pays $60 per every thousand of face value.

U.S. Treasury debt, the largest amount of debt circulating today and the basis for most interest rate futures, can be broken down into three main types: Bonds, Notes, and Bills.

A *bond* is any debt instrument with a term greater than 10 years. *Notes* are all debt instruments that have a term of greater than 2 years and less than 10 years, while *bills* are debt instruments that have a term less than 2 years. Futures contracts are traded on 30-year Treasury Bonds, 10-year Treasury Notes, 5-year Treasury Notes, and Treasury Bills.

def•i•ni•tion

Term is the amount of time from the time the money is borrowed or lent until it matures. For example, a 30-year mortgage has a term of 30 years. **Coupon** is usually expressed as an annualized percentage rate and describes the rate of interest. **Bonds** have a maturity (or term) greater than 10 years. **Notes** have a term of less than 10 years but greater than 2 years. A term of 2 years or less is referred to as a **bill**.

Futures Move Opposite of Interest Rates

Most bonds and notes are quoted in terms of price, using 100 as the par value. For example, let's say you buy a 6 percent 10-year note. You pay $100 for this, and get $6 a year from the treasury for the next 10 years. However, during this time you wish to sell your note. If interest rates go down to 5 percent, someone would be willing to pay more than $100 for the right to collect $100 in the future and earn $6 a year. But, if interest rates rise, you would have to sell your note for less than $100. The buyer can demand the lower price to compensate for accepting the lower interest rate (coupon), which your note pays.

Because bonds and notes are quoted in terms of price, the price of a bond or a note will always move in the opposite direction of interest rates. If interest rates rise, bonds and notes go down. If interest rates fall, bonds and notes increase in value.

Bills are quoted in terms of yield to maturity, or strictly on a coupon basis. Usually, a bill is quoted as this rate minus 100. For example, if a Treasury Bill is yielding 4 percent ($100 – $4 = $96), the price would be quoted as $96. In the Treasury Bill and more popular *Eurodollar* market, these short-term interest rate instruments are quoted this way.

Eurodollar and Treasury Bill futures, like bonds and notes, move in the opposite direction as interest rates. If you expect interest rates to fall, then you would establish a long position in these markets, while a short position would represent a speculation that interest rates may rise.

def•i•ni•tion

The term **Eurodollar,** not to be confused with Eurocurrency, is the term used to describe the yield paid on the deposit of U.S. Dollars in a foreign bank. Eurodollar futures (symbol ED) are one of the most actively traded futures in the world. They are widely used as a proxy and hedge against sudden shifts in short-term interest rates.

Stock Futures

Another major influence on the economy is the stock market. On February 24th, 1982, the Kansas City Board of Trade introduced the first *stock index* futures.

def•i•ni•tion

A **stock index** is an indicator used to measure and report value changes in a selected group of stocks. There are a variety of stock indexes, ranging from the popular Dow Jones Industrial Average, to the S&P 500 Index, and the NASDAQ composite Index. Basically, all of these are a collection of stocks, which are supposed to be representative of a particular group of stocks.

Stocks are closely tied to interest rates and the economy as a whole. A stock's value represents the present value of all future earnings and dividends.

So generally, stock prices tend to go up when the marketplace expects the company to increase its earnings and they decrease when expecting a decrease in earnings.

Because a company's earnings are closely tied to the business environment or the economy in general, it is obvious that stock prices are affected by the economy, at least partially. This is part of the reason why stock indexes, both futures and index mutual funds, have become so popular in recent years. A single stock may be affected by a bad management decision, or other specific company news, but in general, stocks should rise and fall as expectations about the economy change.

Generally speaking, stock prices tend to reflect expectations about the economy six months or more in the future. In fact, stocks have been such a good indicator of future economic levels that the government includes the stock market in its list of leading economic indicators.

Almost daily, the statisticians working for the U.S. government release reports on the economy. These reports can generally be broken down into three main classifications: leading, concurrent, and lagging indicators.

The leading economic indicators imply possible changes in economy in the future and include …

- Average workweek
- New orders for consumer goods and materials
- Delivery time
- Net business formations
- Contracts and orders for plants and equipment
- Building permits
- Inventory changes
- Changes in total liquid assets
- Money supply
- Changes in stock prices

The concurrent and lagging economic indicators show the general direction of the economy and confirm or deny the trends implied by the leading indicators. Some key indicators in this realm are …

- Unemployment
- Trade balances
- Car sales
- Retail sales
- Consumer prices
- Producer prices
- Housing starts
- Industrial production
- Personal income
- Gross National Product

These indicators are watched for signs of economic expansion or contraction, and the effect the changes would have on financial markets.

Because the price of a stock, or stock indexes, are based on the future earning capacity of the company, stock prices generally rise when the marketplace expects the economy to be strong, or increase in strength. A slowdown in the economy generally weighs on stock prices. Increases in interest rates, which often preclude economic slowdown, usually cause stocks to decrease, while declining interest rates, which imply increased economic activity in the future, tend to be supportive of stock prices.

Currency Futures

As you can see, stock prices are a reflection of the economy as a whole, and are affected by changes in the economy and interest rates. Interest rates are affected by the economy and stock prices, creating an intertwined crisscross of cause and effect relationships between these markets. Since the United States economy is increasingly becoming part of the world economy, a trend that has been in effect since WWI, it is only logical that the events that affect interest rates, stocks, and the economy affect the price of the U.S. Dollar versus foreign currencies.

The transition from backing the U.S. Dollar with gold to allowing the dollar to float freely gave birth to interest rate volatility and changed the economy; it also gave birth to *exchange rate risk*.

def•i•ni•tion

Exchange rate risk is the risk that a change in the price of one currency relative to another will be detrimental. For example, assume that you are vacationing for a month in Australia with the profits you made trading commodity futures. Upon entering Australia you convert $1,000 (U.S.) to Australian Dollars at the rate of $1.96 (Australian $ per U.S. $). At the end of your vacation, if you spent nothing and reconvert the $1,960 Australian Dollars back to U.S. Dollars at the going rate of $1.90 (Australian $ per U.S. $), you will have lost about $60.00 (U.S.) because the exchange rate moved. Now imagine Coca Cola, General Motors, or Microsoft and the millions and millions of dollars they could lose when exchange rates fluctuate. Currency risk is very real, especially when dealing with vast amounts of money.

How Currencies Are Quoted

The U.S. Dollar by definition is worth one dollar. But, if one wishes to convert a U.S. Dollar to a Swiss Franc, what is the dollar worth?

def•i•ni•tion

European Terms describes a method of quoting exchange rates such that they represent the amount of a foreign currency to equal one U.S. Dollar. **Reciprocal European Terms,** the method used to quote futures prices, is the number of dollars it takes to buy a foreign currency. For example, one U.S. Dollar is worth $1.16 (Canadian), and $1 (Canadian) is worth $0.86 U.S.

Currencies are quoted in relative terms to each other. For example, it may take 0.77 Swiss Francs to equal one dollar. So one dollar is worth 1.29 Swiss Franc, or it takes 0.77 Swiss Francs to buy one dollar. Typically when you go to the bank to convert currency, you see prices quoted in U.S. Dollars, or 1.29 Swiss Francs to the dollar. This is known as quoting *European Terms*, or representing the amount of currency necessary to buy or sell one U.S Dollar.

In the futures markets, foreign exchange rates are quoted in *Reciprocal European Terms*, or the amount of U.S. Dollars it takes to buy a foreign currency. For example, one dollar will buy 0.77 Swiss Francs.

Factors Affecting Exchange Rates

The value of a nation's currency is affected by the expectations that the world places on the value of that country in the future. Money flows around the world, seeking value and buying goods and services. A country that represents a good value will attract investment, and a country that has lots of goods and services will attract business.

When a country attracts investment, the value of its currency tends to increase as money is converted from the domestic currency by selling it and converting it to the foreign country's currency, "buying it."

Generally, value of a nation is set by the relative attractiveness of its capital markets (stock and interest rate instruments) coupled with the prospects for economic growth and appreciation in its markets, and stability. Generally, when a nation's economy is growing at a rate more attractive to other markets, or its assets are appreciating at such a pace, the value of its currency increases. When the prospects for appreciation diminish, the value of its currency diminishes in relation.

For example, the U.S. Dollar experienced tremendous appreciation from 1995 to 2001 as the U.S. economy grew at a sustainable rate, stocks appreciated, and debt instruments offered a positive return versus political and inflation risk. The dollar lost value beginning in 2003 and continuing into 2006 because of growing trade imbalances, debt, and negative savings ratios.

It's All Tied Together by the Economy

The value of a nation's currency is viewed as a reflection of the chance of appreciation in its capital markets. Its capital markets (stocks and interest rates) are a reflection of long-term outlook for economic growth. Hence, the value of the U.S. Dollar, U.S. stock market, and U.S. interest rates all depend on the perception of how the economy is doing.

Generally, during times of economic expansion, the U.S. stock markets will increase in value as the economic expansion will be viewed as creating an environment where earnings should increase. During moderate economic expansion, interest rates should be steady to increasing slightly, as the demand for money to increase production and for investment increases. The prospects of capital appreciation generally create an environment where the Dollar should increase in value as well, as U.S. markets offer a good chance for capital appreciation.

At some point in this economic cycle, the cost of money will increase as the demand for it outstrips the supply. At this point, the higher price of money will discourage investment in new plants and equipment. With a lack of new investment in plants and equipment, growth tends to slow and the prospect for future earnings decreases. Decreasing future earnings expectations lowers the attractiveness of stocks to foreigners, who either stop buying Dollars to invest and/or take existing Dollars out of the country, thus lowering the value of the Dollar.

The declining Dollar and the lack of demand for money tend to create an environment where interest rates decline. Rates will decline to a point where the expense of obtaining capital makes investing in plants and equipment appear to be a profitable speculation. Money is borrowed, people are employed, and they spend their money, increasing earnings of companies, and causing stock prices to appreciate. Increasing earnings free up more capital for investment, tightening the supply of money, raising interest rates, and creating another round of capital appreciation to attract foreign investment.

This cycle plays out time and again, with different variations. But generally, the stock market tends to react favorably to signs of economic growth and lower interest rates. Generally, interest rate vehicles tend to react favorably to signs of steady to declining economic growth, while the Dollar tends to react positively to signs of economic growth and increasing stock prices and interest rates. Each has an effect on the other, creating myriad combinations.

Behind this whole cycle is the United States Federal Reserve, trying to guide the economy through interest rate policy to achieve steady economic growth and control inflation. As such, the financial markets view changes in Federal Reserve policy closely. Generally, Federal Reserve policy or comments that point toward lower interest rates are viewed as supportive to financial futures (bullish). Federal Reserve comments or policy that point to higher interest rates tend to be viewed as negative (bearish) for the financial markets.

Because the Federal Reserve watches all of the economic statistics that are released to make their policy, the financial markets tend to react to changes in these economic statistics, anticipating changes in interest rate policy by the Federal Reserve.

The Least You Need to Know

- ◆ Stocks, interest rate instruments, and currencies are commodities because they are homogenous items, only distinguishable by price.

- ◆ The Federal Reserve, the nation's bank, is charged with guiding the U.S. economy along a path of steady growth and controlling inflation by adjusting the supply of money to change interest rates.

- ◆ The interest rate is simply the cost of money. When interest rates are high, future investment is discouraged, while low interest rates encourage spending and stimulate the economy.

- ◆ When the economy is perceived as being strong in the future, increased earnings are anticipated and stock prices go up. When the economy is perceived to be weak in the future, earnings should be lower and stock prices go down.

- ◆ Changes in the economy create changing views of the relative attractiveness of the United States as a place to invest and do business, changing the price of the Dollar relative to foreign currencies.

- ◆ By understanding the basics of the economy, one can hopefully anticipate changes in the price of financial markets and profit through the use of financial futures.

Part 5

Applying Your Knowledge ... Getting Ready to Trade

Part 5 takes you through the steps necessary to develop a trading plan. If your goal is to actually speculate in the futures market, this section will help you to develop a well-thought-out plan on how to profit from these exciting markets.

Futures and options traders are shown how to choose markets, in order to assess the risk of the particular market in advance. In addition, you will learn how to read charts and graphs, using price as a forecasting tool.

Traders are also introduced to the concept of risk—and risk of ruin— and shown how placing smaller bets on market position can lead to larger longer-term success.

Trading is treated as a business in this part. You learn why it is important to treat speculation as a business and not as a gambling venture.

17

Price Analysis: The Technical Approach

In This Chapter

- ◆ Using charts for analysis
- ◆ Understanding market trends
- ◆ The pause that refreshes or reverses
- ◆ Opportunity in inactivity
- ◆ The business of tops and bottoms
- ◆ Beyond charting

In this chapter, we depart from the dry economic production and usage pattern analysis of the futures markets into the realm of the technical analyst or chartist. This form of analysis relies upon basic patterns in price to foretell the future.

In this chapter, we give you an overview of charting and the patterns that market lore holds foretell future price movement. Though this method of analysis may seem like "voodoo" or "black magic" to some, the basic tenets are rooted in the laws of supply and demand, and charting is one of the most popular methods of analysis in use today.

Taking the Technical Approach

Unlike the fundamental approach, which concentrates on interpreting supply and demand, and ascertaining how changes in supply and demand will affect prices, the technical approach uses past price to predict future price.

This is a logical assumption based on the laws of supply and demand. If you remember, price represents the point at which a producer is willing to part with his product and a buyer is willing to purchase it. If producers act upon all their knowledge of supply and demand when selling, and consumers act upon all their knowledge of supply and demand when buying, the price that they reach should be a consensus of current supply and demand. Therefore, all known information should be encapsulated in the price.

The study of price behavior is known as technical analysis. Technical analysts believe that you can obtain more insight into the future behavior of prices by studying *how* prices have acted than by studying *why* prices have behaved a certain way. Because all known factual information regarding production and consumption are reflected by price, technical analysts believe the behavior of prices may yield more pertinent information of the future course of prices than studying the reasons behind price movement.

Trading Tips _____

Technical and fundamental analysts frequently disagree. Technical traders complain that fundamental traders don't time the market and often are bullish or bearish at market extremes. Fundamental traders point out that many of the classic chart patterns could be made with coin flips and may be nonsense. Both fields have successful followers. As the old trading adage goes, "Bulls make money, Bears make money, but Pigs don't!" With this in mind, don't be pigheaded; learn both types of analysis, and incorporate them into your trading.

Technical Analysis and the Bar Chart

The main tool of the technical analyst is the bar chart. A bar chart is a pictorial representation of price and time. On a bar chart, the vertical axis represents price and the horizontal axis represents time—or each trading day. For daily bar charts, a vertical line that connects the highest to the lowest point of the day's trading represents each trading day. A horizontal hash mark to the left represents the session's opening price, while a similar horizontal hash mark on the right represents the session's closing or settlement value (see the following chart).

```
        HIGH
OPEN┤
        ├CLOSE
        LOW
```

Sample bar chart.

Prices for each successive day are plotted going from left to right. Typically, most bar charts illustrate five vertical bars per week, representing the normal number of trading days in a week. In the event of a holiday, the bar chart for that day is omitted.

The same process can be done on different time scales as well. For example, many technical traders keep weekly and monthly bar charts. The open of a weekly chart would represent the opening price of the week, the high would be the weekly high, the low would be the weekly low, and the close would be the closing price on the last trading day of the week.

As price data is plotted, technical analysts begin to see different chart patterns and trends. Analysts have classified these trends and patterns and have found that they tend to recur over time, forming the basis for technical analysis.

Understanding Price Behavior

The study of price behavior requires the technical analyst to look for similar behavior in the past and extrapolate that information into the future. The technical analyst looks for symptoms by examining the price chart. He is trying to diagnose where prices are headed in the immediate future. The analyst is looking at the outward signs of trend, support, resistance, and chart patterns for clues to behavior. Based on his diagnosis, the appropriate action (buy, sell, do nothing) can be taken.

The *trend* of the market refers to its current direction. Has the market been heading higher, or has the market been heading lower? By identifying the trend, the analyst can look back in history at only those situations where the market has displayed a similar trend.

The technical analyst classifies points where price changed from heading lower to heading higher as support. Support is the point (or area) on a chart where the buying of futures contracts is sufficient to halt a decline in price. Support is a price at which sellers refrain from selling, as they believe the price being paid to them is not sufficient to meet their immediate needs.

Resistance is the opposite of support. Resistance is the point (or area) on a chart where the selling of futures contracts is sufficient to halt an increase in price. Resistance is the point at which buyers refrain from buying, as they believe the price they would have to pay is not justified versus the product they are to receive.

The first step in arriving at a diagnosis is defining the concepts of trends and also support and resistance. After these building blocks are defined, we can combine them to create chart patterns that we can use to predict the probable future direction of the market. In this chapter, we use charts from one of the top charting software programs for commodity traders: Track 'n Trade Pro, from Gecko Software (www.trackntrade.com), which includes 25 years of price data.

Trends

The definition of an uptrend (or bull market) is a market making a series of higher highs and higher lows. We define each of the low points as a support point and each of the high points as a resistance point. In a bull market, prices tend to hold support points and violate resistance points.

The definition of a downtrend (or bear market) is a market making a series of lower lows and lower highs. We define each of the low points as a support point and each of the high points as a resistance point. In a bear market, prices tend to hold resistance points and violate support points (see the following example).

Trends of the market.

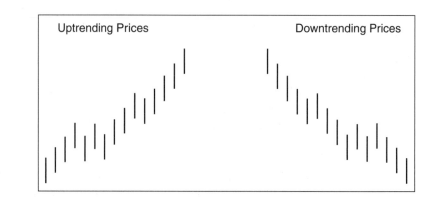

Identifying the market's trend is the first step. By trading with the trend, you follow the general perception of the market. Think for a moment how many significant highs and lows there really are. Most of the time prices dip, rally, and meander upon a path. The general path of the market is the trend. By knowing the market's prevailing trend, one greatly increases his or her odds of success when trading in the direction of the trend and practicing solid trade discipline.

Identifying the trend can be done several ways. Some people use trend lines that connect major lows in an uptrend, or major highs in a downtrend.

Notice how in the trend line that follows, the trend moves steadily downward from January to July.

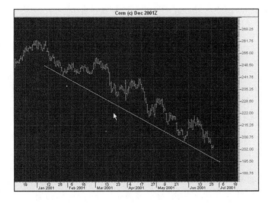

Downward trendline in Corn from Track 'n Trade Pro.

Another method for identifying the trend is to use points where the market has turned previously as guideposts. These points are known as *support and resistance.*

Support and Resistance

Trends are a function of support and resistance. Think of support as a price floor, or a level where prices stop going down—they have found support. Resistance can be thought of as a price ceiling, or a level where prices stop rising—they have found resistance. Think for a moment about going to the grocery store. If you see a product on sale, you usually buy it because it's cheap. If you don't buy two, when you run out and go back to buy more, you say, "Drat! I wish I had bought more." A similar thing happens in the markets. When prices dip down, then rally back up, traders say, "I wish I had bought it down there." If prices return to that level, they say, "Wow, I got a second chance" and they buy near the previous low price, creating support.

Looking again at our definitions of the two primary trends of the market, this becomes clear:

Uptrend (bull market) = higher highs and higher lows

Downtrend (bear market) = lower lows and lower highs

Each high and low is either a support or resistance point. We identify each of the high (resistance) and low (support) points by the fact that prices held these levels. Support and resistance points are simply points where the market has reversed direction (see the following example).

Market support and resistance.

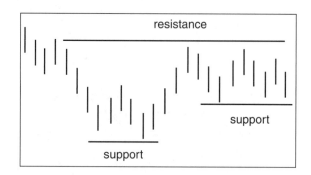

Using the concepts of support and resistance, a technician can put an absolute number to the highs and lows of the trend. Thus, a bull trend can be intact as long as it continues to hold the last major support level, and a bear trend is considered intact as long as it continues to hold the last major resistance level.

Thus a trend, once identified, is considered to be intact until it is reversed. For example, in a bull market, as long as prices continue to make new highs (violate resistance) and continue to make higher lows (holding support) the trend is considered intact. However, if prices violate support, then the trend is suspect.

It is often said in trading lore that a "bull market knows no resistance" and a "bear market knows no support," meaning that once a strong trend is underway, it will probably go further than most anticipate. Many large institutions have designed computerized trading systems around the concept of trend, buying markets that are going higher (in anticipation that upward movement will continue), and selling markets that are weak (anticipating further weakness). Considering that most of the commodity funds (basically, professionally managed commodity accounts) use this technique, some very successfully, it may have merit.

Channels

Prices seldom trend in an orderly fashion straight up or down. Instead they tend to move sideways, vacillating between areas of support and resistance. In technical analysis nomenclature, this is known as a channel or trading range. Channels, or trading ranges, can be spotted very easily by the fact that prices are stuck between areas of support and resistance (see the following figure).

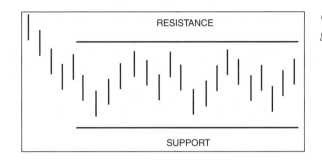

Channels or trading ranges graphically.

In technical analysis lore, these formations tend to foreshadow moves in the market. The sideways channel is a pattern in which the market is building up potential energy before starting another major move.

Between September 28th and October 18th, February Live Cattle futures formed support at 71.40, by hitting this price 6 times. During the same period, February Live Cattle prices formed resistance at 72.00 by hitting this price three times. The area between 71.40 and 72.20 on February Live Cattle could be classified as a channel (see the following figure). The eventual close outside this range on October 18th signaled the end of the channel and start of a new uptrend. A technical trader would have taken this as a signal to buy February Live Cattle futures.

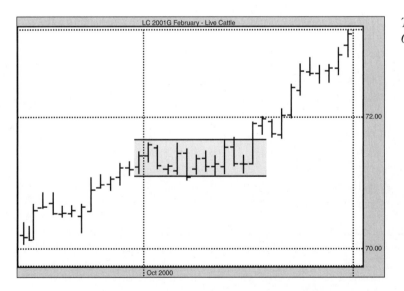

Trading range breakout in Cattle futures.

The longer the channel, the greater the potential move once the market "breaks out" of the channel. A breakout is signaled when the market closes above the resistance of the channel or closes below the support at the bottom of the channel.

Technical lore holds that once the market has broken out of the channel it should continue in the direction of the breakout without violating the opposite extreme of the channel.

When trading in the channel, it is important to note the trend of the market when entering into the channel. Typically, markets tend to break out of the channel in the direction of the trend when entering the channel. For example, if prices are rallying and then go sideways for several weeks, forming a channel, technical lore holds that this market should break out of the upside of the channel, continuing the trend.

Triangles

Sometimes within a trend, a market will stop moving in the direction of the trend, forming only an area of resistance in a bull market or support in a bear market. These instances are known in technical analysis as triangles (see the following figure).

Types of triangles.

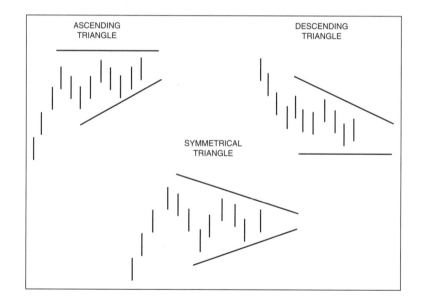

In an upward trend, a market that continues to make higher lows but forms a solid level of resistance, may be forming an ascending triangle. This pattern of solid resistance and rising support levels forms a pattern similar to a triangle, with the rising support levels giving it its name of an ascending triangle.

In a downward-moving—or bear—market, sometimes prices will stop making lower lows, forming support. However, previous resistance points will continue to hold and the market will make a series of lower highs. This setup on the charts is known as a descending triangle.

Technical traders view the penetration of the bottom of the descending triangle as confirmation that the trend is likely to continue downward.

A third type of triangle is formed when the market makes a series of lower highs and higher lows, coiling up into smaller and smaller swings. Unlike the ascending and descending triangles, which have a "flat" side to them, the symmetrical triangle is bounded by both an ascending line of support and a descending line of resistance. What also sets this pattern apart is that the symmetrical triangle can appear in either a bullish or bearish trend, with the breakout of the triangle occurring in either direction, though some chartists prefer it to be in the direction of the previous trend.

In July to August of 2001, corn prices began to contract, forming a symmetrical triangle of lower highs and lower lows (see the following figure). Then corn broke out of the triangle in a downward trend in September 2001.

The basis behind all of the triangle patterns is that the market forms a trend, with the reactions within the trend forming patterns.

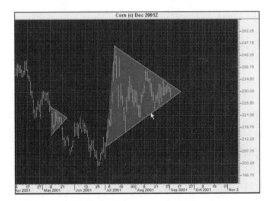

Symmetrical triangle in Corn from Track 'n Trade Pro.

Tops and Bottoms

Up until this point in our study of chart patterns, we have concentrated on identifying the trend and looking for continuation of the trend. Though trend-following is a popular method for trading, some technical analysts also feel that specific patterns can foreshadow a change of trend.

Two classic patterns for forming tops and bottoms are the *double top* and *double bottom*. As the name implies, double tops are formed when two or more roughly matching resistance areas are formed. Typically, technical traders believe that a violation of the lowest support between these two roughly matching highs constitutes a change of trend. Double bottoms are formed when two roughly matching support points are formed, and prices violate the highest resistance area between these points.

Many other complex topping and bottoming patterns exist—like Head and Shoulders Patterns and Rounded Patterns—but generally all major market turning points can be identified by using support and resistance. You can learn more about these more complex tools at www.trackntrade.com/tnt_education.htm.

Remember that an upward trend—or bull market—is characterized by a series of higher highs and higher lows. However, if the market violates support, making a lower low, then the trend is questionable. Simply watching areas of support in a bull market can often clue a trader in to the possible end of that bull market.

The opposite general rules apply to downward trends—bear markets. If a falling market ceases to make lower lows, or higher highs are formed, then the trend is in question.

Using the Technical Approach

Unlike fundamental analysis, technical analysis can easily be applied to the markets to make trading decisions, which is why this method of trading is popular.

For example, if one sees a sideways channel, they can place a buy stop order above the resistance and a sell stop order below the market. If the market breaks out to the upside, then the buy stop order would be elected and the trader would have a long position. Because the bottom of the channel is characterized by support, the technical trader will use that as his initial risk point, using the sell stop order to protect himself from falling prices. Hopefully, after entering the long position, the trader can move his protective sell stop higher as support manifests itself. Given a downward breakout, the sell stop order would be initiated, a short position would be taken, and the protective buy stop order could be moved lower as resistance manifests itself.

Technical trend trading is easy to comprehend as well. In an upward trend, traders typically either buy pullbacks to support or buy breakouts of resistance, risking the position to the closest support level. As higher support levels are made, the speculator would move his sell stops higher, hopefully protecting the open positions profits accumulated in the trade to date. In a bearish trend, the opposite techniques would be used—selling a violation of support or selling pullbacks to resistance.

Future traders can test their ability to read charts and make correct forecasts by using a number of software packages on the market today. These charting programs provide market enthusiasts with historical data, and plot charts right on their computers. Some of the better packages even allow you to step the charts forward one day at a time, and practice your trading, complete with placing fictitious orders and calculating your profit and loss.

Trading Tips _____

One of the best charting programs I have seen on the market is Track 'n Trade Pro, produced by Gecko Software, Inc., which I used in this chapter. Gecko-Charts comes complete with a 25-year database of historical futures data and allows you to play historical charts forward one bar at a time. The software is very easy to use, with controls similar to a VCR. Track 'n Trade Pro has a complete demo version available online at www.trackntrade.com, or you can order by phone at 1-800-862-7193. Cost of their basic package is $197, and includes free nightly data downloads.

The guiding principle of technical analysis is to let the market tell you where it wants to go. If prices truly do represent the collective knowledge of all the participants in the futures markets, then price in and of itself can be used as a forecasting tool for future movements.

The basis of technical trading is to place oneself in a long position in an upward trending market and a short position in a downward trending market. The technical trader believes that prices are never too high to buy or never too low to sell. He lets the market dictate where prices are going, similar to how a boater flows down a river, moving with the current.

One of the key aspects of this is identifying the trend of the market and assuming that the trend will continue. As is often said in trading-related literature, "The trend is your friend … until it ends."

The Least You Need to Know

- The basis of technical analysis is that all the known information about a commodity—supply and demand—is contained in its price.

- The definition of an uptrend (or bull market) is a market making a series of higher highs and higher lows; a downtrend or (bear market) is a market making a series of lower highs and lower lows.

- Support is evident on a chart at the point where prices ceased declining. Resistance is evident on a chart at the point where prices stopped advancing.

- By combining the concepts of trend, support, and resistance a technical analyst can identify particular patterns—such as channels and triangles—that have historically foreshadowed major moves in the market.

Chapter 18

Developing a Trading Plan

In This Chapter

- ◆ Learn to avoid being a market loser
- ◆ Developing trading discipline is essential, but having deep pockets doesn't hurt either
- ◆ Learning to think before trading
- ◆ Risk of ruin and money management
- ◆ See how to plan your trade and trade your plan

Before starting a business it's important to have a business plan and adequate capital. Most new businesses start off with a dream, and the proprietors are willing to work hard. Despite the hard work, they fail because of unforeseen difficulties, poor preparation, or lack of cash flow.

Before trading, it's imperative that you develop a trading plan. Your trading plan should be capitalized with money you can afford to lose, because you might!

Proper planning and adequate capitalization are the cornerstones of any new venture. In this chapter, we develop the criteria for making a trading plan. The first step in developing a trading plan is to make sure you have the discipline to follow it.

Developing Your Style of Trade

Industry lore says that close to 80 percent of all futures traders lose money! This is a figure I have found over the years to hold up, but you have to remember that the same statistics say most new businesses (roughly 80 percent) fail in their first five years as well.

Futures trading closely mimics running a business, so it is not surprising that the success rates of both ventures are similar. You have to be multifaceted, taking calculated risks correctly while finding what works.

Trading Tips

> In an academic study done a few years back, the trading habits of hundreds of people at a discount brokerage were examined. The results of the study indicated a strong bias between success outside the markets (in the business world) and success in the markets. For example, those who held high-paying jobs tended to have better returns than those who had lower-paying jobs. This anecdotal evidence indicates that the business of speculation is similar to business, in that those with the vision and discipline to run companies successfully can run their trading successfully as well.

For example, I live in a small town, and a wonderful new restaurant opened up. The chef was superb, the dining room was well decorated, the wait staff was friendly, and the service was excellent. They went out of business in nine months! Not because they didn't understand how to prepare and serve food—but because (I assume) they were not proficient on the business side of things. The restaurant was always empty, so obviously their marketing was poor. Though I appreciated the abundance of staff always present, for customer flow they seemed to be overstaffed. Also, the location was slightly off the beaten path, and probably bigger than it needed to be.

Though they were proficient in cooking, they failed. In my years of experience working for brokerage firms and trading on the floor, I have seen similar problems with traders. Though some are excellent in calling the market over the long term, short-term swings often knock them out. Others are hopelessly undercapitalized, lacking the finances to weather losses. Others approach speculation more like gambling, betting big for the big payoff, and go broke the first time they are wrong. But the successful traders I have met over the years all have several characteristics in common:

- Discipline
- Attention to detail
- The ability to admit they are wrong

Trading Tips _____

An excellent book on the business of trading is Jack D. Schwager's *Market Wizards: Interviews with Top Traders* (Harper Collins, 1993). This popular book is a series of interviews with America's top traders, delving into what has worked for them and how they approach the markets. Though the book does not attempt to delve into how they actually trade, it does an excellent job of presenting the mindset behind some of the great money managers of our time.

Discipline in Trading

When starting out with any venture, whether speculating in futures and options or opening up a new business, it's important for the entrepreneur to learn discipline in allocating resources. It is the discipline to allocate resources that will ultimately lead to profitability.

In speculating, allocation of resources means time and money. Speculators need to plan for action and have the discipline to follow that plan.

Over the years working for brokerage firms and trading on the floor, I saw many speculators who failed simply because they lacked the discipline to follow their own plans. The ultimate goal of the speculator is to be profitable. The key to profitability is "letting your profits run, and cutting your losses short." Let's look at the second part of that statement first.

Cutting Your Losses Short

Think for a moment about Coca-Cola, a very successful company that has been around for decades. Several years back, Coke started a new cola mixture, aptly called "New Coke." They bought TV advertising, and pushed lots of money into expanding operations for New Coke. As they progressed forward with New Coke, they discontinued "Classic Coke" to free up room for the new product.

Well, consumers ultimately did not like New Coke and clamored for the return of the original "Classic Coke." Coca-Cola scrapped the idea of New Coke, and returned to the original formula for the beloved soda pop in the United States. (New Coke is still marketed outside the U.S. in some locations as Coke II.) As a successful business, Coke had the fortitude to consider "New Coke" a loss in the U.S., write off the idea as bad, and return to what had worked for decades.

Instead of sticking their head in the sand and waiting for people to either acquire a taste for "New Coke" or go bankrupt, Coke accepted the loss, and returned to what has worked for them for decades. They even got a little extra mileage, as consumers rejoiced about the return of "Classic Coke."

Speculators, like the successful businesspeople at Coke, need to try out new things to expand their business, but they also need to accept that they will be wrong. Being wrong in the market is not tantamount to going broke, but simply a cost of doing business if the loss is quickly identified and corrected. For speculators, this means when a position is unprofitable, they need to get out. Not wishing the lost funds will come back, just having the discipline to take your loss.

This becomes difficult, as markets bounce around and you have to leave a trade enough room to grow, while not taking large losses. Most successful traders accomplish this by having a predefined exit strategy, and the discipline to stick to it.

To make matters more difficult, some winning trades start off as losers. Thus it becomes important when setting an initial risk point, that the trader leaves enough room to account for normal market fluctuations, but keeps the amount at risk small enough to preserve capital (easier said than done).

Of course, keeping losses small is an important part of the equation, but you can never be successful only taking small losses—you need to win occasionally as well.

Trading Tips _____

The words "should have," "could have," and "would have" are not part of a successful trader's vocabulary. Speculators need to develop the discipline to act. Set a point at which you're wrong, and if the market hits that point, exit! An old saying on the trading floor is, "If you need to pray, you shouldn't stay!" If you're hoping that a market will come back to profitability—or just break even—then you should exit. Pick a risk level that will allow you to trade again.

Letting Your Profits Run

The purpose of speculation is to take a calculated risk in the hope of garnering a profit. The goal is profits. But profits can be fleeting.

Think for a moment about a horse race. Have you ever wagered on a horse to win, and at the starting gate your horse is in a commanding lead, and you are counting your winnings as the pack catches up and your horse finishes last? Well, in a trade, you can have the same experience. You put the trade on, and instantaneously it is profitable (yeah). However, as days pass, the profits diminish, and your position turns into a loser. This is a risk in trading, which can lead you down a frustrating path.

When trading, holding on to your profits can be difficult. Markets fluctuate! They move from profitable to unprofitable to profitable. Some traders solve this problem by taking profits at a specific amount. For example, assume you're trading corn, and you initially risk 5 cents on every trade ($250 before commissions and fees) and take profits of 10 cents when they appear. In this style of trade, one could be profitable—before commissions and fees—if they are right 40 percent of the time.

Trading Tips

Remember, a stop order is a buy order above the market or a sell order below the market. Stop orders are sometimes referred to as stop loss orders because they are used to exit the market with a loss. For example, a sell stop is used to exit a losing long position, while a buy stop order is used to exit a losing short position. It's always a good idea to place a stop order whenever entering a market, as a means of exiting the market with a controlled loss. As the old adage goes, "A strong defense is the best offense."

But it's impossible to get really big returns if you continually take profits. Some traders prefer to have a few outstanding trades, and a higher percentage of losses. Typically, many successful traders define an initial point of risk, and an initial point of where they are right. For example, assume you buy December Corn at 225 and it goes to 230. At this point, you may wish to move your sell stop order from the initial point of risk to your entry price, removing some of the risk from the market. This allows the trade enough room to grow (prices to increase and account for normal fluctuations).

This style of trade can be difficult to implement as some of those profitable positions will move back to being unprofitable or breakeven trades. However, in the long run, letting your profits run should lead to more profits. For example, assume you initially risk 5 cents ($250 before commissions and fees) in a Corn trade and plan on moving your stop loss to break even if the market moves 5 cents in your favor. Assume on half of the trades you will be wrong, and assume half the trades move to your initial goal. If half of just one trade moves 25 cents in your favor, you will break even before commissions and fees. If two trades move 25 cents in your favor and the other three move back to break even, you can be very profitable by only winning 20 percent of the time if you hold on to your winners much longer than your losers.

Trading Tips

Most professional commodity trading funds implement a trailing stop system. For example, if corn prices move 5 cents in their favor, they place a stop loss order at breakeven to exit the market and continually trail that stop loss behind the market. Most of these large traders have trading batting averages less than 50 percent but manage to rack up impressive returns because the winning trades are far larger than their losses. They practice "riding winners and cutting losers short."

Discipline and Profits and Losses

Perhaps having not traded, many of you will think this sounds easy. Let me assure you that practicing letting your profits run and cutting your losses short is more difficult than it sounds.

Many of the small losses you will encounter will return to profitability, which is frustrating. Many of the profits you will have one day could disappear the next day, making you wish you had exited the position earlier. However, having the discipline to stick with keeping your losses small and letting your profits run is imperative to long-term profitability in the futures and options markets.

Throughout my career, I have witnessed and done the opposite, holding on to a losing position waiting for it to come back and seen a small loss grow into an enormous loss, wiping out months' worth of profits. Many other times I have seen traders exit profitable positions with a small profit just before a big move which would have amounted to sizeable gains. Traders who don't have the discipline to follow this simple rule usually end up "supporting" those who do.

The Technical or Fundamental Approach

In the last several chapters, I explained the virtues of fundamental and technical analysis and how to apply it to your own trading. I personally believe that successful trading is a blend of both styles.

Many traders are devoted practitioners of either fundamental or technical trading. Often, I hear both successful and unsuccessful traders proclaim that either all information is contained in the charts, or charts are simply the presentation of the past and have no predictive purpose. However, the bulk of successful traders that I have known over the years tend to meld both fundamental analysis and technical analysis together to ascertain the future direction of prices. They understand the current supply-and-demand situation as well as what the current price trend is saying. They are successful because they have found what works for them, based on their own risk tolerances and objectives. Your job is to find what meets your needs.

Speculation is the business of drawing conclusions from an incomplete set of facts. Because it is impossible for a trader to know all the fundamental or technical information that is available every day, traders must choose to understand a few things very well.

Traders should use whatever technique or combination of techniques they are most comfortable with. Because this is a personal decision, we designed this book to express our belief that a combination of factors tends to work the best.

For example, by understanding the production and consumption cycle of grains, the informed speculator knows that they have a tendency to rally when production is at risk—such as during planting and pollination. During these times of the year, speculators may wish to watch for bullish chart patterns and trade only the chart patterns that confirm the general fundamental viewpoint of higher prices. During the times of the year when prices tend to fall (like the first quarter and near harvest), traders may wish to take only chart patterns that are bearish in nature, confirming the fundamental bias toward the downside.

By combining the two styles of trades, the serious speculator should be able to understand what is going on in the market. Futures markets tend to be *discounting mechanisms*—meaning they tend to reflect not only what is currently happening but what is likely to happen.

def•i•ni•tion

The price of any commodity or option reflects all market participants' hopes and fears regarding the future. In this sense, very often the futures markets act as a **discounting mechanism** in that they tend to reflect news and events while they happen or even before they happen. Often the futures markets will reflect news before it happens. For example, if a government report is widely expected to be bullish, often prices will go higher in anticipation of this news, and sell off when the news is released as traders "buy the rumor and sell the fact." This is often quoted in the financial press as having been priced into the market.

Much of the choice between fundamental analysis and technical analysis will depend upon the trader's time frame. The shorter the time frame, the more the trader should rely upon technical analysis. The longer the time frame of the trader, the greater she should rely upon fundamental analysis.

Because fundamental analysis is more market specific than technical analysis, traders attempting to master both should limit the number of markets that they are trading, if they decide to incorporate fundamental analysis.

Speculators should look for situations where both the technical and the fundamentals of the market agree. Often at major turning points in prices, the technical and fundamental analysis will yield dramatically different outlooks. For example, during the early part of 2000, when high-tech stocks were skyrocketing, technical analysis portrayed higher prices, while earnings for these companies were lagging behind price (fundamentals). In this case, fundamentals foretold the ridiculous valuation of the stock market, especially the technology-intensive NASDAQ Market, well ahead of technical. But prior to the major run-up in oil prices in 1999, technical analysis pointed to a bottom in prices and a change of trend from down to up about a month ahead of the OPEC announcement that they would curtail production, a move that sent crude oil prices skyrocketing from $14.00 a barrel to almost $38.00 a barrel over the course of the next two years.

It is our feeling that a combination of both the technical and fundamental aspects of trading yield the best results in the long run for most speculators. However, just as in managing the position, discipline in applying your knowledge is crucial. In analysis, one has to draw the logical conclusions from the information, not manipulate the information to present the bias you wish to see. A major help in developing this discipline can be achieved by making a trading plan.

Plan Your Trade, and Trade Your Plan

The first step in building a house is drawing up the blueprints. The workmen who erect the house consult the blueprints when placing walls, sinks, appliances, and electrical outlets.

Trades should be planned with as much detail. Every contingent should be planned for, so decisions are made not in the heat of battle when money is on the line and emotions can be running high, but prior to entering the trade when thoughts should be more rational and calculated.

The goal of your trading plan is to allow you to make decisions before things happen, giving you a blueprint for trading before entering the market. A basic trading plan should include the following features as a minimum:

♦ Trade entry

♦ Initial risk or stop loss point

- ◆ Criteria for stop loss movement

- ◆ Criteria for profitable trade exit, or a point at which you'll abandon the trade if neither a large profit nor loss occurs in a specific amount of time

Trade Entry

The criteria for trade entry should be based on sound reasoning and not left up to a gut feeling. The entire process of trade entry (with criteria) should be spelled out completely. For example, if your trading plan calls for buying a market if the fundamentals are bullish, when the trend is up, you need to clearly state the criteria of both "bullish fundamentals" and "an uptrend."

By clearly stating your rules for entry, you should be able to spot entry criteria without second-guessing yourself. Your trade entry plan needs to be clear enough that if you see A and B, then you will initiate a long position.

Initial Risk or Stop Loss Point

Once you've developed a trade entry technique, you need to assess where your read of the market is wrong. This is your initial risk. For example, if you're buying when fundamentals are bullish and the trend is up, you will set a point at which to place a sell stop order. In this example, it would most likely be the point at which the trend in the market changes.

The initial risk point is where you are wrong. Many traders place this as a mental stop point, saying, "If the market hits this level I will exit." However, beginning traders should strongly consider placing the exit order at the same time as the entry order.

The placement of a stop loss is designed to limit your risk. However, the placement of a stop loss does not guarantee to limit your risk to a specific amount. For example, if a market opens higher than your buy stop, your order to buy will be executed at the opening, not your price. Also, certain market conditions, like limit moves, can make stop losses nonexecutable. A limit move is when the market moves the maximum daily permissible limit. In the event of a limit move, trading ceases until the following day. Remember, a stop loss is a good way to limit your risk, but does not guarantee to limit your risk to a specific amount.

Stop loss placement can be tricky. The idea is to minimize risk by placing the stop loss close to your entry. However, if the stop loss is too close, then normal market fluctuation will take you out of the market, for a loss. If the stop loss is too far away, you can't keep your losses small.

Criteria for Stop Loss Movement

In any trade, you should always be thinking about how to minimize your risk. Obviously, if the reason you are in the trade no longer exists, then exit. But what happens if the trade 1) moves in your favor; 2) moves against you but doesn't move enough to stop you out; or 3) does nothing?

> **Commodity Corn**
>
> An old trading adage is "Never let a winner turn into a loser." Though literal application of this is impossible, traders should set a specific amount of favorable movement that when reached, they will move their stop loss to break even or higher. For example, if Soybeans move 15 cents in your favor, you will move your stop loss to breakeven.

Successful traders work to manage their risk constantly. If the position they are in is profitable, they try to minimize their potential risk by moving their stop loss closer to the entry price and hopefully above the entry price eventually. For example, a trader who is long may move his sell stop order after the market has moved a certain amount in his favor, continually trailing this stop loss behind the market by a specific amount. Technical traders may keep running their stop losses just below support, or above resistance to minimize their risk. The key here is to have a plan set forth for this possibility, giving the market enough room to continue to move in your favor, but not so much as to give back all of your profits.

Criteria for Profitable Trade Exit

Another option can occur when a trade slowly moves against you, but not enough to stop you out of your position (this feels like Chinese water torture). The trader should account for this possibility. Many successful traders also use a time stop, allowing a specific amount of time for the trade to be profitable. For example, after initiating a long position, a trader may say, "If it is not profitable in five days after entry, and my stop loss has not been hit, I will exit at the market on the fifth day." You will find that most of your profitable trades will be profitable very quickly.

Many traders modify the time stop with a specific profit objective as well. For example, "If this trade is not at least $200 profitable by the close of the fifth day, I will exit at the market on close of the fifth day."

The Completed Trading Plan

You will notice that the outline for the trading plan gives you rules to enter the market and accounts for every aspect of the trade and all possible contingents, except exit.

Many trading plans lack when to exit, simply leaving that up to the market stopping them out, with their exit plan being little more than waiting for a signal in the opposite direction. A complete plan should tell you when to get in, when to get out with a loss, when to get out with a profit, and how to adjust your risk along the way.

For example, a sample trading plan may be as simple as to *Sell 1 March Soybean Futures contract at the end of January if*:

- The percentage of soybeans held "On Farm" is greater than or equal to 53 percent as indicated in the January Grain Stocks Report

- Risk 15 cents initially on the trade

- Move the stop loss to *break even* if prices move 15 cents in your favor

- Move stop loss to risk 10 cents at the end of the second week of February

- Exit trade on last trading day of February

This little trading plan has a simple entry rule, based on the percentage of grain held in storage at the beginning of the year. The logic is that when grain stocks are held in large part by farmers (greater than 53 percent), prices will tend to fall as farmers sell their grain to raise money to finance planting and tax expenses due in March. The initial risk is clearly defined at 15 cents per contract ($750 before commissions and fees), as is when to move the stop loss and when to exit the trade. In the 1980s and 1990s, this trading plan generated seven *hypothetical* trades (2000, 1999, 1987, 1986, 1985, 1983, and 1982), yielding an average hypothetical profit 30½ cents per contract ($1,525 before commissions and fees) and a total hypothetical profit of $10,662.50 before commissions and fees.

The term *hypothetical* is used here to describe the system because the trades have not actually been placed in all of the years mentioned. The CFTC requires that research such as this carry the term *hypothetical* in front of anything that has not been actually traded exactly as the results indicate.

Though no one knows for sure if the condition for the trade will exist in the following years, or if the next time it does occur it will work, this plan is based on simple logic and entails strict risk control, and would be simple to follow.

Trading Tips

Be sure to visit the CFTC's Web site (www.cftc.gov) for important news regarding hypothetical trading results and consumer warnings regarding highly optimized systems promising easy riches in the commodities markets.

You must remember, though, no matter how well thought-out the trading plan is, it will not work unless you follow it. Following a plan takes strict discipline, the discipline to enter the market when the plan says so, and the discipline to adjust your risk and take your profits or losses based on the plan.

Trading plans are usually based on past behavior. It is important to also understand that markets do change, and what worked yesterday may not necessarily work today. As all futures and options literature is fond of saying, "Past performance is no guarantee of future results."

Risk Not Thy Whole Account

Because past performance is no guarantee of future results, doing research alone cannot guarantee that you will be profitable in your trading. When you are speculating, you have to learn to accept trading losses, as they are a cost of doing business—unavoidable!

Confronted with this, traders should plan for losses. The old trading adage is "Risk not thy whole account." For example, if you bet on a coin flip and keep doubling your money after each time you are right, you'll go broke with the first wrong flip.

Most experienced and successful traders risk only a small portion of their total equity on any one position. For example, several well-known and successful commodity funds risk between 1 and 3 percent of their total equity on any single trade. Such low risk tends to minimize the *risk of ruin* substantially, but is impractical for most people starting out with $10,000 to $20,000.

def•i•ni•tion

Keeping your risk small is akin to cutting your losses. It also diminishes your **risk of ruin**. This term is typically used to describe the odds of going broke when you have a statistical edge. For example, assume you have a deck of cards, with 20 black cards (6 missing) and 26 red ones. If you bet that a red card will be drawn each time, over the long term you will be a winner. However, you need to be able to withstand 20 losses in a row (it is possible) to ensure that you will come out ahead in the end.

Though it is impossible to calculate an exact risk of ruin for trading, generally it greatly diminishes the less you risk on each trade as a percentage of the whole trading account. For practical trading analysis, traders should try to risk less than 10 percent of their account on any particular trade. If the trade requires more than 10 percent of your account, pass on it—the risk is too high.

Implementing Your Trading Plan

Once you have decided upon a trading plan, you need to implement it. By combining a solid trading plan complete with entry rule, multiple exit rules to account for each market contingent (win, loss, and no change), and strong money management to minimize your risk of ruin, you are well ahead of 80 percent of all traders.

After you have developed this trading plan and money management strategy to minimize your risk of ruin, you should practice it. Most brokerage firms offer paper trading assistance (fictitious trading that is done hypothetically). New traders should paper trade for at least six months, keeping careful track of the orders placed and executed, and being honest with themselves in their performance.

The more computer- and statistically literate individuals may wish to do historical back-testing by purchasing data and programming their own trading systems for simulations. This is a good idea, too, but probably should not replace good old-fashioned real-time testing via paper trading.

Trading Tips _____

There are several software programs available to help you with paper trading. My personal favorite is Gecko Software's Track 'n Trade Pro, which has over 20 years of data in chart form for over 50 commodities, and allows you to practice trading without risking any money. Track 'n Trade Pro is available online at www.geckosoftware.com or by calling 800-862-7193.

After at least six months or 10 transactions of the paper trading variety, you may wish to begin moneyed trading. Obviously, if your paper trading was successful, you will want to try to emulate that trading with money. Therefore it is important that you do your paper trading realistically. Remember, the purpose of paper trading is to practice and learn. Don't paper trade one way, or trade markets you would not really trade, then expect to be successful using real money. Like anything, trading takes practice. And of course, remember to be prepared, as most people who speculate in the futures markets lose money.

The Least You Need to Know

- ◆ Roughly 80 percent of speculators in the futures markets lose money. The common reasons are lack of knowledge, lack of capital, and lack of a solid trading plan or the discipline to carry it out.

◆ Traders should try to let their profits run and cut their losses short.

◆ A well-thought-out trading plan should have an entry signal, an initial risk point, a point to take profits, and an exit plan even if the trade does not have a large profit or loss in a specific amount of time.

◆ Trading should be done with only genuine risk capital, meaning money you can afford to lose! Generally, trading money should be less than or equal to 10 percent of your total net worth.

◆ Just as it is possible to lose a battle but win the war, futures traders need to remember that market losses are unavoidable. Make sure they are small enough so you can live to fight another day in the battle for profits.

Chapter 19

Exploring Single Stock Futures

In This Chapter

- ◆ Why use Single Stock futures?
- ◆ How Single Stock futures work
- ◆ Learn the benefits of Single Stock futures over stock
- ◆ Understand Single Stock futures pricing

If you are an active trader or short-term investor (speculator) in the stock market, this chapter should be of great interest. In this chapter, we examine the latest innovation in the futures markets: Single Stock futures.

Single Stock futures are a unique vehicle specifically designed with the shorter-term speculator in mind. We will discuss the development of this market, and why Single Stock futures may be a better vehicle for short-term trading. The market is still in its infancy, but growing up quickly.

Development of Single Stock Futures

Trading futures on individual stocks in the United States started in December 2001. The introduction of Single Stock futures was a long and arduous battle, involving exchanges, politicians, and regulators. In response to increasing popularity of Index Funds, and increasing volatility in the Stock Market, the sleepy little Kansas City Board of Trade sought to introduce the first Stock Index futures in 1982 to help transfer some of the risk from market funds to individual traders and funds willing to accept this risk. However, this proposal opened up a can of worms.

The Commodity Futures Trading Commission (CFTC) regulates futures and futures exchanges. The Securities and Exchange Commission (SEC) regulates stocks and securities. Because Stock Index futures represented the stock market as a whole, or at least a group of stocks, the CFTC believed that they should regulate this new market. Because the underlying market for a Stock Index futures contract was stock product, the SEC felt they should regulate this market.

def•i•ni•tion

Cash-settled futures contracts require that all open positions be paid out on contract expiry. For example, if you are long at 1022 and it settles at 1042, a payment of 20 points would be made to you and the position closed. Most financial markets are cash-settled, as are some Agricultural markets, like Lean Hogs and Feeder Cattle.

A compromise, known as the Shad-Johnson Accord, was passed in 1982, which allowed for the listing of Stock Index Futures to be regulated by the CFTC as long as the contracts were broad-based and *cash-settled.*

By broad-based index, they meant an index representative of the stock market as a whole, not just a few stocks. This feature allows the SEC to be at ease, because it would be very difficult for a broad group of stocks to be manipulated. Cash settlement, as opposed to physical delivery of the stocks, allowed the futures to not be directly connected to the cash market for the index, causing possible delivery problems. Cash-settled futures pay out the difference between the purchase price and the sale price at contract expiry, with only money, not the underlying commodity, changing hands.

The Shad-Johnson Accord compromise between the CFTC and SEC paved the way for financial futures on Stock Indexes. Following the Shad-Johnson accord, the Kansas City Board of Trade listed futures on the Value Line Composite Index, the Chicago Board of Trade listed futures on the Major Market Index, and the Chicago Mercantile Exchange listed a contract on the Standard and Poor's 500 Stock Index.

Since the listing of Stock Index futures, the playing field has changed dramatically. Major Market Index futures are no longer traded, and the Kansas City Value Line Futures are sparsely traded. But the S&P 500 Index Futures are extremely popular, and the recent introduction of Dow Jones Industrial Average Futures by the Chicago

Board of Trade has been widely heralded as the most successful new futures contract in recent history.

The Need for Stock Market Protection

As more and more money flowed into the stock market, risk increased proportionally. The stock market has several different types of risk, which can be transferred using futures.

Price risk is the simplest to understand. For example, assume you own a collection of stocks, and prices are falling. You wish to exit some of this. Instead of selling each of your stocks individually, you can sell a Stock Index futures contract, which should be fairly closely aligned to your collection of stocks. This is a common practice among many Mutual Fund managers. If they own 350 different stocks, the amount of time it would take to disseminate each of those orders could be prohibitive (for example, due to position size), hence in one transaction they can sell the stock market.

Position size is another risk for large institutions. Mutual funds and large trading houses often have a large percentage of the shares outstanding in a company. If they were to sell all of those shares in one transaction, the price would drop precipitously, decreasing their profitability or increasing their losses in the process. By using a proportional number of futures, they can hedge against further changes in price by taking an opposite position in the futures market.

Stock Index futures allow large institutions and individuals to minimize the risk of their portfolios in a single transaction. As they have gotten more accustomed to using futures to offset their portfolio risk, they are beginning to perceive the need to offset single stock risk, and will most likely become big players in the new Single Stock futures.

The relationship of the individual stocks in their portfolio to the underlying index is known as *beta*. Beta measures the relationship of a stock or a collection of stocks to a Stock Index. For example, if the S&P 500 were to rise 3 percent and your stock portfolio were to rise 3 percent, then your portfolio would have a beta of 100 percent.

def•i•ni•tion

Beta is the correlation of a stock or a collection of stocks to a specific benchmark, such as the S&P 500. Beta measures how much of the change in your portfolio can be attributed to the stock market as a whole. Beta is expressed in a percent, calculated as follows: Beta = Stock Change ÷ Market Change.

If your stocks were to rise only 2.5 percent versus a 3 percent rise in the S&P 500, then your beta would be 83 percent (2.5 ÷ 3).

Single Stock Risks

As we said earlier, stock prices are reported to represent the present value of all future earnings. This is true of the stock market in general, and of individual stocks.

In general, some of the risk to the price of the stock can be attributed to the market as a whole. General macroeconomic behavior, and the business environment, can help or hurt individual stocks and the stock market as a whole. But some things are particular to an individual stock.

For example, a failure of an individual stock to meet analysts' earning expectations can cause the individual stock to fall, while the market as a whole rallies. In addition, changes in management or company-specific news can have a dramatic effect on an individual issues price.

Because price is present on both a market basis and an individual basis there is a need to transfer this risk easily. Risk transference is the main purpose of the futures market—hence the need for Single Stock futures.

Why You Would Use Single Stock Futures

At this point, you might be thinking, "If a stock is risky, just sell the stock." While this is a good point, and an appropriate way for many to minimize risk, the use of futures offers some distinct advantages.

Trading Size and Market Float

Many institutions and large stockholders have more stock in their portfolios than is traded on a single day. In the case of these big players—the mutual funds that probably own some shares fall into this category—they can sell Single Stock futures first, then buy back the futures as they sell the stock off gradually. This keeps large amounts of stock from driving the market down at one time.

They can also use Single Stock futures to better time their purchases. Many of the larger funds buy stock that accounts for the total transactions of several days, or even weeks. If they wish to take a position in a company, they have to spread out their buying over several sessions, sometimes weeks or months to acquire all the stock they want without driving the price up on their own buying. This could be cut in half with the use of stock futures, in which their buying could be spread out between both markets.

Thus by spreading out their buying or selling between multiple markets, large institutions and shareholders may be able to gain better prices and better performance.

Short-Term Protection

Many times, traders have a position in a stock and are worried about an upcoming earnings announcement, economic number, or other event that could have a dramatic effect on the stock's price.

If you are a stock investor, holding periods come into play here. If you hold a stock for less than one full calendar year, you are subject to higher capital gains taxes. However, longer-term holders pay less in taxes. In the case of a stock that never actually expires, taxation can be put off indefinitely.

Futures contracts have a fixed expiry cycle, resulting in regular taxation. However, gains and losses from futures contracts are taxed at a lower rate than short-term gains and losses of stocks. The tax treatment of futures, known as the 60/40 rule, states currently that futures profits are 60 percent taxed at the long-term capital appreciation rate—the lower rate—and 40 percent at the higher short-term capital appreciation rate.

Hence, an individual who owns a stock and fears a short-term break in prices can sell a futures contract against the stock, limiting their exposure without liquidating their stock position and incurring taxation.

Using Single Stock futures as a hedge on your stock positions could be extremely valuable. For example, assume you own XYZ Company at $30 and the stock trades up to $40 prior to an earnings report. You could sell the futures. If the stock price declines back to $30, you could cover your futures, making $10 per share in profit taxed more favorably, and still have your stock, theoretically lowering your entry price to $20. Of course, if the stock rises, your losses on the futures will offset your gains on the stock, limiting the upside.

Selling Single Stock Futures Short

Single Stock futures also offer a more efficient way to sell a stock short. *Short selling* involves borrowing the stock, and selling it in the hopes that the price of the issue will decline.

When you borrow the stock to sell, you have to pay interest on it. Also, any dividend payments made by the company during a short sale are your responsibility. For example, assume you think XYZ Company is over-valued and ripe to decline in price. You borrow 100 shares from your broker, and pay him the broker call rate of interest (currently about 7.5 percent of the stock price). Then if XYZ Company pays a dividend of $0.50 per share, you must also pay that out. Hence on a $30 issue held for one year, your costs would be $225.00 in interest on the borrowed shares and $50 for dividend payment. This means that the stock has to decline to $27.25 during a year before you make any profits.

def•i•ni•tion

A **short sale** in the stock market involves borrowing shares from a broker dealer and selling them in anticipation of a price decline. The payment of dividends on the stock is the responsibility of the short seller, and the short seller has to pay interest on the shares borrowed. Generally, these issues make short selling more complex in the stock market than the futures market, in which a short position is subject to the same rules as a futures contract.

Single Stock futures allow you to establish a short position in a listed stock without incurring these costs. No need to borrow the stock, hence no interest paid out for borrowing. In fact, traders can use a Treasury Bill to post margin requirements, allowing them to collect interest on 90 percent of their margin funds.

Because futures involve physical delivery of the asset or cash settlement at a point in the future, holders of Single Stock futures—either long or short—don't have to worry about dividends, as the present value of the dividend is factored into the price of the future.

Hence, the futures market provides all investors with a more economical and efficient way to speculate on lower stock prices.

Shorting and the Uptick Rule

To avoid market panics and create a more hospitable environment for longer-term investors, the SEC requires that stocks can only be sold short after experiencing some upward movement, known as an uptick.

The uptick rule was established to prevent short sellers from manipulating a market or exaggerating a downward move. When the rule was established in the 1930s, the stock exchange had substantially less volume and large speculators would manipulate prices by selling, with their own selling driving prices lower and causing panic selling, which they would buy into to cover their short positions. With the huge amounts of volume traded on a daily basis on the world's stock exchanges, this type of manipulation is probably no longer feasible, but the rule still exists.

Trading Tips _____

Most brokerage firms allow traders to cover margin requirements by posting a Treasury Bill as collateral. Up to 90 percent of the value of the T-Bill can be used to meet margin requirements. However, be aware that open position losses must be met with cash. For example, if you have a $20,000 account and post $15,000 in T-bills for margin, the remaining $5,000 can be used to cover open position losses. If open position losses are greater than the cash in the account, more money must be sent in, or the T-Bill will be cashed in, which is subject to market losses to meet the required capital needs.

For example, assume you want to sell a stock that is declining in price as follows: 30, 29.80, 29.70, 29.60, 29.40, 29.10, 28.80, 28.60, and then finally trades at 28.70. You may be able to sell it at 28.70, but your order will be placed with all the other orders to sell at 28.70 and you may not get your order executed until another uptick, or at substantially lower prices.

The futures markets have no such uptick rule, and short positions can be established at anytime, as long as a willing buyer exists. Hence, the advent of Single Stock futures make it much easier for individuals to speculate on lower stock prices as well as higher stock prices.

Margin and Leverage

Another advantage of Single Stock futures to the shorter-term trader is leverage. In the stock market, the maximum amount of leverage possible is 50 percent, meaning that you can borrow up to 50 percent of the value of a stock when purchasing it. However, just like borrowing shares, borrowing money for margin on a stock requires the borrower to pay interest.

Margin requirements for futures contracts are much lower. The margin for Single Stock futures is 20 percent of the cash value of the futures contract. Also, when posting margin requirements for a futures contract, you do not have to borrow the funds and can even earn interest on margin money if you use a T-Bill.

Thus in the stock market, to control 100 shares of a stock currently at $30 per share, a trader would have to have $1,500 and could borrow the other $1,500 at the broker call rate of interest.

However, a futures market participant could control 100 shares of the same stock for roughly $6.00 per share or $600 for a predetermined amount of time. The futures trader does not have to pay interest on the remaining $24 per share, and in fact can collect interest on the margin funds by using a T-Bill.

Thus, the futures trader has a smaller barrier to entry into the market, though his time span must be shorter as well. However, such leveraging may be appropriate for short-term traders and day traders especially!

Futures Market Efficiencies

All orders in the futures market are executed on a first come, first served basis. However, in the stock market under the specialist and market maker systems, large orders from institutions can get preferential treatment.

Trading Tips

Orders on the trading floor are filled on a first come, first served basis, but first in priority of order type. The highest priority orders are market orders, followed by stop orders, and finally limit orders. Remember, if you wish to get into or out of a market quickly, use a market order, followed by a stop order.

Special systems, such as the Small Execution Order System (SEOS), have been designed by the stock exchanges to help small retail investors and traders get orders filled quickly. Orders are executed on a first in, first out basis, regardless of size, ensuring a level playing field for all.

OneChicago, a joint venture of the Chicago Board Options Exchange (CBOE), Chicago Mercantile Exchange (CME), and the Chicago Board of Trade, provides a similar advantage to small investors by making Single Stock futures available electronically through CBOE's CBOEdirect and CME's Globex trading platforms. In April 2006, OneChicago reported a 60 percent increase in trading volume over the previous year. In March 2005, the exchange reported that 1.5 million contracts were traded.

When you buy stock, the firm handling your order executes many orders in the stock market. Most major stock brokerage firms have market-making arms that trade against their customers. This creates a potential conflict of interest, as firms may make wider markets, giving their clients worse prices, as they pursue trading and market making profits. It is not required by law that a firm seek out the most competitive bid or offer to execute an order.

This same action on the futures side of the business is a violation of the Commodities Exchange Act and is punishable by prison time and very stiff fines. It is required that all futures contracts be bought and sold on the exchange floor at the single prevailing market price.

Hence, the advent of Single Stock futures helps even the playing field for small speculators, especially short-term and day traders.

Single Stock Futures Pricing Issues

The most basic tenet of pricing a futures contract is that the price of the futures and the price of the underlying commodity will always converge by the expiration of the contract.

For example, assume that you have a December futures contract on XYZ Company and the price of the underlying XYZ stock is at $35 per share. If the futures are not worth exactly $35 per share at the end of trading on the last day of the contract, arbitragers will have an opportunity to profit. (To *arbitrage* is to buy on one market and sell on another market, hopefully benefiting from a discrepancy in prices.)

Assume for a moment that XYZ stock shares are trading at $35 per share and the XYZ Decembers are trading at $35.35 per share on the last day of futures trading. Arbitragers will sell the XYZ December futures at $35.35 and buy XYZ stock at $35.00. When the futures expire they will receive $35.35 per share and relinquish the shares they bought at $35 to the holder of the long futures contract. Hence they will have made $0.35 per share. These arbitragers will continually sell the futures and buy the stock until the spread disappears, as a very small differential can still be profitable to them because of their minimal transaction costs. If the futures were trading at less than the stock, then the arbitragers would buy the futures and sell the stock, until the two were driven back into line, and they would profit on the difference.

def•i•ni•tion

To **arbitrage** is to take a position in one market and simultaneously take an opposite position in another market. In the futures market, this is defined as the simultaneous purchase and sale of similar commodities in different markets to take advantage of price discrepancy.

Cost of Carry

Futures should trade at a premium to the underlying stock price, just as most futures contracts trade at a premium to their physical commodities. This is known as the cost of carry.

Typically in most commodities, the cost of carry is a function of storage costs, insurance costs, and interest rates. Since it is not necessary to store or insure stock certificates, we are left with interest rates.

Because of the opportunity cost associated with money, the futures will price in a premium to the stock. For example, if you did not put up the margin money to buy the stock, you could have put the money in the bank and collected interest. Thus, the cost of carry will be larger the farther away from expiration the futures contract is, diminishing as the futures contract approaches expiration.

Dividends

Dividends are another element that will cause futures to trade at a premium to the underlying stock. If a company pays a dividend, the futures have to reflect the payment of that dividend on its ex-dividend date into carrying charges. For example, if a stock pays a dividend of $.50 per share, the futures will trade a premium to the stock of less than $0.50 per share, incorporating the present value of this future dividend. (Present value is a financial term used to describe the worth today of a payment in the future.)

As time passes toward expiration of the futures contract, this premium based on opportunity costs and the present value of dividends will diminish, and the Single Stock futures price should converge with the underlying stock. If they do not, ever-vigilant arbitragers will bring them into line.

Opportunity cost is typically represented by the prevailing risk-free interest rate. For example, if T-Bills are yielding 5 percent, then a stock futures contract with four months to expiration should trade at roughly a 1.25 percent premium to the underlying asset, as the futures market reflects the missed opportunity to collect this money. However, because you can collect money on margin deposits via the T-Bill market, this can be effectively negated. Present value reflects the current value of a sum of money in the future. Remember that 50 years ago, $1.00 bought a lot more than today, and thus, it is reasoned that $1.00 today buys more than $1.00 will in 50 years.

The present value of dividends paid during the life of the futures contract is reflected in the price of the futures contract. Thus, theoretically, to reflect these factors, Single Stock futures should trade at a price slightly higher than the underlying stock.

What Single Stock Futures Look Like

Single stock futures are set up similarly to other futures contracts. There are a set number of shares, set regular trading hours, position limits, contract months, expiration or final settlement date, rules for settlement, and Last Trading Day.

OneChicago's single stock futures contract includes an agreement for delivery of shares of a specific stock at a designated date in the future, called the expiration date. The size of a OneChicago single stock futures contract is 100 shares of the underlying stock. OneChicago offers over 200 futures on single stocks. Their March 2006 top traders were Wal-Mart Stores Inc., Merck & Co., Inc., Exxon Mobile Corp., U.S. Bancorp, and Citigroup.

Trading Tips _____

You can learn more about trading single stock futures at OneChicago's website (www. onechicago.com).

Contract Size

A Single Stock futures contract size is 100 shares, which is also the common single-lot size traded on a stock exchange floor. This would equate to $100 per contract move for every dollar change in the price of the Single Stock futures contract.

Contract Months

There are no more than three quarterly and two serial contract months at any point in a calendar year, just like most other types of futures contracts.

Settlement

Cash settlement is required upon expiration of the contract. Final settlement price is based on the opening prices of the component securities on the Final Settlement Date. For example, in its contracts, OneChicago sets the third Friday of the expiration month as the expiration date, unless the Exchange is not open for trading, in which case the expiration date is the preceding business day.

Single Stock Futures and Changes in the Industry

Currently, the bulk of trading in futures and options is done in trading pits through open outcry. Open outcry, as explained in Chapter 3, is the guys and gals waving their arms around, yelling and screaming.

For Single Stock futures, however, the new exchange is electronic, similar in nature to the NASD (National Association of Securities Dealers) Exchange. This could change the way all stocks and futures are traded, and generally speed up the nature of doing business on the exchanges.

The Chicago Mercantile Exchange (CME) was at the forefront of electronic trading, introducing the first (and wildly successful) all-electronically traded futures contract—the Standard and Poor's E-mini Stock Index futures. The Chicago Board Options Exchange's electronic order-routing system to execute all market orders of 10 contracts or less was in place before single stock futures started trading.

Besides changing the way futures and options are traded, the advent of Single Stock futures may change the regulatory environment as well. As the market for futures on single stocks grows, the lines between the SEC and the CFTC will be more shaded, and each fiercely independent agency may try to exert power over the other.

Single Stock futures are an incredible innovation allowing greater risk control and increased speculative efficiencies to the world's financial markets. Even if you never trade a Single Stock Future contract, the greater efficiency they will bring to capital markets will benefit you.

The Least You Need to Know

- Single Stock futures increase market efficiency because they offer an outlet for individuals and large institutions to take and transfer risk in a more efficient manner.

- Increased leverage, and a more level playing field, make Single Stock futures an ideal trading vehicle for short-term traders, especially day traders.

- Because futures exchanges operate on a first in, first out execution system, small- and medium-size traders should receive the same executions as large institutions.

- Single Stock futures closely mirror the price of stocks because of arbitrage.

- Because of the nature of the futures market, Single Stock futures can be an ideal way for speculators to take advantage of lower stock prices.

- Single Stock futures are an excellent way for individuals and institutions to take and transfer risk, adding to the liquidity of both markets.

Chapter 20

Picking Markets and Applying Your Knowledge

In This Chapter

- ◆ Look before you leap
- ◆ Choosing markets to trade
- ◆ How to assemble a winning team
- ◆ Learning how to practice trade before you risk your money
- ◆ Educational services that may help you
- ◆ Learn to love and respect risk

Because speculation requires thinking and knowledge, Chapters 11 through 16 extensively covered the driving forces behind commodity prices. In addition, two different styles of assessing a market's probable direction—fundamental and technical price analysis—were discussed in Chapters 10 and 17.

To avoid reckless behavior, developing a structured trading plan was covered in Chapter 18, along with the importance of allocating position sizes to minimize the risk of ruin. The purpose of all of this is to begin to prepare you for speculation and start you on the journey toward profit. This chapter helps you understand how to put it all together.

Speculating Versus Gambling—a Big Difference

By now you understand that the futures and options markets offer incredible opportunities for both risk taking and risk transference. The leverage involved in futures allows speculators to control large amounts of a product versus the small (percentage-wise) margin deposit. You also know by now that leverage is a dual-edged sword, and it is very possible to lose more than your initial investment when speculating in the futures and options markets.

There are two types of risk takers: gamblers and speculators. Throughout this book we have used the term speculator to describe a participant in the futures markets who has no commercial interest in the underlying commodity.

Gambling is part of speculation in that the outcome is always uncertain. However, the speculator engages in a course of reasoning, while the gambler takes the risk in the hope of gaining an advantage or a benefit. Speculation is synonymous with thinking, while gambling is synonymous with hazardous behavior.

Choosing Markets

The first step in beginning to speculate is to choose which markets are appropriate for you. For some, these may be the Stock Index futures, or Single Stock futures. These markets are generally thought to be the home of professional speculators, offering tremendous profit potential and incredible risk.

Trading Time Bomb

Some markets are extremely volatile, and known to have multiple limit moves. The limit is the maximum daily permissible movement. In the advent of a limit-up move, you would not be able to buy this contract; with a limit-down move, you would not be able to sell it. Such extremely volatile markets include Pork Bellies, Lumber, Coffee, and Palladium futures. Though these markets may be suitable for some who truly understand the risk involved, generally, newer speculators should avoid them.

We suggest starting off by looking at the margin requirements of the commodities. Generally the lower the margin requirement, the lower the profit potential, but the lower the risk as well. Just as you have to learn to walk before running, we strongly suggest that you start off with lower-risk futures contracts when you begin your foray into speculation.

If you remember back to Chapter 1, margin requirements are set by the exchanges based on the volatility and size of the underlying contract. The more volatile and risky a market is, the larger the margin requirement will be. However, most markets go through periods of volatility based on supply and demand imbalances, so a steady and placid market today may be tomorrow's rollercoaster ride. But as a general guideline here are some markets we feel beginners should look at initially.

Choosing Your Poison—or Your Pot of Gold

We all have different interests, and will be attracted to different markets for different reasons. Some may prefer the more agrarian markets, while others may prefer to trade more exotic markets, or the fast-moving financial markets. Because trading involves a lot of work, you should choose a market that interests you, as that should make the necessary research a little easier. As such, from each of the seven major futures groups we chose the particular futures markets that may be the most appropriate.

The Metals Market

For the metals enthusiast, we suggest the Gold and Silver markets. Personally we prefer Silver to Gold, as it is more of an industrial metal and has less central bank influence over it. The Platinum, Palladium, and Copper markets are left off the following list as being too volatile, and prone to violent sharp moves. However, it is worth noting that none of the metals have daily trading limits.

Metals	Initial Margin	Maint. Margin	Symbol	Contract Size	Units	$/Unit	Minimum Fluctuation
COMEX GOLD	2,363	1,750	GC	100 TROY OZ	$/OZ	1PT = $1	10 PT = $10
COMEX SILVER	3,038	2,250	SI	5,000 TROY OZ	CTS/ OZ	1CT = $50	½CT = $25

For the currency enthusiast, we strongly recommend trading the Canadian Dollar contract. Though this market is not as liquid as some of the other currencies, like the Japanese Yen, the Canadian Dollar is less prone to overnight fluctuations than the rest of the currencies.

Because Canada generally shares the same time zones as the United States, news regarding the Canadian economy is released during United States business hours. Hence much of the important economic releases and news stories affecting prices are tradable. Japanese and European business hours occur while we are tucked in bed, and much of the movement in the price of these futures occurs in the overnight markets, and is not tradable by many, except those who wish to stay up all night.

Currencies	Initial Margin	Maint. Margin	Symbol	Contract Size	Units	$/Unit	Minimum Fluctuation
CANADIAN $	608	450	CD	100,000 CD	CTS/ CD	1PT = $10	1PT = $10

The Financials Market

In the financial sector, two markets really jump out as great trading opportunities: Eurodollars and the S&P E-mini. Eurodollars are short-term deposits of U.S. Dollars in foreign banks, not the currency. They are the most actively traded futures contract in the world, and are a key interest rate to watch. They also tend to be a slower-moving market with an extremely attractive margin requirement. This is an ideal market for newer traders.

Financials	Initial Margin	Maint. Margin	Symbol	Contract Size	Units	$/Unit	Minimum Fluctuation
EURO-DOLLARS	675	500	ED	1,000,000	BASIS PT	1PT = $25	.5PT = $12.50
S&P 500	6,093	4,875	ES	50 × INDEX	PTS	1PT = .50	25PTS = $12.50 E-MINI

Many readers of this book may be day traders moving over to futures to trade their stocks. Consider looking at the S&P E-mini to get your feet wet. This market is extremely active, easy to get into and out of, and has enough volatility to make it a good candidate for day traders.

The Grains Market

One of the best markets for the beginning futures trader is the Grains market. The ease of getting information combined with enough activity to make this market attractive makes for a great combination for beginning traders.

Grains	Initial Margin	Maint. Margin	Symbol	Contract Size	Units	$/Unit	Minimum Fluctuation
WHEAT	608	450	W	5,000 BU	CTS/ BU	1CT = $50	¼CTS = $12.50
CORN	338	250	C	5,000 BU	CTS/ BU	1CT = $50	¼CTS = $12.50

Corn and Wheat are highlighted because as you know from Chapter 11, these two markets have opposite planting and harvesting cycles. By watching these two unrelated markets, you should always have exposure to longer-term trends caused by supply problems, while the demand trends set on the macroeconomic level should be similar. The Soybean complex has been avoided due to the volatility, as well as Oats, because the volume of trade is so small that the market is prone to some wild shorter-term swings.

The Softs Market

In the Food and Fiber, or Softs, market, consider Cocoa and Sugar. These sweet markets provide exposure to exotic locations such as Africa and South America, and are generally liquid markets that are not too volatile.

Softs	Initial Margin	Maint. Margin	Symbol	Contract Size	Units	$/Unit	Minimum Fluctuation
COCOA	980	700	CO	10 MET. TONS	$/ TON	1PT = $10	1PT = $10
SUGAR	1,400	1,000	SB	112,000 LBS	CTS/ LB	1PT = $11.20	1PT = $11.20
ORANGE JUICE	980	700	OJ	15,000 LBS	CTS/ LB	1PT = $1.50	5PTS = $7.50

Cotton and Lumber have been left off the list because these markets are extremely volatile. Lumber is a notoriously thin market that frequently *locks limit*, giving the trader more risk exposure.

def•i•ni•tion

> **Locks limit** refers to the maximum advance or decline from the previous day's settlement price permitted for a contract in one trading session by the rule of the exchange. Not all contracts have daily trading limits, so be sure to check the contract specifications for the markets that you intend to trade. Limit trading is important because it can open up more risk. For example, if prices lock limit up, you cannot buy unless prices trade lower. However, very frequently, once prices lock limit, they tend to stay there during the trading session, making many orders unexecutable. This increases your risk, and can result in much larger losses than previously estimated. Be warned: trading can be dangerous, as risk and reward are truly commensurate.

Orange Juice is on the list of recommended markets because it is generally a very tradable market. However, frost scares in the spring and fall in Florida can really affect this market and cause excessive volatility, so be warned.

The Livestock Market

In the Livestock market, beginning traders should stick to Live Cattle and Lean Hogs.

Meats	Initial Margin	Maint. Margin	Symbol	Contract Size	Units	$/Unit	Minimum Fluctuation
LIVE CATTLE	945	700	LC	40,000 LBS	CTS/ CWT	1PT = $4	2.5PTS = $10
LEAN HOGS	1,050	800	LH	40,000 LBS	CTS/ CWT	1PT = $4	2.5PTS = $10

Live Cattle and Lean Hogs tend to be less volatile than the Feeder and Pork Belly markets (note: Pork Bellies are on the avoid list because of volatility). Also neither Live Cattle nor Lean Hogs have overnight trading sessions, because these are primarily a U.S.–dominated market.

The Petroleum Market

Last, but not least, is the Petroleum market. Generally, the least volatile component of this segment is Crude Oil, which is why we recommend it to beginning traders.

Energies	Initial Margin	Maint. Margin	Symbol	Contract Size	Units	$/Unit	Minimum Fluctuation
CRUDE OIL	4,725	3,500	CL	1,000 BBL	$/BBL	1PT = $10	1PT = $10

Choose a Stable of Markets

Now that you have nailed down a list of markets that have affordable margin requirements, are generally liquid, and that you have an interest in, you may consider narrowing your field even more, especially if you wish to be an active trader.

There are two schools of thought when trading:

> One mindset thinks, "You should not put all your eggs in one basket" and diversify across markets.

> The other thinks, "You should put all your eggs in one basket, and watch the basket very closely," meaning you should learn to specialize.

Most traders are better off taking a moderate approach, seeking middle ground and choosing a portfolio of markets to watch for patterns in, and have a basic understanding of the supply and demand themes affecting price.

Be careful not to choose all the markets from one market group. For example, though Corn and Wheat are planted at different times of the year, one general event, such as a drought or a change to government loan programs for farmers, could radically affect both, not giving you much diversification.

By choosing just a few markets, you will also avoid the "jack of all trades, master of none" syndrome. With just a few markets, you can devote enough time to understanding what makes them tick.

Trading Tips

When establishing a portfolio of futures markets, keep in mind that you really want to be able to study them, so limit the number. For the beginning trader, we recommend two to four futures. For example, Corn, Eurodollars, and Live Cattle may be a good starting portfolio. Because the Corn and Cattle markets are related, as corn is a cattle feed, one market may affect the other. Almost all markets are related, as even interest rates affect corn and cattle prices. But by choosing one from a different market segment, you should always have a market that offers good opportunity.

The Perfect Business

It has often been said that speculation is the perfect business. You have no customers to please, no inventory to worry about, overhead is minimal, and the profit potential is unlimited.

The trader does not have to worry about pleasing customers, as his job is to position himself in front of the market and to correctly anticipate future price movement. No worrying about customer payments, or if they will buy again next year or such. Just you and the markets, where your skill and discipline will determine how much you earn or lose.

The speculator has no inventory to worry about turning over or paying for. The only restriction on the size of your operation is the size of the bankroll you have for margin. But, remember the rules from Chapter 18 about money management, allocating risk, and not betting your entire account on one play.

The only overhead a speculator has to worry about is commissions and fees. With the advent of electronic trading, these costs have dropped precipitously. Also the more experienced you get and the larger you get as a speculator, the lower these costs will be. Most firms give volume discounts, and reward experience.

The only employee you have is yourself and your broker (or brokerage firm). Brokers are more like independent contractors than employees, though they can be very important in starting your business.

Go back to Chapter 7 and reread the section on choosing a broker. Price isn't always the deciding factor, as an experienced broker can help you tremendously in your preparation for trading as well.

Understand the Risks

Before risking your hard-earned money in the markets, be sure that you understand all of the risks involved. Armed with your observation regarding the markets, you can put them to the test for a period of several months by paper trading.

One of the benefits of paper trading with an experienced broker is that the broker may be able to spot any serious errors in your plan.

Besides allowing you to test and refine your trading plans before actually risking money, paper trading with your broker allows you to get to know them, before money is involved. Obviously, if he is not very accommodating to you before he has your business, it may be a clue that he will be less than accommodating after he does.

The whole purpose of paper trading is to be as realistic as possible when doing it. It does no good to practice trading with a million dollars if you're going to start with $10,000. Don't practice your trading in the S&P if you intend to trade Corn. Keep your practice as realistic as possible.

Most full-service brokers can help in your paper trading, as well. They can give you a good, realistic idea if and where your order would have been executed, and also provide you with the firm's research on the markets that you follow.

The one major downfall to paper trading is that it does not involve real money. It is very easy to live through a fictitious *draw down* but quite different to live through it when your money is on the line. Emotions tend to creep up when real money is involved.

def•i•ni•tion

> The term **draw down** is used to express losses, both realized and unrealized. For example, assume you make $2,000 during the month of June trading commodities in three trades. If the first two trades were each $500 losers, then you would have made $2,000 with a $1,000 draw down at month end. Draw down is also used to describe unrealized losses. For example, assume you bought July Corn at $1.90 per bushel, and prices went down to $1.80 per bushel before rallying up to $2.30 per bushel. You would have had a draw down of $0.10 per bushel and a profit of $0.40 per bushel. Draw down is also known as "heat" and if you have lived through it you will know why!

On most research and hypothetical trading records you will find the following disclaimer mandated by the CFTC, which does an excellent job of explaining the downfalls of paper trading or hypothetical trading:

HYPOTHETICAL PERFORMANCE RESULTS HAVE MANY INHER-ENT LIMITATIONS, SOME OF WHICH ARE DESCRIBED BELOW. NO REPRESENTATION IS BEING MADE THAT ANY ACCOUNT WILL, OR IS LIKELY TO, ACHIEVE PROFITS OR LOSSES SIMILAR TO THOSE SHOWN. IN FACT, THERE ARE FREQUENTLY SHARP DIFFERENCES BETWEEN HYPOTHETICAL PERFORMANCE RESULTS AND THE ACTUAL RESULTS SUBSEQUENTLY ACHIEVED BY ANY PARTICULAR TRADING PROGRAM.

ONE OF THE LIMITATIONS OF HYPOTHETICAL PERFORMANCE RESULTS IS THAT THEY ARE GENERALLY PREPARED WITH THE BENEFIT OF HINDSIGHT. IN ADDITION, HYPOTHETICAL TRADING DOES NOT INVOLVE FINANCIAL RISK, AND NO HYPOTHETICAL TRADING RECORD CAN COMPLETELY ACCOUNT FOR THE IMPACT OF FINANCIAL RISK IN ACTUAL TRADING. FOR EXAMPLE, THE ABILITY TO WITHSTAND LOSSES OR TO ADHERE TO A PARTICULAR TRADING PROGRAM, IN SPITE OF TRADING LOSSES, ARE MATERIAL POINTS WHICH CAN ALSO ADVERSELY AFFECT ACTUAL TRAD-ING RESULTS. THERE ARE NUMEROUS OTHER FACTORS RELATED TO THE MARKETS, IN GENERAL, OR TO THE IMPLEMENTATION OF ANY SPECIFIC TRADING PROGRAM WHICH CANNOT BE FULLY ACCOUNTED FOR IN THE PREPARATION OF HYPOTHETICAL PER-FORMANCE RESULTS AND ALL OF WHICH CAN ADVERSELY AFFECT ACTUAL TRADING RESULTS.

In essence, what this warning states is that paper trading or hypothetical trading records can be useful, but they should also be viewed with some skepticism. When real money is not at risk, it is very easy to think and act rationally. However, when your hard-earned cash is at risk, you can act emotionally.

Simulated trading also does not take into account execution risk. For example, a buy stop placed at 210 in Corn may be actually executed at 212 or even 214 during certain market conditions. A simulated record cannot account for that, either.

However, a well-tested hypothesis is better than not having any testing. Just check what you are doing with a professional (like a broker) to be sure that you are not making any drastic errors, and accept the fact that the real world of trading will be different. When preparing a business plan, you cannot account for every possibility or potential pitfall, and in trading you can't either. But a well-thought-out plan, even if it is hypothetical, can help you avoid some costly errors.

Don't be sold on actual track records either. Some system developers actually trade their systems, which is commendable. However, past performance is no guarantee of future performance, so be sure you understand what they are selling and how it has reacted in the past.

Though It Isn't Perfect, It Definitely Helps

Though paper trading and testing your trading rules is definitely not perfect, it helps. Just as athletes practice before a game or an event, traders should practice before actually trading.

Being prepared, by practicing and using a plan, will put you miles ahead of most speculators. Hopefully this process should make you feel more comfortable about the money at risk in the market, and give you the faith to follow your plan.

Practice will also help give you the discipline to cut your losers and ride those winners. By knowing that the markets can actually move much further than you thought in either direction, you will be able to see the importance of discipline, and playing a good defense.

Continuing Education

As you decide which markets to trade and develop a trading plan, you will need some help along the way. Here is a list of major sources of information about the futures and options markets.

One of the first places to start looking for educational materials is the exchanges. Here is a list of exchange websites, and all have a plethora of free brochures and study materials available:

- ◆ www.cbot.com—Chicago Board of Trade—Trades Corn, Wheat, Soybean Complex, Treasury Bonds and Notes, and the Dow Jones Stock Indexes.

- ◆ www.cme.com—Chicago Mercantile Exchange—Trades Eurodollars, S&P Stock Index, NASDAQ Stock Index, Cattle and Hogs, Foreign Currencies, and Lumber.

- ◆ www.nymex.com—New York Mercantile Exchange—Trades Gold, Silver, Platinum, Palladium, and Petroleum Products (Crude Oil, Heating Oil, and Gasoline).

- ◆ www.nybot.com—New York Board of Trade—Trades Coffee, Sugar, Cocoa, Cotton, and some financial indexes.

- www.kcbt.com—Kansas City Board of Trade—Trades Wheat and Value Line Stock Index.

- www.mgex.com—Minneapolis Grain Exchange—Trades White and Spring Wheat futures.

Government agencies are another great source of information. Here is a list of major government agencies that deal with commodities or the underlying economy:

- www.usda.gov—The U.S. Department of Agriculture is the granddaddy of all agricultural data ranging from supply and demand to weather and livestock data.

- www.doe.gov—The U.S. Department of Energy's website contains all sorts of useful information on the Petroleum markets.

- www.doi.gov—The U.S. Department of the Interior's website contains a plethora of information regarding U.S. energy, mines, timber, and other natural resources.

- www.ustreas.gov—The U.S. Treasury Department's website has all sorts of useful economic analysis and statistics regarding the United States and world economy.

- www.doc.gov—The Department of Commerce keeps records on factory orders and industry in the United States and the world. A must for financial and metals traders.

- www.dol.gov—The Labor Department keeps the employment data for the United States; a key site for interest rate, exchange rate, and financial traders.

- www.cftc.gov—The Commodity Futures Trading Commission governs the exchanges and has a plethora of useful brochures for new traders.

- www.nfa.futures.org—The National Futures Association is the regulatory body of the futures industry. Visit for background checks on brokers and useful guides to avoiding swindles in the futures markets.

The government and the exchanges are not the only ones who have useful information for traders and speculators. The private sector has published a plethora of books and courses on trading. Here are just a few of the many Internet sites available for trading related information:

- www.futuresalmanac.com—A complete listing of the supply and demand figures and analysis for the futures markets.

- www.pitnews.com—Market news, trading tips, charts, quotes, and other information for traders.

- www.commoditycafe.com—A question and answer forum on the web where traders often talk about the markets.

- www.futuresource.com—Great source for quotes and up-to-the-minute news regarding futures and options.

- www.traderspress.com—Great source for further reading on the markets. Very comprehensive book selection for speculators.

Lastly, brokerage firms are an excellent source of information regarding the futures markets. Most offer research, news, quotes, and many other services to help you in your decision making. Here is a brief list of some of my favorites:

- www.gptc.com—Great Pacific Trading Company provides Paper Trading Assistance as well excellent research, quotes, charts, and news.

- www.auberontrading.com—Auberon Trading is an excellent firm specializing in the Livestock markets.

- www.pricegroup.com—The Price Group has been at the forefront of electronic trading for a long time, and probably will remain there.

- www.findbrokers.com—A comprehensive listing of brokers, specialties, and rates; worth a visit.

You will find that the more you study about the markets, the more you have to learn. Trading is a fascinating and difficult business. The markets are always changing and evolving, yet the same basic principles still guide them.

No one has the foolproof "money tree" or the Holy Grail of trading. Each individual has different risk tolerances and return expectations, and different trading styles and horizons fit with different personalities. However, what all successful speculators have in common is the deep passion for learning, the ability to adapt, and the discipline to respect their risk and accept the rewards.

Futures Trading Is Not for Everyone

Hopefully some who read this book will:

♦ Discover that futures trading is not for everyone before losing money in the markets, and in such a case, we will personally consider this book to be extremely useful.

♦ Understand the risks involved and decide to venture into speculation with their eyes wide open, and succeed gloriously.

♦ Find the futures market the ideal place to offset the risk involved in their businesses by hedging, which would be a wonderful delight as well.

♦ Take away from it a new understanding of how the markets operate and the relationships between risk and reward.

It was once penned that the greatest risk ever taken is taking no risk. We agree with this statement wholeheartedly, and just hope that all who decide to enter into speculation do so understanding the risks involved, as well as the potential rewards.

The Least You Need to Know

♦ Speculators take calculated risks to seek a profit, while gamblers take blind risk hoping for a reward. Gambling is best done in casinos and in Las Vegas, not in the futures markets.

♦ Newer traders should choose markets that tend to be slower moving and more forgiving of errors.

♦ New speculators should strongly consider working initially with a full-service broker. They can save you money in the long run by helping you avoid errors.

♦ Those interested in speculating should strongly consider paper trading before risking money in the markets.

♦ Some excellent resources for more information on futures and options and their underlying commodities can be found at the exchanges, the government, in the private sector, and through your broker.

♦ Keen knowledge of the markets, coupled with the discipline to cut your losses and maximize your winners, are the speculator's greatest assets.

Glossary

against actuals   A transaction generally used by two hedgers who want to exchange futures for cash positions. Also referred to as *exchange for physicals* or *versus cash.*

arbitrage   The simultaneous purchase and sale of similar commodities in different markets to take advantage of price discrepancy.

assign   To make an option seller perform his obligation to assume a short futures position (as a seller of a call option) or a long futures position (as a seller of a put option).

associated person (AP)   An individual who solicits orders, customers, or customer funds (or who supervises persons performing such duties) on behalf of a Futures Commission Merchant, an Introducing Broker, a Commodity Trading Adviser, or a Commodity Pool Operator.

at-the-money option   An option with a strike price that is equal, or approximately equal, to the current market price of the underlying futures contract.

average farm price estimate   Marketing-year weighted average price received by farmers.

balance of payment   A summary of the international transactions of a country over a period of time, including commodity and service transactions, and gold movements.

bar chart A chart that graphs the high, low, and settlement prices for a specific trading session over a given period of time.

basis The difference between the current cash price and the futures price of the same commodity. Unless otherwise specified, the price of the nearby futures contract month is generally used to calculate the basis.

bear Someone who thinks market prices will decline.

bear market A period of declining market prices.

bear spread In most commodities and financial instruments, the term refers to selling the nearby contract month, and buying the deferred contract, to profit from a change in the price relationship.

beginning stocks Grain and Oilseed commodities not consumed during the previous marketing year. These are the stocks "carried over" into the current marketing year and added to the stocks produced during that crop year. *See also* carryover.

bid An expression indicating a desire to buy a commodity at a given price, opposite of offer.

broker A company or individual that executes futures and options orders on behalf of financial and commercial institutions and/or the general public.

brokerage fee A fee charged by a broker for executing a transaction.

brokerage house An individual or organization that solicits or accepts orders to buy or sell futures contracts or options on futures and accepts money or other assets from customers to support such orders. Also referred to as *commission house* or *wire house*.

bull Someone who thinks market prices will rise.

bull market A period of rising market prices.

bull spread In most commodities and financial instruments, the term refers to buying the nearby month, and selling the deferred month, to profit from the change in the price relationship.

buying hedge Buying futures contracts to protect against a possible price increase of cash commodities that will be purchased in the future. At the time the cash commodities are bought, the open futures position is closed by selling an equal number and type of futures contracts as those that were initially purchased.

calendar spread The purchase of one delivery month of a given futures contract and simultaneous sale of another delivery month of the same commodity on the same exchange. The purchase of either a call or put option, and the simultaneous sale of the same type of option with typically the same strike price, but with a different expiration month.

call option An option that gives the buyer the right, but not the obligation, to purchase (go "long") the underlying futures contract at the strike price on or before the expiration date.

canceling order An order that deletes a customer's previous order.

carrying charge For physical commodities such as grains and metals, the cost of storage space, insurance, and finance charges incurred by holding a physical commodity. In interest rate futures markets, it refers to the differential between the yield on a cash instrument and the cost of funds necessary to buy the instrument. Also referred to as *cost of carry* or *carry*.

carryover Grain and Oilseed commodities not consumed during the marketing year and remaining in storage at year's end. These stocks are "carried over" into the next marketing year and added to the stocks produced during that crop year.

cash commodity An actual physical commodity someone is buying or selling, for example, Soybeans, Corn, Gold, Silver, Treasury Bonds, etc. Also referred to as *actuals*.

cash contract A sales agreement for either immediate or future delivery of the actual product.

cash market A place where people buy and sell the actual commodities, as in grain elevator, bank, etc.

cash settlement Transactions generally involving index-based futures contracts that are settled in cash based on the actual value of the index on the last trading day, in contrast to those that specify the delivery of a commodity or financial instrument.

charting The use of charts to analyze market behavior and anticipate future price movements. Those who use charting as a trading method plot such factors as high, low, and settlement prices, average price movements, volume, and open interest. Two basic price charts are bar charts and point-and-figure charts. Anticipating future price movement using historical prices, trading volume, open interest, and other trading data to study price patterns.

cheap Colloquialism implying that a commodity is under priced.

clear The process by which a clearinghouse maintains records of all trades and settles margin flow on a daily market-to-market basis for its clearing member.

clearing member   A member of an exchange clearinghouse. Memberships in clearing organizations are usually held by companies. Clearing members are responsible for the financial commitments of customers that clear through their firm.

clearinghouse   An agency or separate corporation of a futures exchange that is responsible for settling trading accounts, clearing trades, collecting and maintaining margin monies, regulating delivery, and reporting trading data. Clearinghouses act as third parties to all futures and options contracts—acting as a buyer to every clearing member seller and a seller to every clearing member buyer.

closing price   The last price paid for a commodity on any trading day. If there is a closing range of prices, the settlement price is determined by averaging those prices. Also referred to as the *settle* or *settlement price*.

closing range   A range of prices at which buy and sell transactions took place during the market close.

commission fee   A fee charged by a broker for executing a transaction. Also referred to as *brokerage fee*.

commission house   An individual or organization that solicits or accepts orders to buy or sell futures contracts or options on futures and accepts money or other assets from customers to support such orders. Also referred to as *wire house*.

commodity   An article of commerce or a product that can be used for commerce. In a narrow sense, products traded on an authorized commodity exchange. The types of commodities include Agricultural Products, Metals, Petroleum, Foreign Currencies, and Financial Instruments and Index, to name a few.

Commodity Credit Corp.   A branch of the U.S. Department of Agriculture, established in 1933, that supervises the government's farm loan and subsidy programs.

Commodity Futures Trading Commission (CFTC)   A federal regulatory agency established under the Commodity Futures Trading Commission Act, as amended in 1974, that oversees futures trading in the United States.

contract grades   The standard grades of commodities or instruments listed in the rules of the exchanges that must be met when delivering cash commodities against futures contracts.

contract month   A specific month in which delivery may take place under the terms of a futures contract.

convergence   A term referring to cash and futures prices tending to come together (as in, the basis approaches zero) as the futures contract nears expiration.

cost of carry (or carry)   For physical commodities such as grains and metals, the cost of storage space, insurance, and finance charges incurred by holding a physical commodity. In interest rate futures markets, it refers to the differential between the yield on a cash instrument and the cost of funds necessary to buy the instrument.

crop (marketing) year   The time span from harvest to harvest for agricultural commodities. The crop marketing year varies slightly with each agricultural commodity, but it tends to begin at harvest and end before the next year's harvest, for example, the marketing year for Soybeans begins September 1 and ends August 31.

crop reports   Reports compiled by the U.S. Department of Agriculture on various agricultural commodities that are released throughout the year. Information in the reports includes estimates on planted acreage, yield, and expected production, as well as comparison of production from previous years.

cross-hedging   Hedging a cash commodity using a different but related futures contract when there is no futures contract for the cash commodity being hedged and the cash and futures markets follow similar price trends (for example, using Soybean Meal futures to hedge Fish Meal).

crush spread   The purchase of Soybean futures and the simultaneous sale of Soybean Oil and Meal futures. The sale of Soybean futures and the simultaneous purchase of Soybean Oil and Meal futures.

crushing   The act of processing Soybeans into Soybean Meal and Oil.

customer margin   *See* performance-bond margin.

daily trading limit   The maximum price range set by the exchange cash day for a contract.

day traders   Speculators who take positions in futures or options contracts and liquidate them prior to the close of the same trading day.

deferred (delivery) month   The more distant month(s) in which futures trading is taking place, as distinguished from the nearby (delivery) month.

deliverable grades   The standard grades of commodities or instruments listed in the rules of the exchanges that must be met when delivering cash commodities against futures contracts. Also referred to as contract grades.

delivery   The transfer of the cash commodity from the seller of a futures contract to the buyer of a futures contract.

delivery day   The third day in the delivery process at the Chicago Board of Trade, when the buyer's clearing firm presents the delivery notice with a certified check for the amount due at the office of the seller's clearing firm.

delivery month   A specific month in which delivery may take place under the terms of a futures contract. Also referred to as *contract month*.

delivery points   The locations and facilities designated by a futures exchange where stocks of a commodity may be delivered in fulfillment of a futures contract, under procedures established by the exchange.

delta   A measure of how much an option premium changes, given a unit change in the underlying futures price. Delta often is interpreted as the probability that the option will be in-the-money by expiration.

Demand, Law of   The relationship between product demand and price.

differentials   Price differences between classes, grades, and delivery locations of various stocks of the same commodity.

econometrics   The application of statistical and mathematical methods in the field of economics to test and quantify economic theories and the solutions to economic problems.

ending stocks   Grain and Oilseed commodities not consumed during the current marketing year. These are the stocks "carried over" into the following marketing year and added to the stocks produced during that crop year. *See also* Carryover.

equilibrium price   The market price at which the quantity supplied of a commodity equals the quantity demanded.

exchange for physicals   A transaction generally used by two hedgers who want to exchange futures for cash positions. Also referred to as *against actuals* or *versus cash*.

exercise   The action taken by the holder of a call option if he wishes to purchase the underlying futures contract or by the holder of a put option if he wishes to sell the underlying futures contract.

exercise price   The price at which the futures contract underlying a call or put option can be purchased (if a call) or sold (if a put). Also referred to as the *strike price*.

expanded trading hours   Additional trading hours of specific futures and options contracts at the Chicago Board of Trade that overlap with business hours in other time zones.

expiration date   Options on futures generally expire on a specific date during the month preceding the futures contract delivery month. For example, an option on a March futures contract expires in February but is referred to as a March option because its exercise would result in a March futures contract position.

exports   The amount of Grain or Oilseed sold to foreign buyers.

extrinsic value   The amount of money option buyers are willing to pay for an option in the anticipation that, over time, a change in the underlying futures price will cause the option to increase in value. In general, an option premium is the sum of time value and intrinsic value. Any amount by which an option premium exceeds the option's intrinsic value can be considered time value. Also referred to as *time value.*

feed ratio   A ratio used to express the relationship of feeding costs to the dollar value of livestock.

fill-or-kill   A customer order that is a price limit order that must be filled immediately or canceled.

first notice day   According to Chicago Board of Trade rules, the first day on which a notice of intent to deliver a commodity in fulfillment of a given month's futures contract can be made by the clearinghouse to a buyer.

floor broker (FB)   An individual who executes orders for the purchase or sale of any commodity futures or options contract on any contract market for any other person.

floor trader (FT)   An individual who executes trades for the purchase or sale of any commodity futures or options contract on any contract market for such individual's own account.

forward (cash) contract   A cash contract in which a seller agrees to deliver a specific cash commodity to a buyer sometime in the future. Forward contracts, in contrast to futures contracts, are privately negotiated and are not standardized.

full carrying charge market   A futures market where the price difference between delivery months reflects the total costs of interest, insurance, and storage.

fundamental analysis   A method of anticipating future price movement using supply and demand information, as well as other economic indicators.

Futures Commission Merchant (FCM)   An individual or organization that solicits or accepts orders to buy or sell futures contracts or options on futures and accepts money or other assets from customers to support such orders. Also referred to as *commission house* or *wire house.*

futures contract   A legally binding agreement, made on the trading floor of a futures exchange, to buy or sell a commodity or financial instrument sometime in the future. Futures contracts are standardized according to the quality, quantity, and delivery time and location for each commodity. The only variable is price, which is discovered on an exchange trading floor.

futures exchange   A central marketplace with established rules and regulations where buyers and sellers meet to trade futures and options on futures contracts.

gamma   A measurement of how fast delta changes, given a unit change in the underlying futures price.

grain terminal   Large grain elevator facility with the capacity to ship grain by rail and/or barge to domestic or foreign markets.

gross processing margin   The difference between the cost of Soybeans and the combined sales income of the processed Soybean Oil and Meal.

hedger   An individual or company owning or planning to own a cash commodity (Corn, Soybeans, Wheat, U.S. Treasury Bonds, Notes, Bills, etc.) and concerned that the cost of the commodity may change before either buying or selling it in the cash market.

hedging   The practice of offsetting the price risk inherent in any cash market position by taking an equal but opposite position in the futures market. Hedgers use the futures markets to protect their business from adverse price changes.

high   The highest price of the day, week, or month for a particular futures contract.

hog/corn ratio   The relationship of feeding costs to the dollar value of Hogs. It is measured by dividing the price of Hogs ($/hundredweight) by the price of Corn ($/bushel).

holder   The purchaser of either a call or put option. Option buyers receive the right, but not the obligation, to assume a futures position. Also referred to as the *option buyer*.

horizontal spread   The purchase of either a call or put option and the simultaneous sale of the same type of option with typically the same strike price but with a different expiration month. Also referred to as a *calendar spread*.

in-the-money option   An option having intrinsic value. A call option is in-the-money if its strike price is below the current price of the underlying futures contract. A put option is in-the-money if its strike price is above the current price of the underlying futures contract.

initial margin   The amount a futures market participant must deposit into his margin account at the time he places an order to buy or sell a futures contract. Also referred to as *original margin*.

intercommodity spread   The purchase of a given delivery month of one futures market and the simultaneous sale of the same delivery month of a different, but related, futures market.

interdelivery spread   The purchase of one delivery month of a given futures contract and simultaneous sale of another delivery month of the same commodity on the same exchange. Also referred to as a *calendar spread*.

intermarket spread   The sale of a given delivery month of a futures contract on one exchange and the simultaneous purchase of the same delivery month and futures contract on another exchange.

intrinsic value   The amount by which an option is in-the-money. An option having intrinsic value. A call option is in-the-money if its strike price is below the current price of the underlying futures contract. A put option is in-the-money if its strike price is above the current price of the underlying futures contract.

introducing broker   A person or organization that solicits or accepts orders to buy or sell futures contracts or commodity options but does not accept money or other assets from customers to support such orders.

inverted market   A futures market in which the relationship between two delivery months of the same commodity is abnormal.

invisible supply   Uncounted stocks of a commodity in the hands of wholesalers, manufacturers, and producers that cannot be identified accurately; stocks outside commercial channels but theoretically available to the market.

last trading day   According to the Chicago Board of Trade rules, the final day when trading may occur in a given futures or option contract month. Futures contracts outstanding at the end of the last trading day must be settled by delivery of the underlying commodity or securities or by agreement for monetary settlement (in some cases by EFPs).

LDP (Loan Deficiency Payments)   A program that provides producers a financial tool to help farmers market their crops throughout the year.

leverage   The ability to control large dollar amounts of a commodity with a comparatively small amount of capital.

limit order   An order in which the customer sets a limit on the price and/or time of execution.

limits   The maximum number of speculative futures contracts one can hold as determined by the Commodity Futures Trading Commission and/or the exchange upon which the contract is traded. Also referred to as trading limit. The maximum advance or decline—from the previous day's settlement—permitted for a contract in one trading session by the rules of the exchange. According to the Chicago Board of Trade rules, an expanded allowable price range set during volatile markets.

liquid   A characteristic of a security or commodity market with enough units outstanding to allow large transactions without a substantial change in price. Institutional investors are inclined to seek out liquid investments so that their trading activity will not influence the market price.

liquidate   Selling (or purchasing) futures contracts of the same delivery month purchased (or sold) during an earlier transaction or making (or taking) delivery of the cash commodity represented by the futures contract. Taking a second futures or options position opposite to the initial or opening position.

loan program   A federal program in which the government lends money at pre-announced rates to farmers and allows them to use the crops they plant for the upcoming crop year as collateral.

loan rate   The amount lent per unit of a commodity to farmers.

long   One who has bought futures contracts or owns a cash commodity.

long hedge   Buys futures contracts to protect against a possible price increase of cash commodities that will be purchased in the future. At the time the cash commodities are bought, the open futures position is closed by selling an equal number and type of futures contracts as those that were initially purchased. Also referred to as a "buying hedge."

low   The lowest price of the day, week, or month for a particular futures contract.

maintenance   A set minimum margin (per outstanding futures contract) that a customer must maintain in his margin account.

managed account   *See* performance-bond margin.

managed futures   Represents an industry comprised of professional money managers known as commodity trading advisors who manage client assets on a discretionary basis, using global futures markets as an investment medium.

margin   *See* performance-bond margin.

margin call   A call from a clearinghouse to a clearing member, or from a brokerage firm to a customer, to bring margin deposits up to a required minimum level.

market order   An order to buy or sell a futures contract of a given delivery month to be filled at the best possible price and as soon as possible.

marking to market   To debit or credit on a daily basis a margin account based on the close of that day's trading session.

minimum price fluctuation   The smallest allowable increment of price movement for a contract.

moving-average charts   A statistical price analysis method of recognizing different price trends. A moving average is calculated by adding the prices for a predetermined number of days and then dividing by the number of days.

National Futures Association (NFA)   An industry-wide, industry-supported, self-regulatory organization for futures and options markets. The primary responsibilities of the NFA are to enforce ethical standards and customer protection rules, screen futures professionals for membership, audit and monitor professionals for financial and general compliance rules and provide for arbitration of futures-related disputes.

nearby (delivery) month   The futures contract month closest to expiration. Also referred to as the *spot month*.

notice day   According to Chicago Board of Trade rules, the second day of the three-day delivery process when the clearing corporation matches the buyer with the oldest reported long position to the delivering seller and notifies both parties. *See also* First Notice Day.

offer   An expression indicating one's desire to sell a commodity at a given price; opposite of bid.

offset   Taking a second futures or options position opposite to the initial or opening position. Selling (or purchasing) futures contracts of the same delivery month purchased (or sold) during an earlier transaction or making (or taking) delivery of the cash commodity represented by the futures contract.

OPEC   Organization of Petroleum Exporting Countries. Members are: Algeria, Indonesia, Iran, Iraq, Kuwait, Libya, Nigeria, Qatar, Saudi Arabia, the United Arab Emirates, and Venezuela.

open interest   The total number of futures or options contracts of a given commodity that have not yet been offset by an opposite futures or option transaction nor fulfilled by delivery of the commodity or option exercise. Each open transaction has a buyer and a seller, but for calculation of open interest, only one side of the contract is counted.

open outcry   Method of public auction for making verbal bids and offers in the trading pits or rings of futures exchanges.

opening range   A range of prices at which buy and sell transactions took place during the opening of the market.

option   A contract that conveys the right, but not the obligation, to buy or sell a particular item at a certain price for a limited time. Only the seller of the option is obligated to perform.

option buyer   The purchaser of either a call or put option. Option buyers receive the right, but not the obligation, to assume a futures position. Also referred to as the *holder*.

option premium   The sum of money that the option buyer pays and the option seller receives for the rights granted by the option.

option seller   The person who sells an option in return for a premium and is obligated to perform when the holder exercises his right under the option contract. Also referred to as the *writer*.

option spread   The simultaneous purchase and sale of one or more options contracts, futures, and/or cash positions.

option writer   The person who sells an option in return for a premium and is obligated to perform when the holder exercises his right under the option contract. Also referred to as the *option seller*.

original margin   *See* initial margin.

out-of-the-money option   An option with no intrinsic value, as in a call whose strike price is above the current futures price or a put whose strike price is below the current futures price.

over-the-counter market   A market where products such as stocks, foreign currencies, and other cash items are bought and sold by telephone and other means of communications.

payment-in-kind program   A government program in which farmers who comply with a voluntary acreage-control program and set aside an additional percentage of acreage specified by the government receive certificates that can be redeemed for government-owned stocks of Grain.

performance-bond margin   The amount of money deposited by both buyer and seller of a futures contract or an options seller to ensure performance of the term of the contract. Margin in commodities is not a payment of equity or down payment on the commodity itself, but rather it is a security deposit. Within the futures industry, financial guarantees required of both buyers and sellers of futures contracts and sellers of options contracts to ensure fulfilling of contract obligations. FCMs are responsible for overseeing customer margin accounts. Margins are determined on the basis of market risk and contract value. Financial safeguards to ensure that clearing members (usually companies or corporations) perform on their customers' open futures and options contracts. Clearing margins are distinct from customer margins that individual buyers and sellers of futures and options contracts are required to deposit with brokers.

pit   The area on the trading floor where futures and options on futures contracts are bought and sold. Pits are usually raised octagonal platforms with steps descending on the inside that permit buyers and sellers of contracts to see each other.

point-and-figure charts   Charts that show price changes of a minimum amount regardless of the time period involved.

position   A market commitment. A buyer of a futures contract is said to have a long position; a seller of futures contracts is said to have a short position.

position day   According to the Chicago Board of Trade rules, the first day in the process of making or taking delivery of the actual commodity on a futures contract. The clearing firm representing the seller notifies the Board of Trade Clearing Corporation that its short customers want to deliver on a futures contract.

position limit   The maximum number of speculative futures contracts one can hold as determined by the Commodity Futures Trading Commission and/or the exchange upon which the contract is traded. Also referred to as the *trading limit*.

position trader   An approach to trading in which the trader either buys or sells contracts and holds them for an extended period of time.

premium   (1) The additional payment allowed by exchange regulation for delivery of higher-than-required standards or grades of a commodity against a futures contract. (2) In speaking of price relationships between different delivery months of a given commodity, one is said to be "trading at a premium" over another when its price is greater than that of the other. (3) In financial instruments, the dollar amount by which a security trades above its principal value. The price of an option—the sum of money that the option buyer pays and the option seller receives for the rights granted by the option.

price discovery   The generation of information about "future" cash market prices through the futures markets.

price limit   The maximum advance or decline—from the previous day's settlement—permitted for a contract in one trading session by the rules of the exchange. According to the Chicago Board of Trade rules, an expanded allowable price range set during volatile markets.

price limit order   A customer order that specifies the price at which a trade can be executed.

production   The amount of Grain or Oilseed produced during the crop year. Derived by multiplying the harvested acres by the yield per acre.

pulpit   A raised structure adjacent to, or in the center of, the pit or ring at a futures exchange where market reporters, employed by the exchange, record price changes as they occur in the trading pit.

purchase and sell statement   A statement sent by a commission house to a customer when his futures or options on futures position has changed, showing the number of contracts bought or sold, the prices at which the contracts were bought or sold, the gross profit or loss, the commission charges, and the net profit or loss on the transaction.

purchasing hedge or long hedge   Buyer purchases futures contracts to protect against a possible price increase of cash commodities that will be purchased in the future. At the time the cash commodities are bought, the open futures position is closed by selling an equal number and type of futures contracts as those that were initially purchased. Also referred to as a *buying hedge*. The practice of offsetting the price risk inherent in any cash market position by taking an equal but opposite position in the futures market. Hedgers use the futures markets to protect their business from adverse price changes.

put option   An option that gives the option buyer the right but not the obligation to sell (go "short") the underlying futures contract at the strike price on or before the expiration date.

range (price)   The price span during a given trading session, week, month, year, etc.

resistance   A level above which prices have had difficulty penetrating.

resumption   The reopening the following day of specific futures and options markets that also trade during the evening session at the Chicago Board of Trade.

reverse crush spread   The sale of Soybean futures and the simultaneous purchase of Soybean Oil and Meal futures. The purchase of Soybean futures and the simultaneous sale of Soybean Oil and Meal futures.

runners   Messengers who rush orders received by phone clerks to brokers for execution in the pit.

scalper   A trader who trades for small, short-term profits during the course of a trading session, rarely carrying a position overnight.

secondary market   Market where previously issued securities are bought and sold.

selling hedge or short hedge   Selling futures contracts to protect against possible declining prices of commodities that will be sold in the future. At the time the cash commodities are sold, the open futures position is closed by purchasing an equal number and type of futures contracts as those that were initially sold. The practice of offsetting the price risk inherent in any cash market position by taking an equal but opposite position in the futures market. Hedgers use the futures markets to protect their business from adverse price changes.

settle   *See* settlement price.

settlement price   The last price paid for a commodity on any trading day. If there is a closing range of prices, the settlement price is determined by averaging those prices. Also referred to as the *settle* or *closing price.*

short   **(noun)** One who has sold futures contracts or plans to purchase a cash commodity. **(verb)** To sell futures contracts or initiate a cash forward contract sale without offsetting a particular market position.

short hedge   To sell futures contracts to protect against possible declining prices of commodities that will be sold in the future. At the time the cash commodities are sold, the open futures position is closed by purchasing an equal number and type of futures contracts as those that were initially sold.

speculator   A market participant who tries to profit from buying and selling futures and options contracts by anticipating future price movements. Speculators assume market price risk and add liquidity and capital to the Futures markets.

spot   Usually refers to a cash market price for a physical commodity that is available for immediate delivery.

spot month   The futures contract month closest to expiration. Also referred to as nearby delivery month.

spread   The price difference between two related markets or commodities.

spreading   The simultaneous buying and selling of two related markets in the expectation that a profit will be made when the position is offset. For example, buying one futures contract and selling another futures contract of the same commodity but different delivery month.

steer/corn ratio   The relationship of Cattle prices to feeding costs. It is measured by dividing the price of Cattle ($/hundredweight) by the price of Corn ($/bushel).

stop order   An order to buy or sell when the market reaches a specified point.

stop-limit order   A variation of a stop order in which a trade must be executed at the exact price or better. If the order cannot be executed, it is held until the stated price or better is reached again.

strike price   The price at which the futures contract underlying a call or put option can be purchased (if a call) or sold (if a put). Also referred to as the *exercise price*.

Supply, Law of   The relationship between product supply and its price.

supply, total   The total amount of supply of a Grain or Oilseed. Consists of Beginning Stocks + Production + Imports.

support   The place on a chart where the buying of futures contracts is sufficient to halt a price decline.

suspension   The end of the evening session for specific futures and options markets traded at the Chicago Board of Trade.

technical analysis   Method for anticipating future price movement using historical prices, trading volume, open interest and other trading data to study price patterns.

tick   The smallest allowable increment of price movement for a contract.

time limit order   A customer order that designates the time during which it can be executed.

time value   The amount of money option buyers are willing to pay for an option in the anticipation that, over time, a change in the underlying futures price will cause the option to increase in value. In general, an option premium is the sum of time value and intrinsic value. Any amount by which an option premium exceeds the option's intrinsic value can be considered time value. Also referred to as the *extrinsic value*.

time-stamped Part of the order-routing process in which the time of day is stamped on an order. An order is time-stamped when it is (1) received on the trading floor, and (2) completed.

trade balance The difference between a nation's imports and exports of merchandise.

trading limit The maximum number of speculative futures contracts one can hold as determined by the Commodity Futures Trading Commission and/or the exchange upon which the contract is traded. Also referred to as the *position limit*.

underlying futures contract The specific futures contract that is bought or sold by exercising an option.

use, domestic The amount of Grain or Oilseed consumed during a marketing year within the country of origin or production.

use, total The amount of Grain or Oilseed consumed during a marketing year. Total Use consists of all subcomponents of usage—feed, food, seed, sillage, crushing, exports, domestic use, and residual.

variable limit According to the Chicago Board of Trade rules, an expanded allowable price range set during volatile markets.

variation margin During periods of great market volatility or in the case of high-risk accounts, additional margin deposited by a clearing member firm to an exchange.

vega Measurement of how the price of an option changes versus a change in volatility. Typically expressed as a percentage of the change in volatility.

versus cash A transaction generally used by two hedgers who want to exchange futures for cash positions. Also referred to as *against actuals* or *exchange for physicals*.

vertical spread Buying and selling puts or calls of the same expiration month but different strike prices.

volatility A measurement of the change in price over a given period. It is often expressed as a percentage and computed as the annualized standard deviation of the percentage change in daily price.

volume The number of purchases or sales of a commodity futures contract made during a specific period of time, often the total transactions for one trading day.

warehouse receipt   A document guaranteeing the existence and availability of a given quantity and quality of a commodity in storage; commonly used as the instrument of transfer of ownership in both cash and futures transactions.

wire house   An individual or organization that solicits or accepts orders to buy or sell futures contracts or options on futures and accepts money or other assets from customers to support such orders. Also referred to as *commission house* or *Futures Commission Merchant (FCM)*.

writer   The person who sells an option in return for a premium and is obligated to perform when the holder exercises his right under the option contract. Also referred to as the *option seller.*

yield   A measure of the annual return on an investment.

yield curve   A chart in which the yield level is plotted on the vertical axis and the term to maturity of debt instruments of similar credit-worthiness is plotted on the horizontal axis. The yield curve is positive when long-term rates are higher than short-term rates. However, the yield curve is negative or inverted if short-term rates are higher than long-term rates.

yield to maturity   The rate of return an investor receives if a fixed-income security is held to maturity.

Contract Specifications

Australian Dollar

Exchange	International Monetary Market Division of the Chicago Mercantile Exchange
Symbol	AD
Contract Months	March, June, September, December
Trading Unit	100,000 Australian Dollars
Tick Size	0.0001/Australian Dollar ($10.00)
Daily Price Limit	None
Trading Hours	Day Session: 7:20 A.M. to 2:00 P.M. Globex: 5:00 P.M. to 4:00 P.M. Monday through Thursday; 5:00 P.M. to 4:00 P.M. Sundays and holidays.
Last Trading Day	9:16 A.M. CST on the second business day immediately preceding the third Wednesday of the contract month
Delivery	Delivery is made on the third Wednesday of the contract month at a bank designated by the clearinghouse.

Australian Dollar Options

Exchange	International Monetary Market Division of the Chicago Mercantile Exchange
Contract Months	All months. Months not corresponding to a futures contract are based on the next available futures contract—for example, January options on March futures.
Exchange	International Monetary Market Division of the Chicago Mercantile Exchange
Trading Unit	Calls—option to buy one futures contract Puts—option to sell one futures contract
Strike Prices	Stated in terms of U.S. Dollars per Australian Dollar in terms of one cent
Tick Size	0.0001/Australian Dollar ($10.00)
Daily Price Limit	None
Trading Hours	Same as futures
Last Trading Day	Second Friday immediately preceding the third Wednesday of the contract month
Delivery	A long or short position in the underlying futures contract

British Pound Futures

Exchange	International Monetary Market Division of the Chicago Mercantile Exchange
Symbol	BP
Contract Months	March, June, September, December
Trading Unit	62,500 British Pounds
Tick Size	0.0001/British Pound ($6.25)
Daily Price Limit	None
Trading Hours	Day Session: 7:20 A.M. to 2:00 P.M. Globex: 5:00 P.M. to 4:00 P.M. Monday through Thursday; 5:00 P.M. to 4:00 P.M. Sundays and holidays.

Last Trading Day	9:16 A.M. CST on the second business day immediately preceding the third Wednesday of the contract month
Delivery	Delivery is made on the third Wednesday of the contract month at a bank designated by the clearinghouse.

British Pound Options

Exchange	International Monetary Market Division of the Chicago Mercantile Exchange
Contract Months	All months. Months not corresponding to a futures contract are based on the next available futures contract—for example, January options on March futures.
Trading Unit	Calls—option to buy one futures contract Puts—option to sell one futures contract
Strike Prices	Stated in terms of U.S. Dollars per British Pound on 2.50-cent intervals
Exchange	International Monetary Market Division of the Chicago Mercantile Exchange
Tick Size	$0.0001 per Pound ($6.25 per contract)
Daily Price Limit	None
Trading Hours	Same as futures
Last Trading Day	Second Friday immediately preceding the third Wednesday of the contract month; if a holiday, the preceding day
Delivery	A long or short position in the underlying futures contract

Canadian Dollar Futures

Exchange	International Monetary Market Division of the Chicago Mercantile Exchange
Symbol	CD
Contract Months	March, June, September, December
Trading Unit	100,000 Canadian Dollar

Tick Size	0.0001/Canadian Dollar ($10.00 per contract)
Daily Price Limit	None
Trading Hours	Day Session: 7:20 A.M. to 2:00 P.M. Globex: 4:00 P.M. to 5:00 P.M. Monday through Thursday; 4:00 P.M. to 5:00 P.M. Sundays and holidays.
Last Trading Day	9:16 A.M. CST on the second business day immediately preceding the third Wednesday of the contract month
Delivery	Delivery is made on the third Wednesday of the contract month at a bank designated by the clearinghouse.

Canadian Dollar Options

Exchange	International Monetary Market Division of the Chicago Mercantile Exchange
Contract Months	All months. Months not corresponding to a futures contract are based on the next available futures contract—for example, January options on March futures.
Trading Unit	Calls—option to buy one futures contract Puts—option to sell one futures contract
Strike Prices	Stated in terms of U.S. Dollars per Canadian Dollar on 0.50 cent intervals
Tick Size	$0.0001 per Canadian Dollar ($10.00 per contract)
Daily Price Limit	None
Trading Hours	Same as futures
Last Trading Day	Second Friday immediately preceding the third Wednesday of the contract month. If a holiday, the preceding day.
Delivery	A long or short position in the underlying futures contract

Cocoa Futures

Exchange	New York Board of Trade
Symbol	CO (some quote vendors carry as CC)

Contract Months	March, May, July, September, December
Trading Unit	10 metric tons (22,046 pounds)
Tick Size	$1.00/ton ($10.00 per contract)
Daily Price Limit	None
Trading Hours	Day Session: 8:00 A.M. to 11:50 A.M. EST
Last Trading Day	Ten business days prior to the last business day of the delivery month
Delivery	The growth of any country or clime, including new or yet unknown growths. Growths are divided into three classifications: Group A, deliverable at a premium of $160/ton (including the main crops of Ghana, Nigeria, Ivory Coast, among others); Group B, deliverable at a premium of $80.00/ton (includes Bahia, Arriba, Venezuela, among others); Group C, deliverable at par (includes Sanchez, Haiti, Malaysia and all others). Sanchez moves to Group B in May 2007. Delivery at licensed warehouses in the Port of New York District, Albany, Delaware River Port District, Baltimore or Port of Hampton Roads.

Cocoa Options

Exchange	New York Board of Trade
Contract Months	Same as futures
Trading Unit	Calls—option to buy one futures contract Puts—option to sell one futures contract
Strike Prices	Dollars per ton in $100 increments
Tick Size	$1.00 per ton ($10.00 per contract)
Daily Price Limit	None
Trading Hours	Same as futures
Last Trading Day	First Friday of the month preceding the delivery month of the underlying futures contract
Delivery	A long or short position in the underlying futures contract

Coffee Futures

Exchange	New York Board of Trade
Symbol	KC
Contract Months	March, May, July, September, December
Trading Unit	37,500 pounds (roughly 250 bags)
Tick Size	$0.0005 per pound or $18.75 per contract
Daily Price Limit	None
Trading Hours	Day Session: 9:15 A.M. to 12:30 P.M. EST
Last Trading Day	Seven business days prior to the last business day of the delivery month
Delivery	A Notice of Certification is issued based on testing the grade of the beans and by cup testing for flavor. The exchange uses certain coffees to establish the "basis"; coffees judged better are at a premium; those judged inferior are at a discount.

Coffee Options

Exchange	New York Board of Trade
Contract Months	Same as futures
Trading Unit	Calls—option to buy one futures contract Puts—option to sell one futures contract
Tick Size	$\frac{1}{100}$ cent per pound, equivalent to $3.75 per contract
Daily Price Limit	None
Trading Hours	Same as futures
Last Trading Day	First Friday of the month preceding the delivery month of the underlying futures contract
Delivery	A long or short position in the underlying futures contract

Corn Futures

Exchange	Chicago Board of Trade
Symbol	C

Contract Months	March, May, July, September, December
Trading Unit	5,000 bushels
Tick Size	¼ cent per bushel ($12.50 per contract)
Daily Price Limit	20 cents above or below the previous day's settlement price. Spot month has no limit.
Trading Hours	Open Outcry: 9:30 A.M. to 1:15 P.M. Central time, Monday through Friday. Electronic (a/c/e): 6:30 P.M. to 6:00 A.M. Central time, Sunday through Friday hours. Trading in expiring contracts closes at noon on the last trading day.
Last Trading Day	The business day prior to the fifteenth calendar day of the contract month
Delivery	Second business day following the last trading day of the delivery month

Corn Options

Exchange	Chicago Board of Trade
Contract Months	All months. Months not corresponding to a futures contract are based on the next available futures contract—for example, January options on March futures.
Trading Unit	Calls—option to buy one futures contract Puts—option to sell one futures contract
Strike Prices	Integral multiples of 10 cents per bushel
Tick Size	⅛ of a cent ($6.25 per contract)
Daily Price Limit	Twenty cents ($0.20) per bushel ($1,000/contract) above or below the previous day's settlement premium. Limits are lifted on the last trading day.
Trading Hours	Open Outcry: 9:30 A.M. to 1:15 P.M. Central Time, Monday through Friday. Electronic: 6:32 P.M. to 6:00 A.M. Central Time, Sunday through Friday.
Last Trading Day	The last Friday preceding the first notice day of the futures by two business days
Delivery	A long or short position in the underlying futures contract

Cotton Futures

Exchange	New York Board of Trade
Symbol	CT
Contract Months	March, May, July, October, December
Trading Unit	Cents per 50,000 pounds net weight (approximately 100 bales)
Tick Size	$\frac{1}{100}$ of a cent (one "point") per pound below 95 cents per pound. $\frac{5}{100}$ of a cent (or five "points") per pound at prices of 95 cents per pound or higher.
Daily Price Limit	Three cents above or below previous day's settlement price. However, if any contract month settles at or above $1.10 per pound, all contract months will trade with 4-cent price limits. Should no month settle at or above $1.10 per pound, price limits stay (or revert) to three cents per pound.
Trading Hours	Day Session: 10:30 A.M. to 2:15 P.M. EST
Last Trading Day	Seventeen business days from the end of the contract expiry month
Delivery	50,000 pounds of Grade #2 Cotton or equivalent in Galveston, TX; Houston, TX; New Orleans, LA; Memphis, TN; Greenville/Spartanburg, SC

Cotton Options

Exchange	New York Board of Trade
Contract Months	Same as futures
Trading Unit	Calls—option to buy one futures contract Puts—option to sell one futures contract
Strike Prices	One-cent increments
Tick Size	$\frac{1}{100}$ of a cent or $5.00 per contract
Daily Price Limit	None
Trading Hours	Same as futures

Last Trading Day | The first Friday preceding the fifth to last business day of the month prior to the delivery month

Delivery | A long or short position in the underlying futures contract

CRB Index Futures

Exchange | New York Board of Trade

Symbol | CR

Contract Months | January, February, April, June, August, November

Trading Unit | 500 times Index

Tick Size | 0.05 points, or $25 per contract

Daily Price Limit | None

Trading Hours | Day Session: 10 A.M. to 2:30 P.M. EST

Last Trading Day | Second Friday of expiration month

Delivery | Cash settlement at contract expiration

CRB Index Options

Exchange | New York Board of Trade

Contract Months | Same as futures

Trading Unit | Calls—option to buy one futures contract
Puts—option to sell one futures contract

Strike Prices | Integers which are evenly divisible by two (for example, 240.00, 242.00); minimum of nine exercise prices at all times, four in-the-money, one at-the-money, four out-of-the money

Tick Size | 0.05 points, or $25 per contract

Daily Price Limit | None

Trading Hours | Same as futures

Exchange | New York Board of Trade

Last Trading Day | Second Friday of expiration month

Delivery | A long or short position in the underlying futures contract

Crude Oil Futures

Exchange	New York Mercantile Exchange
Symbol	CL
Contract Months	January, February, March, April, May, June, July, August, September, October, November, December
Trading Unit	1,000 U.S. barrels (42,000 gallons)
Tick Size	$0.01/barrel ($10.00 per contract)
Daily Price Limit	Minimum price fluctuation is $0.01 (1¢) per barrel ($10.00 per contract). There is no maximum limit.
Trading Hours	Open Outcry: 10:00 A.M. until 2:30 P.M. Electronic: 3:15 P.M. to 9:50 A.M. the following day Mondays through Thursdays. 7:00 p.m to 9:50 A.M. Sunday. 3:15 p.m to 5:00 P.M. Fridays and the day preceding all major holidays (this session's trade date will be dated for the following business day).
Last Trading Day	The third business day prior to the twenty-fifth calendar day of the month preceding the delivery month
Delivery	F.O.B. seller's facility, Cushing, Oklahoma, at any pipeline or storage facility with pipeline access to Arco, Cushing storage, or Texaco Trading and Transportation, Inc.

Crude Oil Options

Exchange	New York Mercantile Exchange
Contract Months	Same as futures
Trading Unit	Calls—option to buy one futures contract Puts—option to sell one futures contract
Strike Prices	Dollars per barrel in $1.00 increments
Tick Size	$0.01 per barrel ($10.00 per contract)
Daily Price Limit	None
Trading Hours	Same as futures
Last Trading Day	Second Friday of the month prior to delivery
Delivery	A long or short position in the underlying futures contract

Dollar Index Futures

Exchange	New York Board of Trade
Symbol	DX
Contract Months	March, June, September, December
Trading Unit	1,000 times Index
Exchange	New York Board of Trade
Tick Size	0.01 points ($10.00)
Daily Price Limit	None
Trading Hours	Day Session: 8:05 A.M. to 3:00 P.M. EST. Electronic: 7:00 P.M. to 10:00 P.M. then open from 2:00 A.M. to 8:05 A.M.
Last Trading Day	Third Wednesday of the expiring contract month. On the last trading day, trading ceases at 10:00 A.M.
Delivery	Cash-settled

Dollar Index Options

Exchange	New York Board of Trade
Contract Months	Same as futures
Trading Unit	Calls—option to buy one futures contract Puts—option to sell one futures contract
Strike Prices	Intervals of 1.00 U.S. Dollar Index Point
Tick Size	0.01 Index Points ($10.00 per contract)
Daily Price Limit	None
Trading Hours	Same as futures
Last Trading Day	Two Fridays before the third Wednesday of the expiring contract month at 3:00 P.M.
Delivery	A long or short position in the underlying futures contract

Dow Jones Industrial Average Index Futures

Exchange	Chicago Board of Trade
Symbol	DJ

Contract Months	March, June, September, December
Trading Unit	10 times the Dow Jones Industrial Average Index
Tick Size	One point, or $10.00 per contract
Daily Price Limit	Successive 10%, 20%, and 30% limits.
Trading Hours	Open Outcry: 7:20 A.M. to 3:15 P.M. Central Time, Monday through Friday. Electronic: 6:15 P.M. to 7:00 A.M. Central Time, Sunday through Friday. Trading in expiring contracts ceases at 3:15 P.M. Central Time on the last trading day.
Last Trading Day	The business day preceding the final settlement day
Delivery	Cash-settled

Dow Jones Industrial Average Index Options

Exchange	Chicago Board of Trade
Contract Months	March, June, September, December plus months in between (serial months)
Trading Unit	Calls—option to buy one futures contract Puts—option to sell one futures contract
Strike Prices	100 Index Point increments
Tick Size	0.50 points, or $5.00 per contract
Daily Price Limit	Successive 10%, 20%, and 30%
Trading Hours	Open Outcry: 7:20 A.M. to 3:15 P.M. Central Time, Monday through Friday. Electronic: 6:17 P.M. to 7:00 A.M. Central Time, Sunday through Friday.
Last Trading Day	For quarterly expirations: The trading day immediately preceding the third Friday of the quarterly contract month. For serial expirations: The third Friday of the serial contract month.
Delivery	Cash-settled for quarterly contracts, futures delivery for serial months

Electronic Mini-NASDAQ 100 Index Futures

Exchange	International Monetary Market Division of the Chicago Mercantile Exchange
Symbol	ES
Contract Months	March, June, September, December
Trading Unit	$20 times NASDAQ 100 Index
Tick Size	0.05 Index Points or $10 per contract
Daily Price Limit	Set quarterly see http://www.cme.com/trading/prd/equity/pricelimits2549.html
Trading Hours	Globex: 5:00 P.M. to 3:15 P.M. and 3:30 P.M. to 4:30 P.M. Monday through Thursday; shutdown period from 4:30 P.M. to 5:00 P.M. nightly; 5:00 P.M. to 3:15 P.M. Sundays and holidays.
Last Trading Day	The third Friday of the Contract delivery month
Delivery	Cash-settled to the NASDAQ 100 Index

Electronic Mini-NASDAQ 100 Index Options

Exchange	International Monetary Market Division of the Chicago Mercantile Exchange
Contract Months	All months. Months not corresponding to a futures contract are based on the next available futures contract—for example, January options on March futures.
Trading Unit	Calls—option to buy one futures contract Puts—option to sell one futures contract
Strike Prices	In 10.00-point intervals of NASDAQ
Tick Size	0.05 Index Points or $10 per contract
Daily Price Limit	Options trading halted when lead E-Mini Nasdaq-100 future locks limit.
Trading Hours	Same as futures
Last Trading Day	Third Friday of contract month
Delivery	A long or short position in the underlying futures contract

Electronic Mini-Standard and Poor's 500 Stock Index Futures

Exchange	International Monetary Market Division of the Chicago Mercantile Exchange
Symbol	ES
Contract Months	March, June, September, December
Trading Unit	50 times S&P 500 Index
Tick Size	0.25 Index Points or $12.50 per contract
Daily Price Limit	Set quarterly see http://www.cme.com/trading/prd/equity/pricelimits2549.html
Trading Hours	Globex: 5:00 P.M. to 3:15 P.M. and 3:30 P.M. to 4:30 P.M. Monday through Thursday; shutdown period from 4:30 P.M. to 5:00 P.M. nightly; 5:00 P.M. to 3:15 P.M. Sundays and holidays.
Last Trading Day	The third Friday of the contract delivery month
Delivery	Cash-settled to the NASDAQ 100 Index

Electronic Mini-Standard and Poor's 500 Stock Index Options

Exchange	International Monetary Market Division of the Chicago Mercantile Exchange
Contract Months	All months. Months not corresponding to a futures contract are based on the next available futures contract—for example, January options on March futures.
Trading Unit	Calls—option to buy one futures contract Puts—option to sell one futures contract
Strike Prices	In 10.00 point intervals of S&P 500 Index
Tick Size	0.25 Index Points or $12.50 per contract
Daily Price Limit	Options trading halted when lead E-Mini S&P 500 futures lock limit except at the total daily price limit on an option's last day of trading.
Trading Hours	Same as futures
Last Trading Day	Third Friday of contract month
Delivery	A long or short position in the underlying futures contract

Euro Currency Dollar

Exchange	International Monetary Market Division of the Chicago Mercantile Exchange
Symbol	EC
Contract Months	March, June, September, December
Trading Unit	125,000 Euro Currency
Tick Size	0.0001/Euro Currency ($12.50)
Daily Price Limit	None
Trading Hours	Day Session: 7:20 A.M. to 2:00 P.M. Globex: 4:00 P.M. to 5:00 P.M. Monday through Thursday. 4:00 P.M. to 5:00 P.M. Sundays and holidays.
Last Trading Day	9:16 A.M. CST on the second business day immediately preceding the third Wednesday of the contract month
Delivery	Delivery is made on the third Wednesday of the contract month at a bank designated by the clearinghouse.

Euro Currency Options

Exchange	International Monetary Market Division of the Chicago Mercantile Exchange
Contract Months	All months. Months not corresponding to a futures contract are based on the next available futures contract—for example, January options on March futures.
Trading Unit	Calls—option to buy one futures contract Puts—option to sell one futures contract
Strike Prices	Stated in terms of U.S. Dollars per Euro Currency in terms of one cent
Tick Size	0.0001/Euro Currency ($12.50)
Daily Price Limit	None
Trading Hours	Same as futures
Last Trading Day	Second Friday immediately preceding the third Wednesday of the contract month
Delivery	A long or short position in the underlying futures contract

Eurodollar Futures

Exchange	Chicago Mercantile Exchange
Symbol	ED
Contract Months	January, February, March, April, May, June, July, August, September, October, November, December (note: quarterly months most active)
Trading Unit	$1,000,000 worth of three-month time deposits
Tick Size	.01 (1 basis pt.) or $25.00; .005 (½ basis pt.). First four months in the March quarterly cycle plus two serial months.
Daily Price Limit	None
Trading Hours	Day Session: 7:20 A.M. to 2:00 P.M. CST. CME Globex: 5:00 P.M. to 4:00 P.M. and 2:00 P.M. to 4:00 P.M. Monday through Thursday; shutdown period from 4:00 P.M. to 5:00 P.M. nightly; 5:00 P.M. to 4:00 P.M. Sundays and holidays.
Last Trading Day	Second London Bank business day immediately preceding the third Wednesday of contract month
Delivery	Cash-settled based on the yield to maturity of a three-month deposit of U.S. Dollars in an offshore bank

Eurodollar Options

Exchange	Chicago Mercantile Exchange
Contract Months	Same as futures
Trading Unit	Calls—option to buy one futures contract Puts—option to sell one futures contract
Strike Prices	.25-point increments
Tick Size	Same as futures
Daily Price Limit	None
Trading Hours	Same as futures
Last Trading Day	Same as futures
Delivery	A long or short position in the underlying futures contract

Feeder Cattle Futures

Exchange	Chicago Mercantile Exchange
Symbol	FC
Contract Months	January, March, April, May, August, September, October, November
Trading Unit	50,000 pounds
Tick Size	$0.0001 cents per pound or $5.00 per contract
Daily Price Limit	.03 cents per pound ($1,500 per contract)
Trading Hours	9:05 A.M. to 1:00 P.M. CST
Last Trading Day	Last Thursday of the contract month with exceptions
Delivery	Cash-settled at the U.S. Feeder Steer Price as calculated by Cattle-Fax

Feeder Cattle Options

Exchange	Chicago Mercantile Exchange
Contract Months	Same as futures
Trading Unit	Calls—option to buy one futures contract Puts—option to sell one futures contract
Strike Prices	Cents per pound. First two months only: $0.01 intervals, $0.60, $0.61, $0.62, etc. All other months: $0.02 intervals, $0.62, $0.64, $0.66, etc. For spot month: $0.005 intervals, $0.605, $0.610, $0.615, etc.
Tick Size	Same as futures
Daily Price Limit	None
Trading Hours	Same as futures
Last Trading Day	Same as futures
Delivery	A long or short position in the underlying futures contract

Five-Year Treasury Note Futures

Exchange	Chicago Board of Trade
Symbol	FV
Contract Months	March, June, September, December
Trading Unit	One U.S. Treasury Note having a face value at maturity of $100,000
Tick Size	One half of $\frac{1}{32}$ of a point ($15.625/contract) rounded up to the nearest cent/contract; par is on the basis of 100 points
Daily Price Limit	None
Trading Hours	Day Sessions: 7:20 A.M. to 2:00 P.M. CST, Monday through Friday. Electronic: 6:00 P.M. to 4:00 P.M., Central Standard Time, Sunday through Friday. Trading in expiring contracts closes at noon, Central Standard Time, on the last trading day.
Last Trading Day	Last business day of the expiring contract's named expiration month
Delivery	The third business day following the last trading day.

Five-Year Treasury Note Options

Exchange	Chicago Board of Trade
Contract Months	Same as Futures
Trading Unit	Calls—option to buy one futures contract Puts—option to sell one futures contract
Strike Prices	$\frac{1}{2}$ of a full point
Exchange	Chicago Board of Trade
Tick Size	$\frac{1}{64}$ of a point ($15.625/contract) rounded up to the nearest cent/contract
Daily Price Limit	None
Trading Hours	Same as futures

Last Trading Day	Noon on the last Friday preceding by at least two business days the last business day of the month preceding the option month. Options cease trading at the close of the regular daytime open auction trading session for the corresponding 5-Year Treasury Note futures contract.
Delivery	A long or short position in the underlying futures contract

Frozen Pork Belly Futures

Exchange	Chicago Mercantile Exchange
Symbol	PB
Contract Months	February, March, May, July, August
Trading Unit	40,000 pounds (roughly 37 Cattle)
Tick Size	$0.025/hundred weight or $10.00 per contract
Daily Price Limit	$0.025 above or below previous day's settlement
Trading Hours	Open Outcry: 9:10 A.M. to 1:00 P.M. CST
Last Trading Day	The twentieth calendar day of the contract month with exceptions
Delivery	Delivery of Pork Bellies must take place on the third business following the initial tender and calls for delivery of an expectable amount and age of belly.

Frozen Pork Belly Options

Exchange	Chicago Mercantile Exchange
Contract Months	All months. Months not corresponding to a futures contract are based on the next available futures contract—for example, January options on March futures.
Trading Unit	Calls—option to buy one futures contract Puts—option to sell one futures contract
Strike Prices	Integral multiples of $0.02 per hundred weight
Tick Size	$0.025/hundred weight or $10.00 per contract

Daily Price Limit	None
Trading Hours	Same as futures
Last Trading Day	The last Friday of the month preceding the contract month which is at least three business days from the end of the month
Delivery	A long or short position in the underlying futures contract

Gold Futures

Exchange	New York Mercantile Exchange, COMEX Division
Symbol	GC
Contract Months	February, April, June, August, October, December, plus next two months (note: months mentioned by name are most liquid)
Trading Unit	100 Troy Ounces
Tick Size	$0.10 per ounce or $10.00 per contract
Daily Price Limit	None
Trading Hours	Day Sessions: 8:20 A.M. to 1:30 P.M. EST, Monday through Friday. Electronic: Monday through Thursday 2:00 P.M. to 8:00 A.M.; Friday 2:00 P.M. to 4:30 P.M.; Sunday 7:00 P.M. to 8:00 A.M.
Last Trading Day	Third to last business day of the contract month
Delivery	Gold delivered against the futures contract must bear a serial number and identifying stamp of a refiner approved and listed by the exchange. Delivery must be made from a depository licensed by the exchange.

Gold Options

Exchange	New York Mercantile Exchange, COMEX Division
Contract Months	All contract months
Trading Unit	Calls—option to buy one futures contract Puts—option to sell one futures contract

Strike Prices	$10 per ounce if price is below $500, $20 per ounce intervals if price above $500
Tick Size	$0.10 per ounce or $10.00 per contract
Daily Price Limit	None
Trading Hours	Same as futures
Last Trading Day	Second Friday of the month preceding the delivery month
Delivery	A long or short position in the underlying futures contract

Heating Oil Futures

Exchange	New York Mercantile Exchange
Symbol	HO
Contract Months	January, February, March, April, May, June, July, August, September, October, November, December
Trading Unit	42,000 gallons (1,000 barrels)
Tick Size	$0.0001 per gallon or $4.20 per contract
Daily Price Limit	Minimum price fluctuation: $0.0001 (0.01 cents) per gallon ($4.20 per contract) and Maximum price fluctuation $0.25 per gallon ($10,500) per contract
Trading Hours	Day Session: 10:05 A.M. to 2:30 P.M. EST, Monday through Friday. Electronic: 3:15 P.M. to 9:50 A.M. Monday through Thursday; 3:15 P.M. to 5 P.M. Friday (also days preceding major holiday); 7:00 P.M. to 9:50 A.M. Sunday.
Last Trading Day	Last business day of the month preceding contract month
Delivery	F.O.B. seller's facility in New York harbor, ex-shore. All duties, entitlements, taxes, fees, and other charges paid. Requirements for seller's shore facility: capability to deliver into barges. Buyer may request delivery by truck, if available at the seller's facility, and pays a surcharge for truck delivery. Delivery may also be completed by pipeline, tanker, book transfer, or inter- or intra-facility transfer. Delivery must be made in accordance with applicable federal, state, and local licensing and tax laws.

Heating Oil Options

Exchange	New York Mercantile Exchange
Contract Months	All contract months
Trading Unit	Calls—option to buy one futures contract Puts—option to sell one futures contract
Exchange	New York Mercantile Exchange
Strike Prices	$0.02 per gallon incrementally in even numbers
Tick Size	$0.0001 per gallon or $4.20 per contract
Daily Price Limit	None
Trading Hours	Same as futures
Last Trading Day	Three business days ahead of the futures
Delivery	A long or short position in the underlying futures contract

High-Grade Copper Futures

Exchange	New York Mercantile Exchange, COMEX Division
Symbol	HG
Contract Months	January, February, March, April, May, June, July, August, September, October, November, December
Trading Unit	25,000 pounds
Tick Size	$0.0005 per pound or $12.50 per contract
Daily Price Limit	None
Trading Hours	Day Session: 8:10 a.m to 1:00 P.M. EST, Monday through Friday. Electronic: 2:00 P.M. to 8:00 A.M. Monday through Thursday; 2:00 P.M. to 4:30 P.M. Friday; 7:00 P.M. to 8:00 A.M. Sunday.
Last Trading Day	Third to last business day of the contract month.
Delivery	Copper may be delivered against the high-grade copper contract only from a warehouse in the United States licensed or designated by the exchange. Delivery must be made upon a

domestic basis; import duties or import taxes, if any, must be paid by the seller, and shall be made without any allowance for freight.

High-Grade Copper Options

Exchange	New York Mercantile Exchange, COMEX Division
Contract Months	All contract months
Trading Unit	Calls—option to buy one futures contract Puts—option to sell one futures contract
Strike Prices	$0.01 per pound if price is below $0.40, $0.02 per pound intervals if price above $0.40
Tick Size	$0.0005 per pound or $12.50 per contract
Daily Price Limit	None
Trading Hours	Same as futures
Last Trading Day	The fourth to last of the month preceding the delivery month
Delivery	A long or short position in the underlying futures contract

Japanese Yen Futures

Exchange	International Monetary Market Division of the Chicago Mercantile Exchange
Symbol	JY
Contract Months	March, June, September, December
Trading Unit	12,500,000 Japanese Yen
Tick Size	0.000001/Japanese Yen or $12.50 per contract
Daily Price Limit	None
Trading Hours	Day Session: 7:20 A.M. to 2:00 P.M. Globex: 5:00 P.M. to 4:00 P.M. Monday through Thursday. 5:00 P.M. to 4:00 P.M. Sundays and holidays.

Last Trading Day	9:16 A.M. CST on the second business day immediately preceding the third Wednesday of the contract month
Delivery	Delivery is made on the third Wednesday of the contract month at a bank designated by the clearinghouse.

Japanese Yen Options

Exchange	International Monetary Market Division of the Chicago Mercantile Exchange
Contract Months	All months. Months not corresponding to a futures contract are based on the next available futures contract—for example, January options on March futures.
Trading Unit	Calls—option to buy one futures contract Puts—option to sell one futures contract
Strike Prices	$0.0001 Incrementally
Tick Size	$0.000005/Japanese Yen or $6.25 per contract
Daily Price Limit	None
Trading Hours	Same as futures
Last Trading Day	Second Friday immediately preceding the third Wednesday of the contract month.
Delivery	A long or short position in the underlying futures contract

Lean Hog Futures

Exchange	Chicago Mercantile Exchange
Symbol	LH
Contract Months	February, April, June, July, August, October, December
Trading Unit	40,000 pounds (roughly 37 Cattle)
Tick Size	$0.025/hundred weight or $10.00 per contract
Daily Price Limit	$0.02 above or below previous days settlement
Trading Hours	Open Outcry: 9:10 A.M. to 1:00 P.M. CST

| Last Trading Day | The twentieth calendar day of the contract month with exceptions |
| Delivery | Cash-settled based on the Chicago Mercantile Exchange Lean Hog Price Index |

Lean Hog Options

Exchange	Chicago Mercantile Exchange
Contract Months	All months. Months not corresponding to a futures contract are based on the next available futures contract—for example, January options on March futures.
Trading Unit	Calls—option to buy one futures contract Puts—option to sell one futures contract
Strike Prices	Integral multiples of $0.01 per hundred weight in the first two months and $0.02 intervals in the following months
Tick Size	$0.025/hundred weight or $10.00 per contract
Daily Price Limit	None
Trading Hours	Same as futures
Last Trading Day	The last Friday of the month preceding the contract month which is at least three business days from the end of the month
Delivery	A long or short position in the underlying futures contract

Live Cattle Futures

Exchange	Chicago Mercantile Exchange
Symbol	LC
Contract Months	February, April, June, August, October, December
Trading Unit	40,000 pounds (roughly 37 Cattle)
Tick Size	$0.025/hundred weight or $10.00 per contract
Daily Price Limit	$0.030 above or below previous day's settlement
Trading Hours	Open Outcry: 9:05 A.M. to 1:00 P.M. CST

Last Trading Day	The twentieth calendar day of the contract month with exceptions
Delivery	Delivery of Live Cattle must take place on the third business following the initial tender and calls for delivery of an expectable average weight and age of livestock.

Live Cattle Options

Exchange	Chicago Mercantile Exchange
Contract Months	All months. Months not corresponding to a futures contract are based on the next available futures contract—for example, January options on March futures.
Trading Unit	Calls—option to buy one futures contract Puts—option to sell one futures contract
Strike Prices	Integral multiples of $0.01 per hundred weight in the first two months and $0.02 intervals in the following months
Tick Size	$0.025/hundred weight or $10.00 per contract
Daily Price Limit	None
Trading Hours	Same as futures
Last Trading Day	The last Friday of the month preceding the contract month which is at least three business days from the end of the month
Delivery	A long or short position in the underlying futures contract

NASDAQ 100 Index Options

Exchange	International Monetary Market Division of the Chicago Mercantile Exchange
Contract Months	All months. Months not corresponding to a futures contract are based on the next available futures contract—for example, January options on March futures.
Trading Unit	Calls—option to buy one futures contract Puts—option to sell one futures contract

Strike Prices	In 10.00 point intervals of NASDAQ
Tick Size	0.05 Index Points or $5.00 per contract
Daily Price Limit	None
Trading Hours	Same as futures
Last Trading Day	Third Friday of contract month
Delivery	A long or short position in the underlying futures contract

New York Harbor Gasoline Futures

Exchange	New York Mercantile Exchange
Symbol	HU
Contract Months	January, February, March, April, May, June, July, August, September, October, November, December
Trading Unit	42,000 gallons (1,000 barrels)
Tick Size	$0.0001 per gallon or $4.20 per contract
Daily Price Limit	Minimum price fluctuation: $0.0001 (0.01 cents) per gallon ($4.20 per contract) and Maximum price fluctuation $0.25 per gallon ($10,500) per contract.
Trading Hours	Day Session: 10:05 A.M. to 2:30 P.M. EST, Monday through Friday. Electronic: 3:15 P.M. to 9:50 A.M. Monday through Thursday; 3:15 P.M. to 5 P.M. Friday (also days preceding major holiday); 7:00 P.M. to 9:50 A.M. Sunday.
Last Trading Day	Last business day of the month preceding contract month
Delivery	F.O.B. seller's facility in New York harbor ex-shore. All duties, entitlements, taxes, fees, and other charges paid. Requirements for seller's shore facility: capability to deliver into barges. Delivery may also be completed by pipeline, tanker, book transfer, or inter- or intra-facility transfer. Delivery must be made in accordance with applicable federal, state, and local licensing and tax laws. Delivery shall comply with all state laws related to oxygen content.

New York Harbor Unleaded Gasoline Options

Exchange	New York Mercantile Exchange
Contract Months	All contract months
Trading Unit	Calls—option to buy one futures contract Puts—option to sell one futures contract
Strike Prices	$0.02 per gallon incrementally in even numbers
Tick Size	$0.0001 per gallon or $4.20 per contract
Daily Price Limit	None
Trading Hours	Same as futures
Last Trading Day	Three business days ahead of the futures
Delivery	A long or short position in the underlying futures contract

Oat Futures

Exchange	Chicago Board of Trade
Symbol	O
Contract Months	March, May, July, September, December
Trading Unit	5,000 bushels
Tick Size	¼ cent per bushel ($12.50 per contract)
Daily Price Limit	20 cents above or below the previous days settlement price. Spot month has no limit.
Trading Hours	Open Outcry: 9:30 A.M. to 1:15 P.M. Central time, Monday through Friday. Electronic (a/c/e): 6:33 P.M. to 6:00 A.M. Central time, Sunday through Friday. Trading in expiring contracts closes at noon on the last trading day.
Last Trading Day	The business day prior to the fifteenth calendar day of the contract month.
Delivery	#2 Heavy Oats and #1 Oats at par and substitutions at differentials established by the exchange

Oat Options

Exchange	Chicago Board of Trade
Contract Months	All months. Months not corresponding to a futures contract are based on the next available futures contract—for example, January options on March futures.
Trading Unit	Calls—option to buy one futures contract Puts—option to sell one futures contract
Strike Prices	Integral multiples of 10 cents per bushel
Tick Size	⅛ of a cent ($6.25 per contract)
Daily Price Limit	None
Trading Hours	Same as futures
Last Trading Day	The last Friday preceding the first notice day of the futures by five business days
Delivery	A long or short position in the underlying futures contract

Soybean Futures

Exchange	Chicago Board of Trade
Symbol	S
Contract Months	January, March, May, July, August, September, November
Trading Unit	5,000 bushels
Tick Size	¼ cent per bushel ($12.50 per contract)
Daily Price Limit	50 cents above or below the previous day's settlement price. Spot month has no limit.
Trading Hours	Open Outcry: 9:30 A.M. to 1:15 P.M. CST, Monday through Friday. Electronic (a/c/e): 6:31 P.M. to 6:00 A.M. CST, Sunday through Friday. Trading in expiring contracts closes at noon on the last trading day.
Last Trading Day	The business day prior to the fifteenth calendar day of the contract month
Delivery	Second business day following the last trading day of the delivery month.

Soybean Options

Exchange	Chicago Board of Trade
Contract Months	All months. Months not corresponding to a futures contract are based on the next available futures contract—for example, January options on March futures.
Trading Unit	Calls—option to buy one futures contract Puts—option to sell one futures contract
Strike Prices	Integral multiples of 10 cents per bushel
Tick Size	⅛ of a cent ($6.25 per contract)
Daily Price Limit	None
Trading Hours	Same as futures
Last Trading Day	The last Friday preceding the first notice day of the futures by two business days
Delivery	A long or short position in the underlying futures contract

Soybean Meal Futures

Exchange	Chicago Board of Trade
Symbol	SM
Contract Months	January, March, May, July, August, September, October, December
Trading Unit	100 tons (roughly 2,000 pounds)
Tick Size	$0.10 per bushel ($10.00 per contract)
Daily Price Limit	$20 above or below the previous day's settlement price. Spot month has no limit.
Trading Hours	Open Outcry: 9:30 A.M. to 1:15 P.M. Central time, Monday through Friday. Electronic (a/c/e): 6:31 P.M. to 6:00 A.M. Central time, Sunday through Friday.
Last Trading Day	The business day prior to the fifteenth calendar day of the contract month
Delivery	Second business day following the last trading day of the delivery month

Soybean Meal Options

Exchange	Chicago Board of Trade
Contract Months	All months. Months not corresponding to a futures contract are based on the next available futures contract—for example, January options on March futures.
Trading Unit	Calls—option to buy one futures contract Puts—option to sell one futures contract
Strike Prices	Integral multiples of 10 cents per bushel
Tick Size	$0.05 ($5.00 per contract)
Daily Price Limit	$20/short ton ($2,000/contract) above or below the previous day's settlement premium. Limits are lifted on the last trading day.
Trading Hours	Open Auction: 9:30 A.M. to 1:15 P.M. Central Time, Monday through Friday Electronic: 6:33 P.M. to 6:00 A.M. Central Time, Sunday through Friday.
Last Trading Day	The last Friday preceding the first notice day of the futures by two business days
Delivery	A long or short position in the underlying futures contract

Soybean Oil Futures

Exchange	Chicago Board of Trade
Symbol	Bo
Contract Months	January, March, May, July, August, September, October, December
Trading Unit	60,000 pounds
Tick Size	0.0001 per pound ($6.00 per contract)
Daily Price Limit	Two cents per pound above or below the previous day's settlement price. No limit in the spot month.
Trading Hours	Open Outcry: 9:30 A.M. to 1:15 P.M. Chicago time, Monday through Friday. Electronic (a/c/e): 6:31 P.M. to 6:00 A.M. Central time, Sunday through Friday. Trading in expiring contracts closes at noon on the last trading day.

Last Trading Day	The business day prior to the 15th calendar day of the contract month
Delivery	Last business day of the delivery month

Soybean Oil Options

Exchange	Chicago Board of Trade
Contract Months	January, March, May, July, August, September, October, December
Trading Unit	Calls—option to buy one futures contract
	Puts—option to sell one futures contract
Strike Prices	Stated in terms of ¼ cent per pound when the strike price is less than 30 cents per pound; 1 cent per pound when the strike price is 30 cents per pound or greater
Tick Size	0.00005 per pound ($3.00 per contract)
Daily Price Limit	2 cents per pound above or below the previous day's settlement price. Limits are lifted on the last trading day.
Trading Hours	Same as futures
Last Trading Day	The last Friday preceding the first notice day of the corresponding Soybean Oil futures contract by at least two business days
Delivery	A long or short position in the underlying futures contract

World Sugar #11 Futures

Exchange	New York Board of Trade
Symbol	SB
Contract Months	March, May, July, October
Trading Unit	112,000 pounds (roughly 50 long tons)
Tick Size	$0.0001 per pound or $11.20 per contract
Daily Price Limit	None

Trading Hours	Day Session: 9:30 A.M. to 12:00 P.M. EST
Last Trading Day	Last business day prior to the delivery month
Delivery	Growths of Argentina, Australia, Barbados, Belize, Brazil, Colombia, Costa Rica, Dominican Republic, El Salvador, Ecuador, Fiji Islands, French Antilles, Guatemala, Honduras, India, Jamaica, Malawi, Mauritius, Mexico, Nicaragua, Peru, Republic of the Philippines, South Africa, Swaziland, Taiwan, Thailand, Trinidad, United States, and Zimbabwe

World Sugar #11 Options

Exchange	New York Board of Trade
Contract Months	Same as futures
Trading Unit	Calls—option to buy one futures contract Puts—option to sell one futures contract
Strike Prices	Cents per pound
Tick Size	$0.05 per pound if price is below $0.15, $0.10 per ounce intervals if price above $0.15
Daily Price Limit	None
Trading Hours	Same as futures
Last Trading Day	First Friday of the month preceding the delivery month of the underlying futures contract
Delivery	A long or short position in the underlying futures contract

Index

G

T

U

V-W-X-Y-Z